"BRANDS ON THE READER'S MIND AN IMAGE THAT IS HARD TO SHAKE OFF."
Publishers Weekly

Monty. Classically handsome, extraordinarily gifted—and dedicated to his own destruction. From his smashing screen successes: *The Search, From Here to Eternity, The Misfits,* to his man-to-man showdown with John Wayne in *Red River,* through the behind-the-scenes clashes with directing giants Alfred Hitchcock and John Huston, to his intense relationship with Liz Taylor begun on the set of *A Place in the Sun,* and finally, through his slow drowning in a river of vodka and pills—MONTY captures the truth of a tragic life.

"The entire field of film biography takes a major step forward with the publication of this superb book."
Cinema Booklist

"A detailed, disturbing portrait of a tortured, gifted, self-destroyer."
Chicago Daily News

"Amazing . . . remarkably accurate."
Truman Capote

★★

MAIN SELECTION OF THE MOVIE BOOK CLUB

Monty
A BIOGRAPHY OF
MONTGOMERY CLIFT

Robert LaGuardia

AVON
PUBLISHERS OF BARD, CAMELOT AND DISCUS BOOKS

AVON BOOKS
A division of
The Hearst Corporation
959 Eighth Avenue
New York, New York 10019

First Avon Printing, June, 1978

AVON TRADEMARK REG. U.S. PAT. OFF. AND IN
OTHER COUNTRIES, MARCA REGISTRADA,
HECHO EN U.S.A.

Printed in the U.S.A.

For my father, Rocco LaGuardia

A NOTE TO THE READER

This first biography of Montgomery Clift could not have been written without the elaborate co-operation of many people, who granted, in all, hundreds of hours in interview time. They helped make Monty, both the man and artist, truly come alive. To each one of the individuals who contributed their knowledge and time, I offer my heartfelt thanks.

In particular, I wish to thank the following group of Monty Clift's confidants for giving me their priceless special understanding of the man, and thereby, "allowing" this book to be written: Marjorie Stengel (a big hug to her for putting up with my unending phone calls and visits), Kevin McCarthy, Mira Rostova, William LeMassena, Phyllis (Mrs. Theron) Bamberger, Fred Zinnemann, Doris Langley Moore, Wolfgang Reinhardt, Rex Kennamer, Jack Larson, Bill Gunn, Lehman Engel, Morgan James, Geraldine Kay, Nancy Walker, and Mr. and Mrs. Ray Buckingham.

The interview granted by Mrs. Ethel Clift, Montgomery Clift's mother, is deeply appreciated.

Much thanks also to: Dorothy Aldrin, Edward Anhalt, Robert Ardrey, Noah Beery, Jr., Charles Bonniwell, Freddie Bradlee, Vanessa Brown, Duke Callahan, Truman Capote, Ben Chapman, Janet Cohn, Jack Clareman, Robert Cromwell, Rosalie Crutchley, Desmond Davis, Olivia deHavilland, Doc Erickson, Clarence Eurist, Carlo Fiore, John Fiedler, Neil Fitzgerald, Joel Freeman, David Garfield, Richard Goldstone, T. Edward Hambleton, Howard Hawks, Frances Heflin, William Hornbeck, Norris Houghton, Lorenzo James, James Jones, Millard Kaufman, Stanley

vii

Kramer, Harding Lemay, Frank LaRue, Arthur Laurents, Dorothy Levi, Betty Levin, Barbara Long, Alfred Lunt, Mercedes McCambridge, Jim McCloud, Dr. George Gordon McHardy, Aline MacMahon, Arthur Miller, Ivan Moffat, Jarmila Novotna, Tom Palmer, Edward Parrone, Mary Patton, Donna Reed, Lee Remick, Dore Schary, Walter Shenson, Cornelia Otis Skinner, Ned Smith, Stewart Stern, George Stevens, Jr., Sherry Shourds, Sam Spiegel. John Springer, Maureen Stapleton, Shepperd Strudwick, Bob Surtees, George Tabori, Dan Taradash, Frank Taylor, Phyllis Thaxter, Robert Thom, William Tuttle, Lynn Ungefer, Edith Van Cleve. Peter Viertel, Salka Viertel, George Voskovec, Michael Wilding, Eddie Woehler. Jake Wright, Saul Wurtzel, William Wyler, and Susannah York.

Thanks to Michael Leech for assisting me with a portion of my London research.

I am also indebted to the people of the Theater Collection of the New York Public Library at Lincoln Center for allowing me to plow through the noteworthy Montgomery Clift collection there, and for making available to me numerous valuable photographs, seventeen of which are reproduced in this book. (Credit Astor, Lenox, and Tilden Foundations—Theater Collection, New York Public Library at Lincoln Center—for first photo insert: all photos appearing on first page; Vandamm photo, top of second page; all three Vandamm photos on third page; photo, with Mira Rostova and Augusta Dabney, top of sixth page; full-page photo of Monty on eighth page. Second insert: prank photo by Kevin McCarthy on first page; group photo with Libby Holman, bottom of fifth page; Vandamm photos of *The Sea Gull* on seventh page; *Raintree County* photo, bottom of eighth page. Third insert: Monty, Marlon Brando, and Dean Martin photo, top of first page; and photo of Monty and Judy Garland, third page.) Thanks to MGM, United Artists, Paramount, Twentieth-Century Fox, Warner Brothers, Columbia, and Universal-International. Thanks also to UPI and World Wide Photos, Cinemabilia Inc. and Movie Star News, Kevin McCarthy, Morgan James, Janet Cohn, Ray and Ann Buckingham, and Anthony Crickmay for supplying other valuable photographs.

With any celebrity, especially a romantic figure like Montgomery Clift, there will always be a number of individuals falsely claiming to have had relationships, even intimacies. There were a number of such people who approached me and managed, I hate to say, to take up my time with their fantasies. However, none of their lies or exaggerations became part of this book because I employed, with strict adherence, the multiple-source rule of journalism —"Get corroboration from more than one person." Stories, facts, and claims of relationships were always double- and triple-checked with the recollections of other people, and either accepted—or rejected—as though this volume were a kind of courtroom of truth. The reader is thereby assured of the veracity of the facts contained in this biography.

A side note here: Some names of living people were not used because of possible social embarrassment to them. "Rick," "Jean," and "Dino" are pseudonyms for Monty's male lovers.

Robert LaGuardia

Contents

Chapter One

Images

THE public remembers him as a splendid screen presence, glamorous and vulnerable. He floats by on that giant screen, the image of the intensity of youth, in its most beautiful guise. He was an overnight sensation. Men and women loved him for the promise offered by his unthreatening masculine grace and looks. Bobby-soxers screeched and pounded the floors when his magnificent, sensitive face loomed in darkened movie theaters. Fan clubs popped up all over the country. Hollywood moguls found themselves forced to accede to his demands, their rigid control over actors shattered. He was a total enigma: a polite, well-brought-up young man who achieved great power in Hollywood passively, without deviousness.

But for those people who saw Monty, the real Monty, close up—who lived with him and ached with him—the images are very different. Like a series of takes arriving at the editing laboratory, these memories of an older Monty flicker, out of sequence, with haunting power: Monty walking against the wintry Manhattan wind, his shoulder and hunched body leaning heavily against a black man, his male nurse. Collapsing over and over, in a state of drugged drunkenness, on the floor of a Fire Island summer house, as the homosexual boys and men, fatigued with picking him up, let him lie, and walk over him as if he were a piece of inanimate junk. Waking up in a semi-coma from drugs and liquor in a bedroom of his sepulchral townhouse on Sixty-first Street; being picked up bodily by his nurse and put under a cold shower, in order to face another dose of the life which drove him to this state. His hands and body

1

sometimes shake with tetany, because of a rare hormonal disease. His legs cannot hold him steadily—the drinking has brought on phlebitis. A thyroid condition has made him pop-eyed. Cataracts cause him to wear bottle-cap glasses. An automobile accident and too many pills have ruined his looks, made them scary, and a plastic surgeon with a criminal background begins to make them worse. He has been blackballed from the motion picture business. He sits in his bedroom, vacantly watching television, tears drenching his cheeks. He has destroyed his sexual life. He will not eat. He makes tearful, desperate calls, but his best friends have left him. He shoots Demerol into his arms to anesthetize himself to the pain of his existence. And he drinks . . . and he drinks.

At the age of forty-five, his heart stops.

The personal story, with its riveting horrors, seems locked in combat with his unique professional achievement. Montgomery Clift was, and still is, one of the more important influences on contemporary motion picture acting. Few of today's younger generation of moviegoers realize, when they sit back in awe at the intensity and truth of an Al Pacino or Robert DeNiro or Dustin Hoffman or Jack Nicholson, that these actors' roots can be traced back, in large part, to the strivings of Monty Clift. Many people, when confronted with these so-called "rebel" actors, tend to think "Method" or "Actors Studio," or credit an actor by the name of Marlon Brando with having started it all, but that is a misconception.

The facts speak for themselves. Monty had no predecessor for his screen presence. He did not use the Method, and it was Brando and James Dean and the rest who followed and often built upon Monty's achievement.

Many of his present-day disciples are aware of their debt to Montgomery Clift. "Tell me about him," ask Richard Harris and Warren Beatty whenever they run into someone who knew Monty well. James Dean, too, was aware of Monty's influence before he, ironically, became the legend that Monty should have become. If Monty had died right after making *From Here to Eternity* at the age of thirty-two, he would have become an even greater cult figure than Dean. But Monty lived thirteen years longer—"the slowest suicide in show business," as one of his teachers, Bobby Lewis, put it. For most of the public, the slow, painful process of self-destruction was a secret one. He appeared simply to have taken his money, at the height of his fame, and retired into obscurity. Few eyes saw the greatest drama of his life. The public hardly paid attention to his death.

The pages which follow recount the journey of an "intellectual" movie star into darkness. Some people, unfamiliar with the man or the evolution of his extraordinary psyche, would try to reduce his strange progress into clinical terms: Hebephrenic schizophrenia. Oedipal breakdown. Death wish. These are not necessarily incorrect terms; to the degree that they are helpful, they are used in his biography. It is only that, in the end, Montgomery Clift transcended *all* the labels with his overriding wholeness, his accomplishment, with the fascination he holds for us.

Here, then, is the mystery of the man; the immense and unforgettable presence—the passing images of a life that dazzles, horrifies and puzzles us in breathtaking simultaneity.

CHAPTER TWO

Mother and Son

NEAR the peak of his career, at the time when success began to turn to terror, Monty must have struggled to understand what was happening. It must have been a gnawing curiosity that took him back to the beginning, to the house at 2101 South 33rd Street in one of Omaha's most fashionable sections. The woman who came to the door and saw the haggard young stranger loitering in her garden certainly did not recognize the movie idol who made young girls' hearts flutter all over the country.

"Get out! Get out of the garden!" she shouted.

He could not bring himself to make the awkward declaration, "Please . . . I was born in this house. I'm Montgomery Clift." Too well-bred, too well-mannered, he simply hunched his shoulders and walked off to take the next plane out.

Throughout his life, Monty was never able to reminisce about Omaha or about the strangely nomadic childhood he led thereafter. The Clifts were an emotionally "chilly" family. Supersensitive Monty felt that coldness to his very bones. No damaged child ever knows the exact reasons for the parental neuroses which mar his formative years and Monty, too—brilliant and analytical as he became—could never say what went wrong with the Clifts. Only a dream-like chain of murky childhood events—painful, frozen, loveless—remained to haunt the adult gazing at the mysterious childhood house. By that time, Monty was on the verge of functional collapse.

William Brooks Clift—Bill to his friends—and his wife, Ethel, arrived in Omaha just before the start of that wild

4

decade F. Scott Fitzgerald called "the greatest, gaudiest spree in history." Everyone, in 1920, was making money, hoards of it. Gracious salesmen who called themselves "financiers" were the new post-war mode, with their pretentious wives, their lust for status, their manufacturing, stocks and bonds. The mingling of upper and lower classes caused great social strains: old-monied families tried to distinguish themselves from the newly monied; the newly monied busily aped the old line.

Bill Clift was one of those gracious, golden salesmen. He had been born in 1886 into a proud old Chattanooga, Tennessee, family of Scottish-English descent. They were Old Money; they lived in fine houses with Negro servants; their sons were distinguished doctors and lawyers—Bill's own father had been a judge. But then, shortly before Bill entered Cornell, the Chattanooga Clifts lost all of their wealth. Bill had to work his way through college by selling ads for the college newspaper—and quickly displayed that odd combination of genuine Southern gentility and a born salesman's get-up-and-go which was to characterize him for the rest of his life. At Cornell, he met Ethel Fogg Anderson, a girl from a fine Philadelphia family—old line, like Bill's—courted her and married her in 1914. She was Quaker and Bill, Presbyterian. When they married, it was Bill who converted.

They were both short, small-boned people—Bill was no taller than 5'8", a rather plain-looking man, distinguished only by the softness of his features. He was extraordinarily gentle and sincerely well-mannered, so even-tempered that it was hard to dislike him, or even get angry at him. Ethel, in contrast, was an extremely beautiful woman, with big eyes, a small, lovely nose, and a finely tooled mouth, but somewhat high-strung. Reared by conservative Quakers, she would never dream of emphasizing her attractiveness with other than the most simple, tasteful clothing and minimal makeup.

Bill had majored in mining engineering in college, and that, combined with his selling experience, catapulted him into the frenzied new investment branches of banking called trust companies. Mining firms were booming and the banks needed investment salesmen who understood them. Bill's break came in 1918 when the First National City Bank of New York sent him to open its first bond-affiliate trust company in Omaha. Bill quickly noticed that Omaha's

5

biggest local bank—the Omaha National—had no investment department and approached the president with the idea of starting one. The president bought the idea and Bill Clift, too; suddenly, Bill was the high-salaried vice-president of the Omaha National Trust Company.

While Bill was not good at organizing other salesmen, he was a phenomenal solo performer. His combined qualities of Southern charm, enthusiasm, and total know-how made the Omaha National formidable competition for the other trust companies, and by 1920 Bill had the wherewithal to move Ethel and one-year-old William Brooks, Jr., into a fine house in the most exclusive part of town. He was quickly becoming the ideal of the era: the self-made financier—but he was still far from well-heeled. Most of his salary went to keeping up the elegant home and the staff of servants his lifestyle required.

The year, 1920, was an incredible one. Not only did it mark the beginning of the most socially harried decade this country had ever witnessed, it also saw the beginnings of sensational new strivings in the arts. Fitzgerald's first novel, *This Side of Paradise,* became the first of many books about a class of people for whom wealth, or the need to ape it, would lead to tragedy. Eugene O'Neill's first important production, *The Emperor Jones,* marked the start of a theater that would rip open the age's social hypocrisy. Writers and artists, no longer able to bear their salesman fathers and smothering mothers, fled from the Midwest to Greenwich Village and the Left Bank. Hart Crane sold his first poem and began to cruise the waterfront around the Brooklyn Bridge. And, on October 17, riots broke out in Belfast, Londonderry, and Dublin; the Poillon sisters captured the man who had stolen $45,000 worth of diamonds from Enrico Caruso; and twins, Roberta and Edward Montgomery, were born to Ethel and Bill Clift. William Brooks, Jr., was now eighteen months old. Bill and Ethel had as many children as they wanted.

Jim McCloud, one of the bright young men Bill hired to work with him in the trust company, remembers dinners at the Clifts' as being extremely formal, with an elegance and style which Mr. McCloud feels reflected Ethel's tastes rather than Bill's: Bill was a much more casual, relaxed person who could have done without all the trimmings.

Mr. McCloud also remembers something much more ominous for the future of Montgomery Clift. "Mrs. Clift was a lovely lady but a nervous person who had a penchant for things happening to her. Once she claimed that the maid had set fire to a clothes closet and the house almost went up in flames. She was timorous about staying alone at night when Bill traveled, and, I think because she asked him to, he used to recruit young men from the office to stay with her overnight in his house while he was out of town. Mrs. Clift was afraid of everything. One night while I was staying over, I was awakened in the middle of the night by having a flashlight and a gun pointed at my face, and I saw that it was she. She said that she thought there was somebody in the house. I said: 'For God's sake, put the gun away and let's go see.' I think the truth of the matter is that she had a vivid imagination." These indications of instability were not to be the last.

Perhaps Ethel's extravagant fears abated, or, more likely, whatever was disturbing her intensified, for when the twins were hardly a year old, she left Omaha, and Bill, and began to take frequent extended trips with the three children. During a recent interview for this book, Ethel recalled the reasons for these trips as having to do with the extreme heat of the summertime in Omaha, but soon these excursions to the Berkshires, to Switzerland, to Great Barrington, Massachusetts, began to take place at all times of the year.

By 1925, Bill had left the Omaha National Trust Company and joined the New York Stock Exchange firm of Ames, Emmerich & Company, but the move did not prove much of a change for Ethel or the children. They were now with Bill only a few months out of the year, and the rest of the time, Ethel, little William, Roberta, "Monty" (as everyone now called Edward Montgomery) and the children's "wonderful, horse-faced" governess, Wilkie, lived abroad in rented houses. It was a peculiar family situation, even for a time when people made so much of traveling and living abroad.

Shortly after Bill moved to New York, he took time off from work to sail to Bermuda to rent a house for Ethel and the children. On the ship, he met Phyllis Bamberger, a lively young woman married to a press agent named Theron Bamberger. Bill liked them both immediately, but it was Phyllis's best friend, Maria, who made the greatest impact on him. Maria, about twenty-eight, was single, extravagantly beautiful, of Northern Italian descent, with jet-black hair and olive skin, and extremely bright and candid. She and

7

Bill—who, for all practical purposes, was "single," too—became instant good friends. In New York, during those long months when Bill's family was away, they spent most of their free time together. In fact, they would remain close until the day Bill died, some thirty-nine years later.

In those early years in New York, Bill had bachelor apartments in Greenwich Village, although most evenings would find him at Maria's place. It was really through her and the Bambergers that Bill began to acquire a taste for the theater. The Bambergers were professionally involved with actors, and Maria, a writer and editor, was au courant with big-city theatrical doings. Bill, despite his conservative roots, was delighted with all the theater talk, as well as with the novelty of his Greenwich Village life.

"Bill was quiet, gentle, very sweet, always soft-spoken," says Maria. "He couldn't handle temper. If I raised my voice with him he would put on his hat and coat and he'd be out the door. But the next night he would be back. I think one of the things I liked best about Bill was that he was unlike most of the men I had known in the city. He was a complete gentleman, every inch of him."

By this time, a pattern had been established. Bill would stay in New York, with Maria. Ethel and the children would travel. One cannot help but wonder why Ethel chose to keep herself and the children apart from Bill for so many years. Mrs. Clift parried the question this way: "My husband, Mr. Clift, was an investment banker and his work made it necessary for us to move around a lot. We lived all over—France, Germany, Switzerland. It was unusual for us to live in one place for longer than eight months. Bill had to travel because of his business. He of course couldn't take us for a week here and a week there, so he preferred that we stay in one place for long stretches."

Maria says this is nonsense, that Bill Clift hardly ever left New York City on business trips before the Depression. Something had obviously gone wrong in the marriage. Bill Clift was not the sort of man who would have been inclined to stray from the hearth under ordinary circumstances or, as was the case, have the hearth stray from him. Meanwhile, the separation must have had its effect on the children. Bill talked a lot about the children with Maria, but he seldom speculated on the probable damage that was being done to them, perhaps because he felt that in financ-

8

ing those elaborate trips, and in giving them private tutors and instructors of every sort, he was making up for their uprooting. He may have been too naive to realize that he was condoning, and, in part, creating, a situation which would cause tragedy in later years.

Monty was an incredibly sensitive child and, from all the evidence, he, of the three children, was the most deeply wounded by those early fatherless peregrinations. Shortly after Bill met Maria on that boat to Bermuda, Ethel, Wilkie, and the others moved into the house Bill had rented for them there. The children were reserved, but not unplayful. The twins were about five. One of the adults took movies of the children. Many years later Brooks (as William, Jr., later preferred to be called) showed them to his brother Monty. By then Monty had been alienated from most of the Clifts for almost a decade, and the course of his own self-destruction had entered a terminal stage. When he saw the eerie projected ghosts of those three children playing in the sun, looking like millions of other children, he became dry-mouthed and agitated, as he did whenever something disturbed him in the extreme. At other times, when his childhood was brought up, he might burst into tears, go into a stony, brooding silence, or simply pretend that he hadn't heard the allusion.

Monty hated to talk about what happened back then, undoubtedly because he never fully understood it himself. The closest he ever came to it was to say, in a mid-fifties interview, "Traveling is a hobgoblin existence for children. Why weren't roots established? My brother has been married three times now." Privately, Monty would lash out at his mother and attack her character to his friends—but this would not happen until he was a grown man.

Years later, Monty's friend and physician, Dr. Rex Kennamer, would say, "I'm sure it can all be traced back to the mother."

Yet Ethel, with Bill's money, made sure that Monty and his brother and sister received the kind of upbringing that only nobility could once afford. She dressed them in the best European clothing and gave them private lessons in riding, swimming, tennis, skiing, fencing, and music. Wilkie and various maids saw to their well-being. The few playmates they had were handpicked by Ethel from the "right" families. The effect on the Clift children was an imploded

9

one: they were more or less stuck with themselves and with their mother.

After the season in Bermuda, Ethel, the children, and the governess moved to St. Moritz, Switzerland, where they would spend the next several winters until the twins were about eight. There was a school nearby, but the children never went there because, as Mrs. Clift recalls, the Swiss children there were being taught in a dialect that her own children would not have understood. In any case, it was not a fashionable school. Ethel made an arrangement with the principal to tutor her children privately after school hours. The principal did not know English and so he taught them in German. "I'm not sure how good their German was at the time," says Mrs. Clift, laughing rather charmingly, "but whether they liked it or not they had to learn in German. And they always did their lessons well. We wanted them to have the atmosphere of a school, even though they were being tutored at home, so we rented desks from the St. Moritz school and put the desks in a special spot in the house which was to be thought of as *their* school."

Ethel would also emphasize books and reading, a sense of culture and the world of ideas. She would read works of literature aloud to them and, although some of the words and phrases must have been incomprehensible to them, the children would listen, captivated, whether they understood or not. Some of her methods were most startling and progressive. At the dinner table one night, when the twins were six, she read Lord Byron's *The Prisoner of Chillon* aloud. Monty responded to Ethel's dramatic reading and the torment of the prisoner by leaving the dinner table in tears.

As for Roberta, Monty's twin, the two of them were and would always remain close, even though their personalities showed signs of diverging sharply at an early age, and Roberta's conservatism deepened with the years: As an adult, she even changed her name to Ethel in honor of her mother! Monty and Roberta, though, would always somehow be complements of one another. Perhaps that sense of "incompleteness" that so many would see in Monty later on had its roots, at least in part, in this unique relationship with Roberta, his "other half."

Because of his over-sensitive nervous system, Monty was certainly the most prone toward physical ailments of the three children. His first encounter with doctors and the

10

world of medicine, which would obsess him in later years, came when he was nine years old. The family was on board a ship on its way to Europe once again. A boy held Monty's head under water in the ship's pool for so long that, in his desperate struggle to escape, a gland burst in Monty's neck and caused a severe infection. After Ethel and the children reached Germany, he was hospitalized for weeks with a cast around his head, so the infected gland could drain. The result was a long, ugly scar of three to four inches on the right side of his neck, where the jaw and neck muscles meet. Later, the scar would become the flaw in an almost perfect diamond—all the more revered because it would remind millions that Monty's glamour was indeed real and not the concoction of a makeup department.

By the end of the twenties, prolonged if illusory prosperity and the dream of the good life had brainwashed millions of Americans into spending too much money on material goods, and putting too much faith into mere pieces of paper with the words "stock" and "bond" written on them. In October 1929, lightning struck. Millions were wiped out in the stock market crash. Bill Clift and thousands of other Wall Street financiers saw their savings disappear in a matter of hours.

It was a tragic time, but Bill went on as best he could. Instead of recalling the family from Europe, he moved to Chicago to take a higher paying job with the Greenebaume Investment Company, and moved into a small bachelor apartment with a roommate. It wasn't enough, however. By 1933, Bill simply couldn't afford to keep Ethel and the children in fancy European houses any longer, and so he moved them to a less expensive house in Sarasota, Florida. The next few years were to be, comparatively speaking, the Clifts' roughest.

A great actor's first time in front of an audience is supposed to be a noteworthy event, and it would be nice if we could all be forewarned by regal thunderstorms or other natural phenomena. Invariably, however, biographers find those first steps on the stage to be horribly mundane and Monty's debut was no exception.

Monty first showed interest in acting at the age of eight. The Clifts had just moved from St. Moritz to Les Touches, France, and Monty developed an enthusiasm for pasting to-

11

gether crepe paper costumes and acting out stories, and for going to plays with his mother. By the time the family moved to Sarasota, thirteen-year-old Monty had decided to take the next step. He went to the head of an amateur theatrical company in Sarasota and asked if he needed a boy for one of his plays. There was nothing unusual about it; he had seen other boys, just like himself, on the stage and he figured he could do at least as well. What was unusual was that when, a few weeks later, the head of the summer theatrical company actually offered Monty a small non-paying role in a play called *As Husbands Go,* Ethel Clift permitted her son to take it. As she says, "I had, like the rest of my family, always thought actors superficial. In my family, we had doctors, lawyers, and other professionals, but *never* an actor. At first I tried to discourage my son from going on the stage." Apparently Ethel was swayed by her son's strong will, which would often match her own, and by the thought that having him take a part in a little amateur play was harmless enough. And perhaps she was already beginning to enjoy the thought of her son in the limelight.

It was Bill Clift who was, by far, the more skeptical about the idea of a career in the theater for their son, but Monty had adored being on the stage in Florida, and he kept talking about it with a serious little boy's earnestness. So when, the next summer, Ethel and the children moved to Sharon, Connecticut, a town neighboring Stockbridge, Massachusetts, Bill went scouting around for a play for Monty. Quite by chance, Theron Bamberger had that same summer left his press agentry business and started a theater in Stockbridge (later he also began the famous Bucks County Playhouse). His first play in his theater was a comedy by Dorothy Bennett and Irving White called *Fly Away Home,* and a fourteen-year-old boy had suddenly dropped out of the cast. Theron asked Bill to bring Monty for an audition. Monty was suddenly in his second play.

But this was not like *As Husbands Go. Fly Away Home* was a big-time show on a pre-Broadway tryout; its star and director was Thomas Mitchell; and Monty was cast in an important part as one of Mitchell's four mischievous children.

Phyllis Bamberger remembers Monty well in that play: "We had great pride in Monty," she says. "He gave Theron and me the impression that he was having a great deal

12

of fun being around all these theatrical people, and that he hadn't had much fun before. He was such a charming child and his performance *made* that play."

She also had the distinct impression that well-bred Monty wanted a stage career not so much out of a desire to exhibit himself in front of an audience, as so many child actors do, but in order to escape the strained hothouse atmosphere engendered by Mrs. Clift. Monty, with a charming blend of subdued cockiness and a love for exact description, would delight Phyllis and Theron with accounts of the places he had been to in Europe and America, but he talked about these places with no real sense of enjoyment or personal involvement. Phyllis felt that Monty was a bored little boy who was, quite intelligently, trying to vanquish his isolation with this colorful new theater adventure.

But the boy still had to deal with his mother's smothering ways. Monty was irritated. He wanted to be left alone with his new theater friends, to express himself freely—to have fun. Ethel wouldn't permit it. As Monty, in adulthood, complained to a friend, "She was always with me. She never wanted me to socialize with the other members of the company."

Geraldine Kay, who played one of the other children, remembers something similar. "Mrs. Clift was a small, slender, rather unobtrusive little lady. But you always knew she was there. You felt her presence and her influence on Monty, because when she was not there he seemed to blossom and be himself, and the moment she appeared he would withdraw."

What was it with Monty? He was obviously strong-willed, but around Ethel he would submit totally to *her* will. He was annoyed by her oppressive presence, yet never once did he ever show a sign of rebellion toward her—strange, in view of the fact that Monty was not a submissive boy. What is even stranger is that Monty was at an age when most children go through a kind of identity crisis, in which they often pout and complain about always being told what to do. Why wasn't Monty going through the same kind of overt adolescent rebellion? His obviously repressed resentment would bear violent fruit later on.

Fly Away Home was a light-hearted affair about a divorced couple—Thomas Mitchell and Ann Mason—and their four zany adolescent children—Monty, Joan Thompkins, Georgette McKee, and Lili Zehner—who conspire to

13

reunite them on the eve of their mother's wedding to another man. It opened on Broadway at the 48th Street Theater on January 15, 1935, to fine reviews and ran a healthy (for those days) six months. Brooks Atkinson in particular praised the way a comedically blustering Thomas Mitchell played off the compelling, believable adolescents.

All the children were quite talented, but it was fourteen-year-old Monty whom one especially noticed. He was *so* serious, anxious to learn, respectful of his elders, well-mannered, and, above all, involved. Often, instead of "wasting" time mingling with the children before curtain calls, he would sit quietly in his dressing room reading Shakespeare and other plays. He told Geraldine Kay how anxious he was to study acting formally, but she could see that even now he was *always* studying. "The remarkable thing about him was that he revered the people with whom he worked, who were older than he, and absorbed everything he could absorb. He watched Thomas Mitchell intently; it just all soaked in. We all loved Monty dearly, and everyone knew instinctively that this boy had a wonderful career ahead of him if he could just stay with it. His charms were obvious."

His sense of responsibility was also highly developed for a fourteen-year-old. Phyllis Bamberger remembers that, at the start of the rehearsal period in Stockbridge, Monty had, in his excitement, left his script behind in her home and showed up at the first day's rehearsal without it. None of the children were expected to know their lines yet, but Monty was so anxious that he had memorized every line and cue days ahead of time. He was too thoughtful, however—or too unwilling to appear different?—to show up the other actors by admitting that he already knew the script by heart, so he picked up some blank sheets of paper and pretended that he was reading his lines. Phyllis, meanwhile, had found Monty's script and rushed to the theater with it, only to find the little boy going through his noble pretense. She slipped him the script when no one was watching. She thought to herself that this, indeed, was no ordinary child actor.

Meanwhile, the range of his sensitivities was being extended and deepened. One night Helen Keller came to a performance of *Fly Away Home*. She sat in the fourth row, and well before the performance began she had been spotted and all the actors knew she was there. From the

14

stage, the actors, when they could, would steal glances at Helen Keller and her translator who was, with her hands, giving Miss Keller all the words. Later, the great lady came backstage to meet the cast. As she was introduced to each player, her hands gently felt the features of each face, and through her translator she would then tell the actor which character he played. When she came to Monty, she lingered a moment or two longer than with the others. As soon as her hand left his face, tears burst from his eyes and he could not stop them. With still wet cheeks, Monty later confided that it had been the most touching moment, literally, he had ever lived through.

For the first time since Monty had been a little over a year old, both Ethel and Bill were now settled permanently in the same apartment—a high-rise at 116 East 53rd Street. Unquestionably, it was Monty's career on Broadway that made Ethel decide to stay in New York with Bill. The traveling had ended. Most people who had any contact with the Clifts during this period had the impression that the family's efforts were now aimed primarily at cultivating this obvious talent within their brood.

Monty's career in the theater became Ethel's primary means of social expression and upward mobility. It was her one opportunity to display to others her "learned" refinements, to prove herself socially superior, despite her lack of ability, or interest, in making friends. Her control over Monty, whom everyone saw as genuinely charming, gained for her a certain respectability, a power. Everyone in the company used the expression, "Monty and his mother," whenever referring to Monty alone. (Question to company member Charles Brokaw: "Do you remember Montgomery Clift in *Jubilee?*" Mr. Brokaw's answer: "Oh yes, I remember Monty and his mother very well.") Monty, at this age, had no idea of the complexity of his mother's social and psychological involvement with him—nor of his own forced involvement with her.

Just before *Fly Away Home* began, Ethel made a fascinating move in another relationship, as well. She paid a call to Bill's friend, Maria, whom she had only met a few times, and asked: "Do you think it would be proper for me to let my son Monty go into the theater?" Ethel had developed a unique speech pattern; she used softly elongated vowels which seemed deliberate and affected, and, Maria recalls, "She spoke to me as if butter wouldn't melt in her mouth. I already knew from Phyllis that she was pushing to get Monty into the theater . . . and Bill certainly wasn't keen on the idea. I said, 'I don't think I could advise you on that.' I knew she had already made up her mind." Why did Ethel come to Maria? Was it her own way of putting a subtle, ironic pressure on the two of them?

Bill was still seeing Maria, but more discreetly. He would come over to her apartment after work. While he was there peculiar things would often happen. Maria remembers, "Suddenly the fire department would show up saying, 'Where's the fire?' Someone had called them to report a fire in my apartment, *always* when Bill was there with me. Now Bill never answered the phone, so I don't know how anyone could have known he was with me, unless we were being watched. Bill and I didn't know for sure, but we suspected who was responsible."

At this time, Ethel began to invite various actors with whom Monty became friendly to have tea with them at the apartment. Occasionally Monty would initiate the invitations because he knew his mother liked to meet his theater friends. Geraldine Kay came to the apartment a few times, and became convinced this was not the happiest of situations. "I was a child of the professional theater myself, but I had a great deal of freedom and love and encouragement from my parents—not push. I felt that Monty was being pushed into something, and that he felt it without realizing what it was. Not that he didn't love acting, but he wasn't free to pursue it in his own orbit. I never sensed a warm or close relationship between Monty and his mother, but then perhaps the three children were too well-mannered to show this directly. It seemed to me that Mrs. Clift dominated the household and around her there would be no exhibitions of any kind."

Once Geraldine's parents gave a birthday party for her and invited the entire cast of *Fly Away Home*. The late drama critic George Jean Nathan, an eccentric, showed up in an elaborate disguise, using an assumed name, but everyone recognized him immediately. He became the center of attention. The ambience was jolly. Ethel wasn't there, and Monty suddenly seemed just a young boy, fourteen, having a good time. Nathan, however, watched him and must have seen something in the boy beyond the laughter. Some of the cast began fooling around at the piano, but Nathan, who

16

was an accomplished musician, soon upstaged the lesser pianists in the room by challenging everyone to a little game. He would play a piece of music, usually some well-known excerpt from the classical repertoire, and then tell which member of the cast the music represented. Geraldine got some bright, bouncy piece. Then Nathan played a slow, somber Grieg selection, and said: "That is Montgomery Clift, the oldest person in this room."

One episode during the *Fly Away Home* period may have had distressing significance for Monty.

He was, by this time, the handsomest of the three Clift children by far. He had dark brown hair, a slender, wiry physique; his face was a boy's version of his mother's stunning face, every feature finely detailed. While the play was still in rehearsal in Stockbridge, two English actors who were not in the play but somehow connected with the theater began to hang around Monty constantly. "These two were homosexuals," says Mrs. Bamberger, "a fact which was pretty obvious to me but not to the Clifts. They were in their thirties, attractive, and they would wait for Monty at the theater a lot. I told Bill Clift about the two men. I told him that he ought to be worried about these two actors' relationship with Monty because they were old enough to be his parents and were obvious. Mr. Clift couldn't believe that legitimate men could work on a child. He was naive and too trusting." Bill did not take any action and there is no real evidence, aside from Mrs. Bamberger's fears, that a seduction took place. Yet the matter disturbed her and stuck in her mind.

The Clifts' living conditions at this time were comfortable. Their apartment was spacious. Each of the children had his own room. Ethel installed wall-to-wall bookshelves, which quickly filled with books and classical records. There was a sense of decorum and intelligence about the routine of family life—a routine which was allowed to be interrupted only by the important events of Montgomery's career. Significant issues were discussed at the dinner table and the children freely joined in.

Bill knew that his children had been given—and were still being given—the best of everything. He was concerned that all that European education would make them snobs and braggarts. "My husband always said to them, 'Don't go bragging about what you know. Remember, the fellow you brag to might not know the thing you know, but he might know something else that you don't.' That was something we both felt," says Mrs. Clift. "That it was wrong to brag or be showy about yourself, and I dare say that the children have always lived up to what we felt." It is true that Monty never bragged, or discussed his education with his young peers, or even revealed the fact that he spoke fluent French, German, and Italian. He had totally absorbed the family code of behavior. It is also true that Monty was taught to become secretive about the Clifts' domestic problems. He would never discuss them with anyone in the following years, even when he cursed his parents as if they were demons. Monty, of course, knew about Bill and Maria. The two of them spent time with the children in her family's country house and it is likely the children guessed that Bill's attachment to her was stronger than just friendship—and in later years, Bill would show up with Maria, not Ethel, at Monty's plays.

Young Monty also had a sense of precision born of thoroughness. If he decided to read one Shakespearean play, he would have to read them all; when he became interested in Proust, he read every word of the enormous *Remembrance of Things Past.* A few years before, he attended the Dalton School for a season—a progressive school where the students worked at home with the books that were assigned as the year's curriculum. Monty read them all before school started and then went on to read and study as his fancy led him. Photography became a passion. He would take pictures with his Leica wherever he could. He built a darkroom in the apartment, developed his own film, made his own enlargements, and then used the family bathtub to wash them. Occasionally, some of the Clifts would have to wait an hour or so before they could bathe.

Word got around fast about especially bright child actors, and a few months after *Fly Away Home* closed, Monty was cast without benefit of agent in the Cole Porter-Moss Hart musical-comedy satire of English court life, *Jubilee.* The show tried out in Boston to mixed reviews before it opened on Broadway on October 12, 1935, just before Monty's fifteenth birthday. It starred Melville Cooper and Mary Boland as the king and queen, and June Knight, who danced the famous "Begin the Beguine."

The show had two fifteen-year-olds, who were type-cast as the sweet, well-mannered nonesuch, Prince Peter, and the ruffian Prince Rudolph. Monty, of course, played Prince Peter, and a toughy by the name of Jackie Kelk, who later became a movie actor, played the antagonist, Rudolph. They were put in the same dressing room, and soon were at odds off—as well as on—stage. Both boys, remembers E. John Kennedy, the stage manager, were images of their mothers. Monty would speak in an obviously educated way, always going out of his way to follow the polite amenities, saying "Please," "Yes, sir," "Thank you, sir." Jackie Kelk, on the other hand, was the hail-fellow-well-met type; you always knew when he was around. Similarly, Mrs. Kelk was the more obvious stage mother, pushy with Jackie and others and forever in view, while Mrs. Clift always stayed out of the way—although her presence was very much felt.

The show closed after five months. About this time, Ethel became concerned that Monty did not have any particular best friend. He was not, at the age of fifteen, permitted to run around the city at will; therefore he had only casual peer-acquaintances from his various shows. Now that the Clifts were settled permanently in New York City, it seemed the right time to make a friend for Monty. In the summer of 1936, she took him to Rhode Island to meet the Smith family, and especially Ned Smith, the fifteen-year-old son. The Smiths were conservative Quakers, like her own family, and she had met them several years before in Philadelphia. "Mrs. Clift practically chose me as Monty's best friend," Ned Smith says. "She liked the idea that I was as well-read as he was, and she did her best to encourage our relationship"—a relationship which lasted for twelve years.

Ned today is a chemical engineer and has no connection with the theater—in fact, he blames what happened to Monty both on Monty's upbringing and on the sinister, destructive world of the theater and cinema. His recollections of Monty, especially between the ages of fifteen and eighteen, are vivid and extremely personal.

"I always saw two sides of Monty—the side that was over-sensitive and made him want to sit around and read books and go into the theater and act, and the side that was manly and active. For years I tried to bring out the manliness in Monty. I'd take him on camping trips, and long

19

hikes, and we'd go boating and live out in the woods for days. In the end it didn't work. The other side of him won out and helped to destroy him.

"I'd meet Monty's theater friends sometimes, but he usually saw me apart from them. He could only relate to an individual; he really had no circle of friends, just friends in corners. He was so childlike in the way he related. He would sit across from me, and watch me like an amazed child. He'd absorb everything I did, every facial expression I made, every word I said. Monty never grew out of that; he never learned to see people in an adult way. Maybe that's why he was never able to mix his friends and gain a good perspective on himself versus all the people around him. He was too absorbed in a child's world of sensations.

"Monty's upbringing was totally abnormal because of his mother's dominance in forcing him into the theater. Mrs. Clift—wonderful, brilliant person that she is—is a central figure in the tragedy of Monty's life. Monty influenced me in many, many ways. Yet I'm never sure whether the influence on me was from his mother or him, because his mother told him what to do. He was never able to be a person on his own, and when he tried, he lost.

"Monty had been brought up in a secluded way by Mrs. Clift. Most boys at the age of sixteen or seventeen were laying girls, but not Monty—he was reading books. Of course Monty would have sexual problems later on; he wasn't brought up to be normal."

Ned took Monty fishing and sailing; he brought Monty into a world of sports and traditional "masculine" pursuits and expectations that provided relief from the world of theatrical make-believe—and may inadvertently have also helped set the stage for Monty's later sexual conflict. Monty brought Ned an array of sensitive qualities and a world of glamour, which partly disturbed and partly interested him.

"As time went on I felt offended by the way he was living —I had inherited very strict standards of conduct, very much the same ones he had, although at the time I wasn't always sure he still had them. Looking back, I realize that he always did. I think his standards—our standards— caused him great pain when he had to join all the phoniness around him . . . He began to speak in this whispery, pansy voice and I hated it. I hated all the pansies that went along with being in the theater. Through Monty, I was involved with it and I always felt out of place."

After *Jubilee* closed, Monty did not work on Broadway for a year and a half, which must have pleased his father, who always half hoped that Monty would follow in his footsteps and become a banker or a lawyer. Bill would constantly warn his son that most actors wound up penniless and without the respect of the world. Still, he was rather fond of Montgomery's stubbornness. He would give Maria running reports of Monty's new plays. At least Bill had an open mind. Neither the Chattanooga Clifts nor the Philadelphia Foggs would deign to come to New York to see the awful sight of a young member of the family on the stage. Ethel found herself constantly explaining to her side *what*, in heaven's name, she thought she was doing with her son. "Whenever they would say anything," says Ethel, "I would tell them that it was a good profession and that my son was dedicated to it. I think the trouble was that they did not think much of any of the actors that they saw in the movies and so they just assumed they were all bad."

Right after his seventeenth birthday, Monty went into a new play. He had already appeared with Thomas Mitchell and Mary Boland; now he was fortunate enough to be cast with Fredric March, his wife, Florence Eldridge, and Dame May Whitty. The play was a modern take-off on an 18th century comedy of manners, *Yr. Obedient Husband*, and was March's baby. He financed it, produced it, and, of course, starred in it with his wife.

Ethel went with Monty on the long pre-Broadway tour of the Midwest. Fifteen-year-old actors were normally expected to have their mothers around, but not seventeen-year-old ones. With Ethel occupying adjoining hotel rooms, Monty was never able to sow wild oats with cronies or girls, or do any of the things that seventeen-year-olds have always needed to do. The prince, at seventeen, was still being chaperoned.

In Cincinnati, Monty came down with the flu. Running a fever of 103 degrees, on the verge of pneumonia, he remained determined to go on stage that night. He had no understudy; he might be the cause of shutting the play down! This was in the final cold days of November 1937. When Ethel finally got a doctor to order him to bed, the boy was heartbroken. When the Marches heard, a few hours before curtain time, that Monty was sick, they along with the director John Cromwell, and his actress wife Kay Johnson, went into shock. After a few minutes of despair,

Florence Eldridge turned to Kay Johnson and said: "Here is our Lord Finch! You can do it, Kay, I know you can." "But it's a boy's part," Miss Johnson protested. Florence went on blithely about how boys used to play women's parts in Shakespeare's day, and why the hell not the reverse. Kay was talked into it, learned Monty's part in a few hours, and, when she made her entrance at the beginning of the second act, the already-alerted audience applauded up a storm, and then gave her a bigger hand at the final curtain for her courage. The story ran in all the Cincinnati papers, and a few New York papers even picked it up. Monty saved all the clippings about the transsexual event, and neatly filled up many pages of his official scrapbook with them.

The show opened at the Broadhurst on Broadway in January of 1938, got loathsome notices, and eight days later closed. To mark the occasion, Fredric March contritely took out a full-page ad in one of the trade papers that contained only the words "Oops! Sorry!"

Monty was not long out of a job, however. That summer he undertook his first starring role, in a delicate French comedy entitled *Dame Nature*. The impression he made was so good it opened door after door for him in the next few years.

For the first time in his acting career, Monty's role in *Dame Nature* confronted him with technical difficulties. Up until then, he had gotten by simply by playing himself. It was so easy, in fact, that he had never felt the least sting of stage fright. It was even a mystery to Mrs. Clift, who was amazed that Monty could calmly walk onto an opening night stage as if it were his own living room, while some of the adult actors around him suffered nausea and cramps. Ethel used to try to fathom her son's incredible equanimity. "Aren't you nervous onstage?" Ethel would ask him. He would answer very honestly and simply, "No."

In *Dame Nature,* however, he was not so secure. For the first time he had to create a character. The play (by André Birabeau, freely translated from the French by Patricia Collinge) told the story of a sixteen-year-old boy and a fifteen-year-old girl, both from nice families, who suddenly discover they have made a baby after doing "something" one night, before they fell asleep—"something" that the boy has forgotten. It was a fantastic premise, and rather silly, but it was vital that the audience accept it. With director

22

Worthington Miner's help, Monty achieved a difficult dramatic feat. He was actually able to convince the audience that he was innocent enough to have forgotten what he had done. Another actor telling an American audience about only remembering a "oneness" with the girl would have been thought ludicrous, but Monty's sincerity made the absurd idea somehow credible. Perhaps even more difficult for Monty was the fact that he had to handle outright comedy, and use the audience's laughter at his plight. This posed problems because, as Norris Houghton, the set designer, noted: "Monty had no inherent sense of humor." Monty also had to learn to change the audience's mood after a funny exchange by suddenly showing serious concern. In all, the part required complex and thoughtful acting, and it is interesting to see the result. *Dame Nature* opened at the Booth Theatre to tepid reviews, but Richard Watts commented: "As the boy, young Mr. Clift has an enormously difficult characterization to manage, and on the whole handles it excellently, although there are times when he makes the youthful father too neurotic for comfort." In his first test of independent skill, Monty was already displaying the stylistic tendencies which were to characterize his later work.

Some of the younger people in the cast found him remote and uncommunicative. His inherent politeness and aristocratic bearing had somehow developed into an intriguing put-down of people he did not know well or did not care to know better. He was too honest to pretend affection he didn't feel and too gentlemanly to offend with a cold snub, so he would simply act as nice and undemanding as he could with everyone—and quietly separate the gems from the nonentities. A true prince does not snub, he quietly selects. Freddy Bradlee, who was Monty's understudy and quite taken with the young gentleman's complete dedication to his craft, tried numerous times to get close to Monty and failed. "Monty had a fence around himself. He told you in certain ways, 'Just don't come too close to me.'" Actor Fitzroy Davis had the same experience. He once went backstage to speak with members of the cast. "Monty was just coming off the stage and I was bubbling with enthusiasm about him. I remember quite well that during our talk he was offended that I did not know that he had been in other Broadway shows before this, and rather cut me down by telling me what they were." The problem was less Monty's

23

offense at Mr. Davis' ignorance than his instant recoil at Mr. Davis' strong approach. One could not gain this prince's trust by simply asking for it. You had to be chosen.

And at last he did choose one boy in the company to be his friend: Morgan James, a nineteen-year-old. When he did so, it was no minor episode; Monty befriended with a passion. As Morgan says, "When Monty liked someone, he *liked* that person, and he made sure that person knew it." Morgan was fun to be around, a warm, outgoing young man who, like Monty, was sensitive, but who had one thing that Monty didn't have—a good sense of humor. Monty obviously worshipped that part of Morgan's personality. He himself was so serious that he hadn't the vaguest idea of how to handle a joke when it was told to him. He would always laugh much louder and longer than the joke warranted, as if he were trying to persuade himself and others: "Yes! I get it!"

Morgan quickly became one of the charmed circle invited to have dinner with the Clifts. His impression of Mrs. Clift was vivid: "I first saw her as vivacious and almost false, almost like a Billie Burke type. Later she revealed more of herself and I could see there was more to her than just a pretentiously ingratiating Southern lady." Leaving poor first impressions with Monty's friends and acquaintances seemed to be something Ethel did a lot. Freddy Bradlee says: "I remember her as r*aaaa*ther precious and r*aaaa*ther slightly phony when I saw her backstage. I remember the stage doorman didn't know who she was and wouldn't let her in, and she said, 'Oh, but you don't understaaaand. I am M*iii*sus Cl*iii*ft . . .' Very sort of *aaa*tificial. I said to myself, 'Honey, where did you ever learn *that* accent?' "

Her relationship to Monty continued to be complex. For instance, there is no easy answer to why Monty did not—or was not *permitted* to—date girls by the age of eighteen. "I understood that whenever he brought a girl home there was always some sort of problem," Morgan recalls. "The girl had to go through some sort of screening. Mrs. Clift would question the girl. But she did that out of her understanding that Monty was going to be somebody and that he shouldn't make up his mind or do anything that would cause him to be taken in by a nobody. Mrs. Clift was domineering, but I don't thing she was destructively domineering. She was like a manager who tells the artist, 'I

24

don't want you to go out drinking, I don't want you to go out using your energies with these women until four in the morning.' But Monty was dying to stay out all night with girls."

Monty was sensationally impressed with Morgan's head start in doing all those mad, wild things that he ached to do, if he only could. Morgan, from a fine family himself, would never brag about laying girls; nevertheless, Monty began to relish the picture he received of Morgan's accomplishments.

Some of these accomplishments were professional. Monty was *deeply* impressed by the story Morgan told him about how he had once portrayed a rough sailor type who had been out on an all-night binge for an acting class. Morgan told how he had deliberately stayed out all night, wandering around the docks like his sailor character, and then come to rehearsal, still unshaven the next morning, to play the role.

Monty was infatuated with the whole idea of what Morgan had done. Instantly he said: "Oh, I'm going to do the same thing!" Whenever something really impressed him, Monty would hurry to imitate it.

But it was mostly Morgan's social accomplishments that Monty envied. Morgan let little things slip out about girls and parties he had been to, and Monty used to tell him, as if his whole body and soul were chiming in, that Morgan was more of a man of the world than he was. "You are such a bon vivant," Monty would say. But it wasn't all ingenuousness on his part. Morgan had once said that he knew how to get to Newark, New Jersey, and the burlesque houses there ("You know how to get to *New Jersey!*" exclaimed Monty), and he was buttering Morgan up with the "bon vivant" stuff so that Morgan would take him there. There were no such dens of iniquity in New York, not since Mayor LaGuardia had decided that burlesque shows were breaking up too many families and closed down every one of them.

Monty wanted to see naked girls, and Morgan took him by train all the way to Newark to see them. Morgan would say, "Let's sit in the back." But Monty would demand: "No! We've got to sit in the first row! I want to see everything!" Then he would watch legs, thighs, and big bosoms, the bumping and grinding, like a starved young hawk watches prey.

It developed into a little routine. Whenever Monty had a hankering to see female flesh, he would start by saying what a "man of the world" Morgan was and the next thing Morgan knew, they were on their way to Newark. Had Mrs. Clift known that her prince was being led astray, she would have put her foot down. But she approved of Morgan—he had nice manners, his father was a New York doctor—and whenever Monty went out with Morgan there were no questions asked.

That year with Morgan changed Monty enormously. His horizons expanded. Somehow he came closer to understanding that art was his life, and life his art. Somehow now, for the cause of both, he was willing to take risks. Perhaps it was all those stories Morgan told him about the incredible things he did to prepare for roles . . . perhaps it was sitting in the front row of burlesque houses, or meeting aggressive girls like Diana Barrymore who smoked and drank, or everything all together, that gave Monty the sudden impulse to live and behave as if everything were a preparation for a role. He began going up to total strangers and talking with them. Ned Smith would watch him approach drunks in bars and down-and-out characters in railway stations. They would all amaze Monty. He would come back to Ned and mimic them with devastating accuracy.

The best agents in town were now competing wildly for Monty. Just to be glanced at by agent Maynard Morris was, to the young actor of the day, like being touched by the Pope, and here was Maynard Morris waiting patiently for Monty backstage on many nights, along with another top agent, William Levine. Monty was becoming quite a prize. Maynard Morris wound up handling Monty, though not exclusively.

All this time, Monty still lived in the Clift apartment. He certainly didn't have to. He was making good money on Broadway and could have left his parents and his mother's strictures anytime he wished. But he still needed her, for a role model, for her dominating support. So there he stayed.

Lehman Engel, another friend of Monty's, sheds more light on the relationship. Engel was fast gaining a reputation as a talented musical conductor when he first met Monty, and happened to make a reference to a lecture he was scheduled to give at a Stamford, Connecticut, YMCA. Two weeks later, Engel walked out onto the Stamford platform and there in the very first row was Montgomery Clift. Lehman was surprised; he and the young man hadn't exchanged a word since that first meeting in New York. Later, Monty deliberately waited until everyone had left before quietly approaching Engel and asking, "How are you going back to New York?" "By train," Lehman said. "Then," said Monty, "would you mind if I rode back with you?"

Of course Lehman Engel did not mind at all. One cannot help but notice how calculatingly Monty had planned the situation. He had known for weeks how he was going to flatter the twenty-eight-year-old musician by making a pain-staking two-hour trip to attend a relatively unimportant talk. It was Ethel all over again, making a special trip with Monty up to Rhode Island just to betroth him to a friend.

Practically the first thing Monty did was to introduce him to his mother and father. It was as if Ethel and Bill came packaged with Monty as a single social entity. By now there was every indication that Ethel had become Monty's "other self," his alter ego. In order to truly make a friend, Monty was compelled to have the new friend become involved with those "other parts" of his personality —his coterminous existence with Ethel.

Another time, Monty and his mother planned a special trip to Philadelphia for days and sprang it on Engel only hours before the departure. Monty was just like a little child going to the circus. It was an extravagant expedition involving theater tickets, museum visits and a suite at the most expensive hotel in Philadelphia, and Ethel had organized it all for Monty and Lehman Engel. Monty just thought she was being very kind and generous, but, at twenty-eight, Lehman could sense a disturbing reality that Monty, at eighteen, could not. "Mrs. Clift thought that my relationship with Monty was the greatest thing in the world, and I think I know the reason for that. He would occasionally date Fortune Ryan, one of the big Ryan million-aires, and she was wild. He would see Diana Barrymore, who was already a big lush. Mrs. Clift would make catty remarks about them, and I think she felt that he was safe when he was with me because then he wasn't about to run off and get married to one of those girls. Mrs. Clift was Monty's girlfriend, his mother, his everything. She would skip down the street with Monty. She never had this kind of relationship with her daughter or with her other son.

They would skip down the street because that's the way Monty was, and the way *he* was, she was; she followed him. Monty was on top of the world in those days. He didn't know what sadness was."

Nevertheless, the first signs of ambivalence toward his mother began to appear. As Lehman notes: "There was something very strange about Mrs. Clift which Monty and I often discussed. Apparently, she didn't have a bank account. Instead, she walked around with her handbag filled with rolls of hundred dollar bills, and paid the light and telephone bills by hand. I knew that his father wasn't successful and that Mrs. Clift wasn't wealthy, but neither Monty nor I could figure out where she got all this money. Monty had been taking piano lessons and Ethel asked me, 'What kind of piano do you think Monty should have?' I told her that it depended, but that the best pianos were made by Steinway. And she went out and bought a Steinway grand, the most expensive. She went to Jensen's and bought a set of silver flatware to put on the table—it cost a fortune. It was very mysterious, where she could have gotten this money. Once upon a time she told me—with Monty there—that she frequently went up to Boston, because there was a very kind man there who owned a large factory or mill of some sort, and she was ghosting his biography. Now, anyone who's talked with Mrs. Clift knows that she doesn't use the King's English; she doesn't know a verb from a pronoun. She couldn't write an English sentence. Both Monty and I wondered if there wasn't something between them."

Monty never brought up the subject of Ethel and those rolls of hundred dollar bills or the "biography" she claimed to be writing. It was Lehman who always made the initial observations. But Monty would shrug his shoulders and look just as amazed as Lehman at the bizarre and almost unthinkable solutions to the mystery of Ethel. At those times he showed no animosity toward her, but he showed no inclination to defend her, either. In retrospect, Monty's diffident interest about his "other self" was a warning signal.

The transition Monty was now making from a quiet, charming, shy boy into a bubbling, enthusiastic, talkative soul—though only with certain select people, like Lehman or Morgan James, of course—occurred within a period of no more than a year. Lehman felt, however, that beneath that ebullient exterior there was a distressing sense of self-obliteration. He had no real ego to speak of. Monty was "high, high, high . . . having a wonderful time," but one couldn't be sure that Monty's inner self had anything to do with his outside behavior, that he had developed enough sense of self, at the age of eighteen, to match the demands made on him by his complex artistic life. He not only had to exhibit what appeared to be a "nautral" self onstage, he had to deal with a full complement of complicated older personalities, and absorb the compelling suggestions of the bookish intellectual ideas which occupied him now with more than average frequency.

That spring Monty appeared in a new play—Karel Capek's *The Mother,* starring the legendary, aging Nazimova. It was a decidedly inferior work, an allegory about a mother who has lost all but her youngest son—Monty —in senseless wars. The audience had to sit for two hours while flashbacks of the dead sons and husband haunt the stage, until a surge of patriotism overtakes Nazimova in the last scene and she hands Monty a gun.

The play opened on Broadway on April 25, 1939. Tom Palmer, one of the actors, remembers the curtain call: "The theater just went wild. There was the usual applause, and then people started coming down the aisles and banging on the footlights. I was green and I felt: 'My God! The play's a sensation!' But Nazimova was muttering as the curtain was going down: 'I do not like this . . . I do not like this.' And she was right, because instead of a straightforward ovation, it was hysteria—a cult audience. They were going wild over her, not the play, and she was aware of it." Indeed, Nazimova was more than right. The next morning the critics slaughtered the play, which closed four nights later.

Mr. Clift warned Monty again that perhaps he should reconsider his choice of a career. The warning had no effect.

That summer Monty became very ill. Lehman Engel, exhausted and in need of a rest, decided to go to Mexico, and booked the cheapest accommodation possible on an old tanker, the S.S. *Orizaba,* famous because seven years earlier Hart Crane had jumped from it to his drunken death on the way back from Vera Cruz.

Shortly before the *Orizaba* was to depart New York,

Mrs. Clift called Lehman. "Lehman, would you mind if Monty went along with you? Monty tells me you already have your ticket. Well, give him your ticket, and I will exchange it for one so the both of you will be in the same quarters—that is, if you're *sure* you don't mind. Of course Monty will pay his own way."

When they arrived at the ship, Lehman had a slight shock. Ethel Clift had booked them the *only* suite on the boat, with a private bath and a shower—luxuries Lehman didn't even enjoy in his own New York apartment. And there, piled in the suite, was a mind-boggling display of liquor, books, candies, flowers, cookies, and other expensive goodies. "They must have cost hundreds of dollars. I had a feeling that she had gone there at dawn to arrange the flowers and everything."

In Cuernavaca, Mexico, the two moved into a cottage in the back of the Hotel Marik. It was dreamlike. The cottage stood before a tropical orchid garden and a swimming pool. Two snow-covered volcanoes rose in view. No one was about.

Lehman was a good friend of the Garfields, Julie ("John") and his wife Robbie, who were then in nearby Mexico City to publicize his new film, *Juarez*. Lehman found out that Garfield was miserable in Mexico City—he could not breathe; he was sick with diarrhea; all he wanted to do was die or leave. Lehman persuaded the Garfields to visit the Marik and they were so enchanted they instantly moved in. Monty and John Garfield hit it off well. Garfield instantly liked this educated, pleasant boy who was so terribly willing to please, and Monty returned the feeling, though he was by no means impressed with him because he was a movie star. Monty had worked with many well-known actors by now and, more importantly, he did not look to the cinema for his models—an element of his training that would make his future screen impact so explosive.

After four days in Cuernavaca, the Garfields had to get back to Hollywood, and Monty and Lehman rode with them to Acapulco (which didn't really "exist" in those days), where they could get a ship back. The auto trip was a nightmare. For five hours, dust flew in their faces, the road jolted and bumped every bone; diarrhea kept them in cramps. The heat in Acapulco was unbearable. After the Garfields left, Monty and Lehman decided to return instantly to Cuernavaca, but not, for God's sake, by car again. They were told they could take a plane to Mexico City, but had no idea what "plane" really meant. It landed in the middle of a field, and to enter it a cow had to be pushed out of the way. The plane was small, "open," and unpressurized, with empty holes in the dashboard where there had once been a compass and other guiding instruments. The pilot flew out over the ocean to gain altitude and was completely lost when he came back over land. Monty remained absolutely silent, his face white as a sheet. At first Lehman thought it was simply fear—their lives were certainly in great danger—but it became clear that something in Monty's intestines was killing him. There was no toilet in that plane, of course, and without making a sound he sat there and suffered. Finally Lehman spotted Cuernavaca and pointed out Mexico City to the pilot. After they landed, Monty and Lehman drove to the Marik. Monty got sicker and sicker. Two days later he flew back to New York.

When Lehman himself came back to New York a week later, he found Monty still in agonizing pain. The diarrhea was so bad he could hardly walk, and it was finally diagnosed by a young doctor in New Orleans as amoebic dysentery. The doctor put Monty in a clinic, treated him with drugs and a special diet, and nearly had to operate, but the treatment finally took and in two weeks Monty was discharged.

The dysentery had taken its toll, however. His intestines had suffered severe damage and after returning to New York, Monty was stricken by acute colitis. It would come and go for the rest of his life, and few people realized that the reason Monty took to eating practically raw steak —and little else—was that it was one of the few foods that would not cramp him.

Another terrible disappointment awaited him. About the time of his nineteenth birthday, he was cast as the serio-comic Clarence Day, Jr., in the original *Life With Father,* which was to open in early November. Anyone on Broadway with a little savvy knew the comedy was going to be a smash. Monty prepared to have his hair curled and dyed red, and rehearsed in the play for weeks, when, suddenly, at ten o'clock at night, he received word that he was canned. No one told him why, so Monty assumed the worst: They hated his acting. In point of fact, authors Howard Lindsay and Russell Crouse had found that Monty wasn't ordinary enough for their character, that his manner was a little "special." It was quite a compliment, actually; they were saying that Monty could never be taken for a run-of-the-mill comic juvenile, but he never knew that, and he left the theater that night ready to head for the nearest gas pipe.

It turned out to be lucky, however. Had he not been fired from *Life With Father*, he would not, several months later, have been called to a room at the Theater Guild for a monumental first meeting with Alfred Lunt and Lynn Fontanne. They were casting Robert Sherwood's new play, *There Shall Be No Night;* it would turn out to be Alfred's greatest single acting achievement to date, and Monty's most important experience on the stage. Monty walked into the rehearsal room, Lunt took one long look at him, walked over to his wife and said, "That's the boy." Lynn Fontanne looked at the young man, then turned to her husband and said, "Yes, I guess that's the boy." It was as simple as that. Neither one of the Lunts had ever even heard of Montgomery Clift, let alone seem him perform, and Monty had not yet read for them. The "boy" they were referring to was the key part of Lunt's son, Erik Valkonen. They had Monty go through the motions of reading for them, but it was unnecessary—his eyes, his intensity, his appearance, were all as the Lunts had imagined "their son" to be. Two days later, Monty had the part of Erik.

There Shall Be No Night was hot off Sherwood's typewriter. Sherwood wrote the play in a heat of anger and passion directly after the Russian invasion of Finland in late 1939, and the Finnish patriots' valiant resistance. He argued for mankind's need to fight for its sanity, for the inherent dignity of all those who would take up arms against militant evil. The plot was simple. Lunt, a Nobel Prize-winning psychiatrist wed to an American played by Fontanne, is a pacifist who feels the world can only be saved by the defenses of the inner mind; he tries to dissuade his patriotic son, Monty, from rushing off to fight for Finland against the marauding Russians. Erik is killed, and soon Dr. Valkonen realizes that guns are necessary for the survival of the mind. He makes several eloquent speeches on the raison d'être of "righteous" warfare, and goes off to be killed himself, leaving his wife to face certain death in

32

defense of their home. It was exciting in its topical immediacy but, as a play, dramatically flawed by that unrelenting single theme.

When it opened at the Alvin Theatre on April 29, 1940, the New York critics unanimously agreed that Sherwood had written too hastily, but that Lunt saved him by giving an unparalleled performance filled with contagious conviction. *There Shall Be No Night* was noted as one of the season's most important productions and ran for two years.

Monty, by now, had played with some of the greatest, but never before had he worked so closely with an achiever like Alfred Lunt. Lunt and his wife were strict disciplinarians in all of their companies. Laughs Lunt today: "A friend once said, 'Once in our hands you're in the hands of the Gestapo,'"—and with him as both director and star of *There Shall Be No Night,* there was never a wasted or flippant moment during rehearsals. Monty was so impressed by this actor that he began to ape Lunt's mannerisms, Lunt's very style. Lunt had an intense, thoughtful, slightly hesitant manner of stage speech—some of his words would run quickly together in mid-sentence, while between others would be extraneous pauses. He acted with tactility, often choosing to run his finger along the cheek of an acting partner to emphasize the deep contact of his character with the other. Afred had quietness, emotional sureness, simplicity.

Suddenly, one was sure one saw a younger version of Lunt in Monty. He used Lunt's oddly syncopated, rhythmical readings, the somewhat higher than ordinary pitch of voice, the extra pause-beat during which he would look deeply into the eyes of another actor. Monty's was no mere imitation; it was a genuinely felt influence and, in effect, completely correct in *this* play because Monty was playing Lunt's son, and some sons *are* like their fathers.

During the run of *There Shall Be No Night,* Monty often went for weekend jaunts to Janet Cohn's house in Pound Ridge, Westchester, usually taking along his new friend, Billy LeMassena, a member of the company just out of college. Janet Cohn was a literary agent whom Monty had often bumped into in the theaters during the last few years, and her place in Pound Ridge was legendary. In the late thirties and forties it became a mecca for the playwright clients of her famous boss Harold Freeman, her own writer clients, and for various striking young talents about town. Janet's gentle manner and informality inspired friendships. Monty and Billy had only to jump into the Buick and tear up to Pound Ridge to find all sorts of combinations of New York's most provocative personalities, all like themselves having just dropped in on Janet.

Toward the end of the summer of 1940, Lunt and Fontanne started closing down the play for three-day weekends to give themselves a rest. Monty, in love with the atmosphere in Pound Ridge, rented a big converted barn just down the road from Janet's place. Monty and Billy instantly dubbed it "The Red Barn" and went up every weekend. But now Ethel, with her other two children away at Harvard and Bryn Mawr, began to feel somewhat deserted and started paying day- and weekend-long visits to Monty at his Pound Ridge hideaway.

For the first time, Monty's resentment of his mother's presence came out into the open. Everyone around Monty became painfully aware of the tension building up in him toward his mother's unwelcome visits. "When Mrs. Clift came up to see him," says Janet Cohn, "Monty just blew up. He would come over to my place to get away from her and growl about her being there. Ordinarily, Monty was very exuberant and expressive, but whenever his mother came up, he withdrew. He would try to get her to go back to the city, but I don't think she took his objections too seriously. When he would talk to her brusquely, she would just go on as if nothing had happened. She would fix things up around the barn for him, but the more she tried to have Monty depend on her, the more he would resent it. Once she came up from New York with a lot of expensive lilies, and planted them in his garden. As soon as she went back to New York, he tore up every single one of them and threw them in the lake. It just broke my heart."

Billy had a similar experience. Ethel showed up with a load of marigolds one day and instructed Billy on how to plant them. "But I didn't *want* to plant them," says Billy. "I didn't know anything about planting flowers, and I didn't like doing it, but she kept insisting. I dug and made all these mistakes and she told me that this was wrong and that was wrong . . . and finally I just started crying. Monty stood there watching the whole thing, just shaking his head, and I could see he felt sorry for me. He consoled me later and said, 'You just can't talk her out of anything.' "

Ethel made the grievous tactical error of not taking Monty's rebellion seriously. In her eyes, he still needed her now as much as he had during *Jubilee*. In reality, Monty did not need her then as much as she needed *him*. But he did need her now. The fact that he was still willing, as an adult, to remain so unnaturally a part of her domain proves that he had to cling to her. Ethel's mistake was in not giving her grown son more breathing space; as a result, she pushed the truth of their relationship into his face. The mistake would cause her boundless grief.

The problem for Monty now was that although he resisted his mother's strong ego, he had little else to take its place. His sense of self was so hazy and incomplete that one minute he would be full of great ambition, the next he couldn't care less what happened to him. He often talked to Janet Cohn as if he weren't serious about acting, as if he were doing it simply because of lack of anything better to do. "He gave me the impression," says Janet, "that he would have been just as happy being a bricklayer." It wasn't that Monty lacked dedication, but that the underlying personality structure for his dedication lacked reinforcement. As he approached twenty, the weakness of the personality foundation would occasionally appear obvious.

About that time Monty became friends with a young girl in the company named Phyllis Thaxter. She, too, was from a sophisticated family. Mrs. Clift was crazy about her—Phyllis was the kind of girl Ethel could see Monty marrying.

Phyllis would go out to The Red Barn with Monty and Billy, or sometimes just with Monty. Janet Cohn says, "We all liked Phyllis so much and hoped that something would happen between them. She was dark, quite attractive, short; she was crazy about him. I know that. Monty used to bring Phyllis over to my place, and once she told me she loved him, and that she would marry him in a minute if only he would have her. She told me that she was settling for friendship. I thought it was just too bad."

According to Billy, everyone in the company—men and women—was attracted to Monty. It was difficult around Monty to tell where "pure" love left off and sexual feelings began. Monty's boyish fire always seemed so asexual that the picture of him sleeping with anyone of either sex appeared crazily out of focus—at that time.

But appearances were deceiving. Billy, as Monty's closest confidant, already knew that nineteen-year-old Monty was primarily homosexual, and trying desperately not to let anyone suspect that he had had—and was now having—relationships with men. Conceivably, Monty had started with those two Englishmen in *Fly Away Home*. Unquestionably, Monty *was* interested in girls—his trips to the burlesque theater proved that—but he was a late bloomer heterosexually, and he could not, at nineteen, achieve bisexuality.

"Monty was secretive about it," Billy says, "but over the course of three years we bared our souls, and found out everything about each other. I know Monty was worried that anyone should find out, and he was extremely careful about his behavior. It was a hangup; but it's understandable—Monty wanted desperately to be a successful actor, and homosexuality could be dangerous for an actor's career. In those days, people pretended and hid it much more than today, even in the theater. I never felt that Monty was disturbed about the homosexuality itself. He wasn't happy about it, but I think it was just the fact of having to pretend, to make people think he was someone he wasn't, that bothered him. You see, Monty was an extremely moral person, and he had a great sense of ethics. He hated dishonesty of any kind. We would constantly get into discussions about how bad it was to lie—he thought lying was responsible for much of the corruption that was eating away the world. Monty did not believe in making compromises, the way most people do, and having to lie and compromise himself by pretending that he wasn't a homosexual deeply disturbed him. Later on, his distress over this problem grew."

Many years later, Monty got into a discussion about "love" with a young friend, Mary Louise Kitsen. He talked about Phyllis Thaxter as she was when he was nineteen; he described her appearance and personality in detail and made it clear that he had once cared for her very much. "Why didn't you do something about it?" asked Miss Kitsen. Monty simply answered: "It was impossible," and quickly changed the subject.

The touring company of *There Shall Be No Night* was, as Alfred Lunt notes, a "dream." The year-and-a-half tour, including innumerable one-night stands, was exhausting, but everyone liked each other enormously. Those two years had a deep influence on Monty. Although he was always somewhat remote, he was now able to make frequent forays out of himself. He often went out with a colorful character named Richard Whorf for beer-drinking sprees. Whorf had played Sly in the Lunts' production of *Taming of the Shrew*, and loved to do Sly's belch-on-cue for the amusement of cronies. It was a slightly absurd sight, seeing Monty come back from one of the beer sprees doing the belch-on-cue. Everyone knew immediately who had been "at" him.

Billy has films of the company fooling around in the snow, and occasionally shows them today whenever he is in a reminiscing mood. They are delightful. Monty, with a comic exuberance one never sees in any of his films, is seen dressed in an elegant brown suit and red sweater-vest. He slides down the side of a snow and ice-covered bridge; does some lovely ice skating; takes a snapshot of Phyllis Thaxter —all the time hoking it up, like an elegant young man in a Mack Sennett comedy, before the elegant young man gets a pie in the face. He is forever smiling, incredibly beautiful from all angles. His age seems to change from one moment to the next like a chameleon its colors. He looks extremely healthy. One film, taken in the summer, shows him taking off his shirt and sprawling on the grass, displaying a supple young torso. His chest hair has not all grown in yet, and his chest is spottily covered with light brown lion-fuzz. Watching these home movies, it is almost impossible to believe that this carefree young Apollo would soon be haunted by demons.

On the morning of December 7, 1941, kamikaze planes swooped down on Pearl Harbor, murdering and wounding four thousand unsuspecting American boys. The next day, Congress unanimously declared war on Japan. Bully Russia suddenly became an ally of the United States and, shortly before the end of the year, the U.S. government formally requested the closing of *There Shall Be No Night*. Alfred Lunt, part Finnish himself and totally involved with the play's message, was devastated. The last performance took place on December 18, 1941, in Rochester, Minnesota. The Lunts invited the whole cast to come to their home in Genesee Depot, Wisconsin, for a final party. They gave Monty a picture of themselves with this telling inscription: "From your *real* parents."

That winter, after a skiing trip with Billy, Monty's colitis grew worse. By the spring of 1942, his diarrhea had become unbearably painful, and he again went down to the clinic in New Orleans. Mrs. Clift asked Billy to accompany him. For nearly three weeks he visited Monty every day at the infirmary and cooked filet mignon for him on a hospital hot plate—the only food Monty was permitted to eat. Monty was treated with sulfa drugs. Finally, the colitis abated enough to permit Monty to return to New York and work.

Not long afterward, Billy was drafted, Ned was drafted; all of Monty's contemporaries left for the war. Monty felt left out and attempted to enlist in the ski troops, but his history of dysentery and colitis disqualified him. Instead of *being* a soldier, Monty played soldiers on Broadway all through the war years.

"We all went into the front lines and some of us got shot and killed," says Ned Smith. "Monty couldn't go into the war. Instead, he stayed in the theater. And he got shot and killed."

CHAPTER THREE

Changes

H E had a purity of spirit—an image of a Greek god.
He extracted certain ideas from Thornton Wilder,
Alfred Lunt, Alfredo Valente—all the extraordinary people with whom he came into contact—of *what is the perfect person.* He was the personification of the actor's art,
masculine beauty, photogenic personality."

This is how actor Kevin McCarthy described his new
friend, twenty-two-year-old Montgomery Clift. These emerging qualities quickly wrought sweeping changes in Monty's
professional life.

Following his tour with the Lunts, Monty succeeded in
one brilliant role after another. He became Broadway's
top "sensitive" leading man. Casting moguls from every
major studio in Hollywood rushed to offer him long-term
contracts. His hauntingly intense face and stage presence
became *de rigueur* study for every other young Broadway
actor.

Along with these "godlike" qualities, however, emerged
another personality—painfully artificial, acutely dangerous.
The changes swirling within Monty were complicated and
often not visible, but they burned him, they ate at him. In
the end, he was consumed.

During the war, actors and acting teachers became obsessed with a new movement in the theater, a kind of "new
macho." It was a brooding mood, a masculine self-consciousness, that began with the Group Theater and reached
its apotheosis with the sexually neurotic acting style of the
Actors Studio and the Method. Soon, it invaded Hollywood

and then the whole country with strange new masculine images.

They were images totally alien to Monty's sensitive personality, but ones he felt he *had* to adopt, had to emulate. They started a war in his weak and unresisting ego that was so destructive—and yet so surreptitious—that when the tensions in his psyche finally erupted, it came as a total surprise. Everyone wondered how this young man of such great talent and self-discipline could have exploded so, but much of the blame can be laid to this devouring obsession.

In search of the new macho, Monty discarded those qualities natural to him: his princehood, his upper-crust breeding, his good manners, his Brooks Brothers suits, whatever slim continuity of his own he had ever possessed. His vulnerable ego structure had always been bound up with his mother's; it was never whole or self-sufficient. It was therefore easy for him to play intellectual "switch" games with his very foundations without realizing what the perilous consequences could be. Everyone thought he was simply doing what actors always do—playing roles off-camera. How dead wrong they were.

In late 1942, Monty's close association, through Janet Cohn, with Thornton Wilder made him a natural choice for the part of Cain in Wilder's new play, *The Skin of Our Teeth*. However, when playwright Bob Ardrey suggested it to the play's director, Elia Kazan, Kazan said he didn't want to work with a homosexual. "Kazan didn't like homosexuals," says Bob Ardrey. "I explained to him that Monty wasn't, that he was simply a very nice, well-bred boy, and that didn't make him a fairy. I said, 'After you meet him you'll find out that this is a lot of nonsense; Monty is not queer.' At the time, this was one of those gossipy things. They said the same things about Orson Welles when he first began to gain a reputation. It was something that lesser actors said about other actors who were becoming successful. Also, the Group Theater probably thought Monty was a fairy."

The Group Theater: During the great political and intellectual unrest of the Depression, Clifford Odets and Lee Strasberg gathered around them a pack of passionate revolutionaries, intellectuals who demanded that American theater stop pretending and start reflecting the psychological desperation being felt by millions of Americans. These often brilliant but erratic playwrights, actors, directors, scenic designers, and acting teachers attacked capitalism and pummeled Broadway with ill-made plays, wrenching in their compelling anger. They condemned contemporary "technique" acting, advocated the ideas of Stanislavsky, and fought the boredom of poverty by engendering an atmosphere shot with sexual tensions. The product of their anger was a decidedly warped, super-masculine mood—the one image everyone recalls from the heyday of the Group Theater is Elia Kazan, steely and determined, at the end of Odets' *Waiting for Lefty,* shaking his fists violently at the audience, yelling, "Strike! Strike!" with the audience, performance after performance, shaking their fists back at him, answering, "Strike! Strike!" Because the Group's heterosexuality was so unnatural, members were terrified of homosexuals, who were considered subversives. The irony of it all was that several "screaming queens" worked at the center of the Group—but they were accepted because they were obvious and slightly absurd. The big threat lay in homosexuals who were not absurd.

The Group Theater was decimated when its major stars —John Garfield, Franchot Tone, and others—defected to Hollywood, but the Group's brilliant theatrical zeitgeist lingered on Broadway through such strong personalities as Elia Kazan, Bobby Lewis, Lee Strasberg, Cheryl Crawford, Sanford Meisner, and Stella Adler. Monty had already been somewhat influenced by them by the time of *The Skin of Our Teeth.* The Group and its Stanislavsky methods haunted all serious acting classes and discussions.

Bob Ardrey introduced Monty to Elia Kazan, who liked him after all and cast him as Cain. Kazan's presence, the way he always seemed to be searching for a structure for his scenes, his deceptively informal approach: All of this fascinated Monty. Kazan told the actors to come to rehearsals in dirty work clothes, a revolutionary idea. In the past, actors *never* stepped out of their apartments without being dressed to the nines. He worked on a deeply personal relationship with the cast; he felt a director could never be able to encourage real acting unless he got to understand the actor's problems and hangups. All of this was incredibly new to Monty, and impressed him deeply.

Kazan grew fond of Monty and wanted to help him with his career. There was much talk among serious young New York actors about whether or not one should defect to

Hollywood (assuming one were called, and most were not); all the big money was there. Kazan sensed that the West Coast would be after his young protégé fairly soon, and he warned Monty of the folly of signing film contracts just for the money.

Kazan affected Monty's personal life as much as his professional life. Kazan and Ardrey firmly believed that Monty was doing himself great harm by continuing to live at home with his mother. "We thought," says Ardrey, "that he should leave home because the image of the 'nice boy' turned off directors and producers in the theater. He was one of the most gentlemanly people ever—excessively so." The behavioral expectations of the Group Theater now reached out and touched Monty where he lived. In early 1943, Kazan drew Monty aside for a private discussion. It is doubtful he said anything as cruel as "You better leave home because half of Broadway already thinks you're a fairy," but Monty could not fail to understand Kazan's meaning.

Monty said very little during the conversation, except to agree. Almost immediately, he moved out of his parents' apartment. But Monty didn't move far. He took a little sublet walk-up above a laundromat at 127 East 55th Street, between Park and Lexington, about a minute's walk away. Ethel and Bill were dumbstruck. Why did he want to desert them? Monty did come home all the time for dinner, and would sometimes move back for a week or so when he got tired of taking care of himself, but his manner with the Clifts wasn't as before; the seed was planted, the blame already placed. After a week with Bill and Ethel, Monty would get thoroughly disgusted and run out on them. He began to use the term "my Goddamned mother" when speaking of the woman whose hospitality he continued to accept.

Just because he left his mother, however, doesn't mean he lost his need for a mother. Immediately after leaving home, Monty became thickly entangled in relationships with two older women, relationships that lasted the rest of his life. If he couldn't have Mrs. Clift, he would have substitutes for her.

Monty met both women at the same time in what we would today call an off-off-Broadway play, *Mexican Mural*. It was directed by Bobby Lewis as a kind of ultimate artistic conclusion to a series of acting classes.

Mira Rostova was actually only five years older than Monty. Quietly forceful, delicately attractive, she was born in Leningrad. The Bolsheviks considered her father, who owned coal mines and land, to be a subversive capitalist, and in 1933 he and his family fled to Germany. Mira studied acting and at an early age joined the Kammerspiele, a Hamburg repertory company, and went on to act in Berlin and Vienna, but in 1941, war again forced her to flee, this time to New York. Her own poor English plus the competitive nature of the New York theater discouraged her from a career as an actress in America, but acting was still in her blood. She took classes with Bobby Lewis and met Monty.

"Monty and I found that we had many things in common. Our minds were much alike. We had the same taste in literature and theater and films." Monty was attracted to her strength, to her convictions on all aspects of how an artist should live and work. Mira, on her part, saw a well-bred, aristocratic young man who was also, at the age of twenty-one, somehow old-fashioned, sometimes even corny. He saved all his Playbills. He carefully updated precious scrapbooks. He considered it important to go only to a certain Swedish tailor and to wear cashmere sweaters. Such things did not mean much to Mira, but Monty had an eager innocence which, on that beautiful face, somehow legitimized all the squareness and gave it charm.

Despite what people have thought, Mira says there was never any romance between them. She was aware of his homosexual orientation, but they were devoted to each other—and in the years to come she would be a major influence on his acting career.

Needless to say, the few times Mrs. Clift met Mira, she was not exactly overjoyed. Mira describes her reaction as "guarded."

The other older woman was Libby Holman. She had obviously been cast in *Mexican Mural* because of her value as a curiosity. A well-known torch singer and Broadway singing star of the late twenties, Libby Holman gained her greatest fame in 1932 as the center of a sensational murder case. Her husband of eight months, Zachary Smith Reynolds—twenty-year-old heir to a tobacco fortune worth thirty million dollars—had stood in front of her, put a loaded gun to his temple, and pulled the trigger. Under the urging of the Reynolds family, Libby was tried for murder with the state prosecutor trying to prove that Libby had had her eye on Zachary's money. The trial, however, uncovered the fact that Zachary, six years Libby's junior, had had strong suicidal tendencies, and was depressed because apparent homosexual tendencies had made him impotent with Libby. Lack of real evidence and the trial's upsetting revelations convinced the Reynolds to pressure the state into dropping its case. A few months later, Libby gave birth to a son, Christopher Smith Reynolds. The scandal not only ruined Libby's career, it made her a social pariah during the thirties. The $750,000 that she received from Zachary's estate, however, at least gave her financial independence. Her son was to inherit almost seven million dollars.

At the time Monty met Libby, she had just married actor Ralph Holmes—again, much younger than she and a depressive homosexual. It seems to have been a pattern: Libby Holman was attracted to young men whose homosexuality was bound up with weak ego structures. Her instincts were those of a domineering mother; for these tortured young men, close association with her was rather like a promise of new life, new sexual security, a return to the womb. After several years of marriage to Libby, Ralph Holmes, following a separation, went into a depression and took his own life with sleeping pills.

Before Ralph's suicide, she and Monty began seeing one another. No one could say for sure what really went on between them. After Ralph's death in 1945, their relationship became more open—although there would always be a slight mystery over what Monty and Libby "did" when they were alone. She, too, would be a dominant influence in his life in the years to come.

Mexican Mural made another contribution to Monty's life as well: It was there he met actors Kevin McCarthy and Augusta Dabney, a happily maried young couple whom Monty took to instantly. If Mira and Libby were to become mother substitutes, the McCarthys were to become "family" substitutes. *Mexican Mural* itself—a confusing, expressionistic series of contemporary Mexican vignettes loosely structured into one play—bombed. But for Monty, Mira, Libby, Kevin McCarthy and Augusta Dabney, that wretched, short-lived play had special significance. Kevin McCarthy says: "It's like one of those watershed things— you meet a lot of people at a certain moment and they stick with you for the rest of your life."

In this period of extreme change, each new friendship Monty made played a specific part in creating a new person. It was almost as if he had calculated which few individuals in the random environment he would need as either models or support. The McCarthys, churchmouse-poor, were breezy, natural, ordinary people who just happened to be actors. It was a little perplexing, at least to Kevin, why this splendid young man—undoubtedly headed for something great—chose the two of them as friends. Monty was constantly at their place. In a manner very unlike him, he would put his feet up on tables, lean against the refrigerator reciting poetry like a Bohemian, and wobble from room to room as if he had never in his life walked with poise. Sometimes Kevin could even sense Monty studying his ordinary American-ness; Kevin was brought up in Seattle, quite a distance from Les Touches and St. Moritz. Often Monty would slip into Kevin's mode of behavior, his playfulness, and his middle-American sound, and then mix them with the sophisticated, pause-filled Alfred Lunt image. Kevin and Augusta were much too natural to understand, while it was happening, that Monty was studying their spontaneity, their very love lives, with Stanislavskian calculation.

Kevin was straight as an arrow, very much in love with his wife and faithful to her. This was important behavior for Monty to soak up. It was 1943, and Monty still had had no significant heterosexual involvement. He had to gain his experience vicariously, and therefore involved himself with the McCarthys so completely that he was able to observe and feel everything else *but* the McCarthys making love. "When I was out of town Monty would date Augusta, and occasionally I felt jealousy. Augusta is a very circumspect and proper woman and I never imagined anything between them. It was just that Monty had a kind of proprietary way with her, as if he owned her." Once Monty, the McCarthys, and Morgan James were in a nightclub, when Kevin looked up and saw Monty dancing with his hands right on Augusta's derriere. He walked over to the dancing couple and addressed his friend quite coldly: "Get your hands off my wife's ass." Monty was just testing, though.

During the run of *The Skin of Our Teeth*, Janet Cohn would try to get Monty to go to Tallulah Bankhead's house, which, coincidentally enough, was also in Pound Ridge.

Monty had some rapport with her—he was one of the few people in the play she would still talk to—but basically he was frightened of Tallulah's lusty hormones. He had heard all the stories about how she turned her servants into alcoholics, swam naked in front of strange men, and had faggot "caddies" around to service her, and he violently disapproved. Tallulah thought of Monty as a nice, innocuous boy—which meant that she did not find him sexually interesting. Translated another way: Monty did not waste his valuable time charming Tallulah with his newly acquired "happy macho" image.

In May 1942, Monty was forced to drop out of *The Skin of Our Teeth*—his colitis had struck again, as severe as ever. For three weeks he was hospitalized in New Orleans with a condition so severe he might have died of dehydration; even so, he switched on his beguiling alter ego so totally that doctors, nurses, even fellow patients fell over themselves to wait on him hand and foot. Dr. George Gordon McHardy sighs wistfully at the mention of Monty's name and recalls vividly how Monty drew people to him. He and Dr. Donovan Browne used to take turns visiting Monty's bedside every day, and the doctor who got Monty was usually the happy one. Not only was he an extraordinarily good patient, but his playfulness had a way of making others forget the gloomy miseries of tropical diarrhea.

When Monty finally left the clinic, his weight was down, his constitution debilitated, and his spirits, like his intestines, weakened. He had no intention of returning to his parents' place or to his walk-up. Some people he had charmed silly had invited him to stay with them at their Napa Valley ranch in northern California; he wrote to them and flew out. There, he did the first real physical labor he had ever done in his life. His new friends taught him how to ride a horse, and soon he was "riding fence" —repairing fence breaks—and laying eight-inch pipe eight hours a day. In the rejuvenating California sun, his health revived. He returned to New York toward the end of that summer, infatuated with the idea of cowboys. He told his friends that when he made his first film—he was sure by now that he was going into the movies—it would have to be a cowboy flick. He loved the idea of leaping fences on horseback. It was a macho kick. He would not go to Hollywood to play any drooling, sensitive young man.

Right on cue, a film offer from Hollywood fell into his lap. No one can recall who first approached Monty with an offer to play the son in MGM's *Mrs. Miniver*, but undoubtedly the man waving the contract was Joe Pasternak, MGM's chief talent scout in New York in those days. There was no such thing then as a one-shot deal with newcomers. To play in *Mrs. Miniver*, Monty would have to sign away seven years of his life to one of the most ruthless film companies in Hollywood, and move permanently to California. Monty already knew what Kazan would think of it. He went to Lehman Engel for advice, and Lehman told him, "Monty, pay no attention to these offers. Don't do it yet, because you'll be miserable. They'll use you for whatever they want you for. You just wait . . . you'll be a very big success. Just wait until you've done a couple more things in the theater. They'll want you even more. And then you can demand everything—your choice of directors, co-stars, scripts." It was sound advice, and Monty took it. Through the forties, Monty would often turn to Lehman to ask if "now was the time."

An interesting and ominous note at this time was Monty's growing fascination with drugs. His dysentery and colitis could only be treated by diet, rest—and lots of drugs, including powerful opiate painkillers, like codeine. He became academically interested in the nature of drugs in general. Kevin used to go with him to Powders, a big drug store on Madison Avenue and 83rd Street, where Monty would go behind the counter and engage in serious analytic discussions with the pharmacist about the nature and effect of all the medicines he was taking. Monty began stocking up on cough syrups and mild mood elevators like Ritalin, and offering them gratis to friends who were down with something. Mira remembers being slightly amused at Monty's generosity with his drugs. Later, it would not be so amusing.

There were now two distinct Montys: the refined prince and the liberated prankster, an outgoing, man-of-the-world, good-time Charlie. With ease, he would flick back and forth between the two extremes.

He did not waste his energies conjuring his showy, extroverted side for his contemporaries—young actors who were neither good friends nor especially important to him. He was still being supported by his father, and so did not have to do all the things they were forced to do —take jobs on radio (considered the dregs then), wait on tables, haunt agents' offices and auditions. He simply waited for his reputation to bring him his next part, and if months passed before he worked again, he would continue living as an upper-class gentleman, with his acting, photography, and piano lessons. For Monty, it was never a question of survival, as it was for other young men in the theater. He lived apart from them and was envied.

He went to some theater parties, without much relish. A room full of "arty" strangers frightened him. In March of 1944 Fitzroy Davis threw a party and Duane McKinney, then an actor, invited Monty. Somewhere en route to Fitzroy's, Duane told Monty about the ballet dancers, among other ethereals, who would be there, and when the cab stopped at a red light, Monty opened the door in a panic and told his friend: "I can't meet these people." Duane grabbed him back into the cab. Davis recalled his first impression of Monty at twenty-three. "I remember his eyes, as he stood behind Duane at the door, luminous with fright, his mouth half open. Later Duane, talking about Monty and sex, said, 'I don't think he can make up his mind yet how to start a sex life. I've always thought he had some terrible scare very young. Now, you know, he acts about sex as if he were looking at an escalator and saw other people riding up and down, but did not know how to get on.'" Instead of socializing with the guests, Monty stayed in the kitchen talking with two actresses, then, after a few hours fled and went frolicking in Central Park with one of them.

Only with his close friends and the few people who counted did Monty display that new, more flamboyant, overtly sexual personality. This other side of him constantly attempted to approximate a normal sense of humor, but always missed the mark.

At first no one thought those sudden daredevil pranks were anything more pathological than a mild case of an actor showing off or, at worst, Monty's own strange rendition of a normal sense of humor. "He was just a perpetual boy," was Augusta Dabney's observation. But there was something much more worrisome and symptomatic about the pranks. They reflected a macabre sense of desperation which could never be articulated. It was a "sense of humor" which contained a sense of the morbid and perverse as well. His "pranks" always flirted with death. His "humor" involved flying in the face of mortality.

Each prank was different and yet somehow always the same. There was, for example, Monty's "basic" prank—hanging.

Right after Kevin and Monty first met, they happened to be in a room on the thirteenth floor of the New Yorker Hotel. Kevin turned his back for a moment and when he looked around, there was Monty hanging by his fingertips from the ledge of the window, thirteen floors above a bustling street, just a hairsbreadth from death.

"Oh, my God!" thought Kevin, courting a brief impulse to run from whatever sudden madness had overtaken his friend.

Monty just kept dangling by his fingertips, waiting calmly to be rescued by Kevin. After his panic disappeared, Kevin rushed to the window and pulled Monty back into the room. Kevin concluded, from Monty's manner, that it was all a big joke.

Mira saw similar things. She lived a few doors down from Monty on Fifty-fifth Street, and since they lived so close, they constantly wandered in and out of each other's apartments. Monty, one day, went up to his roof, walked over to her building, and hung from the building's edge, so that Mira suddenly saw a head hanging upside down and no body!

These pranks were obviously more than a devil-may-care personality running out of control. If you saw them right, the pranks amounted to a *real* personality crying out for help. They were psychodramas. In each one, Monty appeared as one seeking rescue. But from what? From that impostor he was perfecting? From his Oedipal fears? From the homosexuality he feared would give him away? Or was he seeking rescue, above all, from that intelligent but weak creature—himself?

Monty was brilliant in a brief City Center showcase production of *Our Town* as George Gibbs, then went into Lillian Hellman's *The Searching Wind.* He was cast in the small but pivotal part of a boy returning from the war with a wounded leg and a damaged spirit. The questions he asks of his politically involved family during the course of one evening provoke flashbacks to events prior to the war. The flashbacks force the family to realize their

49

own responsibility for the war. At the end of the play, tragedy comes full circle when news arrives that Monty's leg must be amputated.

On the first day of rehearsal, director-producer Herman Shumlin interrupted Monty during his initial readings. He told Monty that if he closed his eyes while Monty was reading he could hear Alfred Lunt talking. The cadence and rhythms and hesitations were exactly like Lunt's. Monty was taken aback. He told Shumlin that he would go home and work on the problem. After a few more rehearsals, he got rid of the imitation; Lunt was still there, but the similarity was no longer so startling.

Monty was onstage only about ten percent of the playing time, but he had the play's best and most moving dramatic speeches. The opening night audience heard a compellingly attractive voice. Monty spoke with a minimum of vocal stress, yet his manner was so intense that members of the audience actually leaned forward, anxious to absorb every word. The performance was a great feat of concentration, and managed to liberate the play from its awkward structure.

By the next morning, Monty had become a minor Broadway star. Ward Morehouse of the New York *Sun* called Monty's performance "thrilling" and "powerful." The *Journal-American* called Monty "sincerely moving." Howard Barnes of the *Herald Tribune* said: "Clift brings a fierce intensity to the part of the disabled grandson which is the very stuff of fine acting." It is doubtful whether there was one young Broadway hopeful who didn't rush to see this new kind of acting once the word was out.

Things began moving quickly. *The Searching Wind* closed after a year, and Monty was instantly proposed for the lead in another war play, Elsa Shelley's *Foxhole in the Parlor*. Here, again, Monty was a morally wounded, disillusioned soldier returning from the war. His wild, strange rantings against the cruelties of war make his neighbors and sister believe that he is deranged, but at the end of the play, Monty proves that his "madness" is really unique sanity; he makes a stirring speech before Congress and forces everybody, including the audience, to think twice.

Foxhole opened on May 23, 1945, and was Monty's first starring role on Broadway. Not only did he receive top billing, but top salary. The critics, tired of talky and poorly constructed war plays, hated this new effort, but swooned over Monty almost in one voice. The reviews tell it all.

Robert Garland of the *Journal-American:* "Montgomery Clift, recently of *The Searching Wind,* is as touching as he is terrifying in the role of the returned soldier with a Messianic complex gleaming with abnormal brightness in his war-weary eyes. Broadway knows no finer piece of underplaying."

Herrick Brown of the *Sun:* "Montgomery Clift is again cast as a boy home from the front, and his portrayal of Miss Shelley's tortured hero is one of the best performances at present to be found in town. He keeps an excellent rein on the role throughout and at the same time reveals vividly the lad's agony of spirit."

Howard Barnes of the *Herald Tribune:* "Certainly whatever Miss Shelley had in mind is brilliantly illuminated by Clift. This young actor has given several outstanding performances in the past. He has never given so fine a one against such staggering odds. On more than one occasion he picks up a situation, as it were, by the bootstraps, making it ring with eloquence which is not there in the writing. His portrayal of a fighter discharged from an Army hospital for mental cases is something to witness. Not so the play."

And so Elsa Shelley was ravished, and a twenty-four-year-old young man turned suddenly into a matinee idol. Had it not been for the critical paeans to Monty, management would have closed *Foxhole* immediately. Harry Bloomfield kept the play going, hoping that he could hold audiences with the new "critics' darling." Bloomfield's press agent hired a theater claque of fifty to wait outside the Booth Theater to attack the new star with autograph books and applause, while reporters and cameramen just happened to be on the scene. Clued in on what was to happen, Monty covered his face with his jacket and rushed out of the theater. The claque continued to wait until someone chanced to tell them that Montgomery Clift had been gone for an hour.

Monty was aware, naturally, of his sudden value. All that talk about the brooding quality of his acting, the power of his quiet eye-work and strange speech, and his good looks made the studio heads, sitting in their offices, begin to salivate over this fresh, new meat. During the six-week run of *Foxhole,* and right afterward, one Coast offer after another came to Monty. He received scripts, invitations to come to Hollywood, and that invariable seven-year deal that went along with any single script offer. Monty flatly turned down most of the scripts. In a few instances, he went so far as to accept a round trip ticket to Hollywood. He sat across from Louis B. Mayer and explained to him that his artistic conscience would not allow him to sign for a certain number of years; he would rather sign for specific scripts of his own choosing. Mr. Mayer reportedly went berserk upon hearing this from a young nobody. The studio head explained that he had great respect for talent, but could not permit money to be poured into building up a newcomer who would make one film and rush back to New York. Monty refused the seven-year deal politely, sending Mayer to the brink of tears. Like every other major studio, MGM badly needed new romantic young blood. Half of Hollywood's cinematic studs were off fighting the war. On another trip to Hollywood, Monty tested for Warner Brothers' *Pursued,* managed to get Warners to relent on the seven-year deal in favor of less stringent "options," and signed. When he got back to New York, he had a change of heart, and notified Leland Hayward, who was handling him, that the deal was out of the question. The studio threatened to sue, but in the end agreed to tear up the contract.

Lehman Engel was right. The more Monty protested, the more the Coast lusted. With each new turndown, the financial bids grew. There was less and less emphasis on rigid deals. It must have seemed to the moguls that Monty's cool was the most brilliant they had ever encountered, as if he were successfully bluffing his way through a poker game. It was nothing of the sort. There was a part of Monty that simply did not care. It gave him his negotiating power.

Monty had talked about going into the movies since he was nineteen. There was never any doubt in his mind that he was going to be a big cinema star. Billy noted, all along, Monty's drive, his need for success—big success, the kind that only movie stardom could bring. Money per se didn't mean much—Monty never mentioned it; having been brought up as a child of wealth, he disdained the idea of craving it.

But the big dilemma—which, ironically, only worked to increase his negotiating position with the studios—was that something old in Monty, a holdover never quite transformed into his new image, stood in conflict with the big superplan. Mira Rostova was often in contact with that "old" Monty, and she could see that Monty's refusals of studio offers were not simply the work of his artistic conscience. He had definite qualms about the big plan. "The studios were after him, yes," says Mira, "but Monty wasn't all that interested. He was ambitious to do excellent work, but he didn't seem to know whether he wanted to go out to Hollywood and do all that was required of him. I think he could take it or leave it."

Monty's recently acquired prominence made him a bit cocky. One broiling midsummer night during a performance of *Foxhole in the Parlor,* Monty, without notifying the stage manager, had the air-conditioning shut off. The people in the audience fanned themselves; the actors onstage perspired. Monty later explained to the mystified stage manager that the noise of the air-conditioning distracted his concentration. In his next play, *You Touched Me!* the other actors resented Monty's selfishness and his uncommunicativeness. One of them, Neil Fitzgerald, recalls that Monty could be "very naughty."

"If he decided he didn't like the direction, he would change things to suit himself. And he was terribly inconsistent in his performances. He would change the position of chairs and other things to his liking without asking permission. I knew Monty had been reprimanded by the stage manager on several occasions. It was pretty awkward for us. In one scene three of us were seated around a table, center stage. His position was a little in front of us, in front of a whatnot with books and bric-a-brac on it. Guthrie McClintic had directed Monty to stand there while we talked to him, with our faces toward the audience, but he began to move his position away upstage until we'd have to turn around to speak to him. Edmund Gwenn, who wasn't in the scene, suggested: 'Well, you fellows talk to the spot where he's supposed to be. Let him go wherever he likes.' We all spoke, as it were, to the lonely whatnot, and Monty had to come back."

You Touched Me! was an adaptation by Tennessee Williams and Donald Windham of a story by D.H. Lawrence, an interesting if critically unsuccessful play about a sea captain, played by Edmund Gwenn, who conspires with his R.A.F. pilot/adopted son Monty—the personification of virility—to awaken the suppressed lust in his spinsterish daughter, Marianne Stewart. Since Monty's character is an "idea" similar to the gentleman-caller in Williams' *The Glass Menagerie*, not a real person, Monty had an interesting problem. For the first time in his career he was called upon to portray pure macho, an exercise which delighted him. He managed to convince the audience that he was unmitigated male sexuality without making a vulgar display of himself, as most other actors of his age and type would have. How? He used *inner* silence, unusual pauses in his speeches, awkward body movements. He spoke so quietly that at times he was practically inaudible. He shifted his moods erratically, from a brooding pose to a bursting smile. These were extremely unorthodox, risky procedures, and had the effect of involving the audience with *him*, an exceedingly selfish aim if one thinks only in terms of the play, but a daring and stupendously courageous maneuver when one thinks of the ground he was breaking.

The kind of acting Monty did in *You Touched Me!* and *Foxhole in the Parlor* required one step beyond concentration: that process which would come to obsess actors, madden directors, and enflame audiences—"preparation." The very word, even more than the Method, would scare half of Hollywood owing to its intimations of religious self-scourging. Some would see it as a synonym for the hairshirt worn by actors with self-destructive complexes. Indeed, whatever "preparation" did come to mean, Monty was the first—the *very* first—to immolate himself on its altar.

Prior to this time, Mira Rostova had not been a coach; she had simply been an intelligent, dedicated student. Her friendship with Monty, when they first met three years before *The Searching Wind*, was based solely on their personal attraction for one another. In the beginning they talked about *everything*; they laughed a lot. In time, however, as Mira became more aware of Monty's thirst for achievement, and as his extraordinary future became clearer, the thrust of their relationship began to focus on Monty's specific goals. During the rehearsal period for *The Searching Wind*, Mira helped Monty "prepare" for the role. The two of them would engage in endless discussions of choices and character motivation; they would pick apart every line of dialogue. It was Monty who prompted these so-called coaching sessions with Mira—partly out of ambition, partly out of fear. Mira explains it this way: "We found we both loved the process of working on a role, discovering what a part was really all about, making the right choices. Many actors will eventually get tired of this process of preliminary delving, but Monty and I were the same: we could work endlessly studying parts. Actually it was this preliminary probing that Monty really loved; performing on a stage frightened him. He was always so afraid that something would go wrong while he was up there. I remember he said to me several times that he probably should have been doing something else with his life. I had the feeling that acting as a profession dissatisfied him. Monty's enthusiasm and meticulousness and seriousness were things he would have brought to anything he chose to do in life."

Monty was secretive. Only a few people were even remotely aware that he was frightened of the stage. Mira had self-assurance; she was a frail-looking woman who could startle others with a strong display of conviction. She buoyed Monty; helped him believe in himself. He was honest with her, and displayed to her his old, dependent self. Aware that he needed this constant reassurance and bolstering, she "prepared" with him and, in so doing, infused in him her own great sense of self-worth and artistic intransigence. By the time of the actual performance, he was part Monty, part Mira, and his sense of purpose was so magnified, he could not only cope with his own fears, but take great onstage risks.

Evidence for this can be seen in the fact that real stardom did not begin to happen for Monty until they started working together. Monty, of course, continued to develop on his own, but after *The Searching Wind* Mira coached Monty for every role, and with each one he grew more daring, more "internal." The *You Touched Me!* adventure was Monty's most brilliant escape from the ordinary into the realm of psychological projection. After that exciting excursion, there was really no point in continuing to work on Broadway. He had reached a certain juncture. After *You Touched Me!* closed, he looked only at those packages from Hollywood sent by his agent.

Monty's sexual and social lives were fast becoming as complicated as his professional growth.

In early 1946, he met an easygoing young man through a casual acquaintance. Rick, Monty's age and au courant with the New York theater, lived in New Jersey. For several months, they made dinner dates about once a week; Rick came over to Monty's apartment; they'd listen to records and discuss plays—all quite platonic. This was usual for Monty. He was not highly sexed; most of his socializing involved talk, emotional support, and relaxation. No one ever remembers Monty walking into a bar, a party, or even down the street with his eye on a specific man or woman.

One rainy night, Monty and his new male friend came back to Monty's place above the laundromat. Rick was just about to leave. The scene which ensued, had it been between a man and a woman in a first-draft movie script, might have been blue-penciled as Romantic Cliché Number Sixty-two. "I was about to leave," says Rick, "when Monty helped me on with my raincoat. He was behind me. I felt his hands touching me while he helped me on with the raincoat. Some slip must have happened, and we both knew that we wanted each other. He kissed me, and then said, surprised, something like, 'I had no idea . . .' Well, I had no idea about him either. We went to bed."

This was the beginning of summer. For the next three months, they saw each other about twice a week. Rick always drove into New York on Friday; they would spend the night at Monty's and then drive to Jones Beach the next morning. Often one of Monty's friends, a famous homosexual choreographer, would come along. Monty was tender in bed—not passive, but not demandingly aggressive either—and invariably playful the next morning. In the car, Monty would often mortify Rick, who was rather proper and from a good New England family, by hanging his jockstrap to dry on the driver's rearview mirror outside the car.

At the same time, Monty was also seeing and sleeping with several young women! Kevin McCarthy and Augusta Dabney used to spend time with Monty and his girl friends, who were invariably involved with the theater. "Monty used to brag a little about his affairs with women in his own discreet way," says Kevin. "He made innuendos that he had done pretty well with them." Rick says he knew at the time that Monty was bisexual. "Once Monty asked me for a loan of several hundred dollars so that a girl friend of his could have an abortion. I gave him the money and didn't ask any questions."

The question of Monty and Libby Holman is a touchy one; there was much talk at the time. Some of this talk came from Monty himself. Libby Holman is dead now, and what lives on is a series of impressions, rather than facts. Undeniably, she was sexually and emotionally attracted to sensitive homosexual young men like Monty. On weekends, Kevin, Augusta, Billy, and Monty used to go up to her palatial house, Treetops, in Stamford, Connecticut, just minutes away from the Red Barn in Pound Ridge. Based on statements, innuendos and observation of their behavior together, Kevin felt certain there was a sexual involvement between Libby and Monty, despite the fact that she was fourteen years his senior. She was a robust, intelligent woman, but hardly attractive; her face was riddled with premature wrinkles. Billy shuddered to think of them, because the idea of this young god in bed with an unattractive older woman seemed repulsive. Monty told Rick that he and Libby had "wild scenes" with marijuana and pep pills.

Libby, at the time, was strung out. The suicide of Ralph Holmes on top of the murder-scandal had affected her sensitivity and poise. Maureen Stapleton recalls a marvelous dinner at Treetops, at which Libby just sat at the table drinking, not touching a bite of the exquisite food. She didn't know most of the dinner guests and she didn't care to know them. She was almost like a female Jay Gatsby, surrounded by her own wealth—maids, butlers, eye-stoppers such as a white mink throw rug on the bathroom floor—yet uninvolved. Others remember her drinking heavily, and there was much talk—but only *talk*—of drugs. She may or may not have introduced Monty to heavier drugs than he was then taking. A few years later, Janet Cohn saw Monty and Libby coming out of a movie theater laughing, joking, and taking swigs out of a liquor bottle half hidden in a brown paper bag.

Toward the end of the summer of 1946, the Leland Hayward office sent Monty an exceptional new Hollywood offer. Hayward had suggested Monty for one of the two leads in Howard Hawks' first western, *Red River*. The other lead was to be John Wayne. Talk about macho!

Hawks had been impressed with Monty in *You Touched Me!* and, now an independent, liked the idea of signing him on a freelance basis. The script Hawks sent Monty was quite bare, not at all an indication of the sprawling, box-office epic it would become, and Mira didn't like it. Lehman Engel, on the other hand, said: "Do it. Now is the time."

In the end, Monty overruled Mira. The idea of riding horses in the Arizona sun with a lot of cowboys and stunt men, and co-stardom with Wayne, plus a terrific contract which offered $60,000 with no strings attached, overwhelmed him. Before anything was signed, however, Monty had to fly out to Hollywood to talk with Hawks in person.

During the meeting, both Hawks, a fiercely independent man, and Monty, determined not to become studio chattel, treaded gingerly. After some initial polite sallies, Howard Hawks got dead serious. He looked into Monty's eyes and said: "Now look, this is a western. If you can't sit on a horse, you may as well go right home." Monty was far from an expert rider and, cowed, asked, "What shall I do?" That was what Hawks wanted to hear.

Hawks was famous for a kind of ESP instinct about the potential power of unknown actors—his "discoveries." He liked to take command of them, to mold them. For instance, Lauren Bacall was an eighteen-year-old nobody from New Jersey with a high, squeaky voice when she wound up in Hawks' office. She believed, mistakenly, that she had been asked to come all the way from New Jersey to star in Hawks' next film. As soon as he heard her speak, he told her bluntly that her voice made her unsuitable for films. But then he took another look. Perhaps something could be done . . . drastic changes. For weeks, she shut herself up in a room in Hollywood, and by the end, under Hawks' tutelage, her voice had become low and sexy. There was still the problem of her timid manner with men. Hawks took her to parties; men didn't seem to notice her. Hawks suggested that she try stepping on their toes, figuratively speaking, and playing hard to get. In a matter of months she became a sexy, Frances-Farmer bitch-with-a-baritone, and Bogart fell head over heels for her.

On another occasion, Hawks took a rather undistinguished Paramount player, Carole Lombard, and put her opposite John Barrymore in *Twentieth Century*. Lombard was so stiff and unaware of her hidden powers with men that Barrymore tried to get Hawks to fire her. Again, Hawks followed his instincts and schooled Lombard in the kind of comedic bawdiness that was to become her trademark. He advised her to kick Barrymore in the balls with no warning during a key scene and then see what happened while the cameras rolled. Barrymore played the rest of the scene holding his nuts while Lombard wreaked havoc. A star was born.

Now, Hawks knew he would be taking an enormous risk in signing Monty. The script called for two strong men to engage in a lengthy physical and emotional combat. Monty had to have as much strength as the Duke, "or Wayne would blow Monty right off the screen." Monty was small—a slender five-feet-ten. When Wayne first saw him, he asked Hawks how in tarnation he expected to pull off those fight scenes and the test of wills. At first, Hawks honestly didn't know how he could create the necessary balance, but he had an instinct that he could increase Monty's screen "size."

To do that, however, Hawks had to be able to restructure Monty's personality for the camera. Monty was already a stage actor, filled with technique concepts and his own ideas of what he wanted to be on film. Hawks didn't like that, but he *did* like the fact that Monty got worried when he was told to go home if he couldn't ride. There was, then, some insecurity, some vulnerability that Hawks could work with. When Monty said, "What shall I do?" Hawks responded, "You come down to location three weeks early. I'll give you a good cowboy, you'll start at six in the morning and come back in time for dinner." Monty was more than willing. Howard instructed the cowboy to take Monty to steep places, through water, into jumps. Monty literally worked his backside off for three weeks, and became such a crackerjack cowpoke that Hawks rewarded him with an old five-star Texan hat that had once belonged to Gary Cooper.

Red River was based on an undistinguished short story from the *Saturday Evening Post* called "The Chisholm Trail," about the first cattle drive from Laredo, Texas, to Abilene, Missouri. The drive established Texas as the leading national supplier of beef and made millionaires out of a few small-time cattle barons. Hawks got his writers to add elements of the courage and ruthlessness of the very first Texas cattle barons, the King family, and cast Wayne as a man faced with either losing his small cattle empire in Texas, because the market for beef has suddenly dried up, or risking the lives of his men to herd his cattle way up to Abilene. During the drive to Abilene, Wayne's adopted son Monty rebels against Wayne's ruthless executions of his increasingly restless men, seizes control, and takes the herd to Abilene himself. It was a simple story, but with Hawks' imagination it acquired monumental proportions on the screen.

Hawks was pleased to see how quickly Monty learned to ride and was convinced he had not made a mistake. Up until the actual shooting started, however, he kept several replacements for Monty—just in case his instincts had backfired. Hawks' first problem with Monty was "that baloney"—Monty's feeling that he had to prepare for every scene by working out each line of dialogue days ahead of time, leaving no room for spontaneity. Hawks gave him an on-the-spot object lesson. He called Wayne over and told Monty, "You just choose a subject, and Wayne and I will improvise a scene for you." The improvisation amazed Monty and gave him a whole new idea of acting.

Hawks then proceeded to show Monty just how he could be David to Wayne's Goliath. The film's first key scene between the two is a head-on confrontation—and for the first time, everyone realized how right Hawks was in casting Monty. The sequence had Monty stand by, smoldering quietly, while Wayne ordered the execution of some of his men for trying to desert. Monty told Hawks before the scene that he would play every line resolutely, to convince the audience he was a match for Wayne, but Hawks said, "No, don't try to get hard, because you'll just be nothing compared to Wayne. Start by taking a cup of coffee and just watch him all over." Monty understood perfectly: Underplay the first part of the sequence, throw the lines away as if there was something far more important going on in his mind. The effect was electric. Wayne, always quick to admit that he was wrong, went over to Hawks and said, "Any doubts I had about that fella are gone. He's going to be okay." The rushes that night showed Wayne's determination perfectly matched by Monty's eyes, and cool, suppressed, time-bomb manner. Monty's character had been established.

Again, Hawks remembers: "Monty came up to me about a scene in which he says to Duke, 'I'm going to get your herd to Abilene.' That was where the men finally side with Monty and Duke rides off alone in another direction. Monty said to me: 'I have a chance to dominate the scene and I wonder if you have any ideas.' I said: 'Play it the way it seems best.' I went to the Duke and said: 'Hey, Monty thinks he's got a great scene coming up. Now I'm going to put you in a saddle during that scene, and I've got a little suggestion for you: Don't even look at Monty. Just let him talk to your back.' We shot the scene and Monty came out with his line, 'I'm going to get your herd to Abilene,' and Duke said, 'I'm going to kill you.' Well, Duke didn't even look at him while he said that and Monty didn't know what to do. I let him stand there looking dumbfounded just as long as I wanted, and then I said, 'Get the hell out of there, Monty!' and he turned and walked away. I knew my voice could be cut out. Monty came over to me and said: 'My big scene didn't amount to much, did it?' 'Well,' I said to Monty, 'that's exactly what I've been talking to you about. He didn't even have to look at you when he said, 'I'm going to kill you.' Monty said: 'I didn't have a chance. He was just marvelous. You just showed me there are other ways of doing it.' Oh, Monty was learning! Really rapidly! He was a damn fine actor."

As best he could, Monty had a good time during the five months of filming in Arizona, but he would often go off by himself in depressed moods. People around the set did not dislike Monty, but it was difficult for them to get wildly warm and friendly toward a young man who took his work so seriously he would often lapse into speechlessness. One who did become friends with him was Noah Beery, Jr., who shared a tent with him and Walter Brennan. As Mr. Beery explains: "It did take us a long time. Monty and I turned to each other in self-defense after a while, because dear Walter, who was one of the world's great entertainers, ran out of material, so he was repeating on us, you know. We had no way but to turn to each other for friendship. Monty was actually a very cute fella. Certain things would strike him funny that wouldn't strike you as funny. Oh, we became good friends. I remember the thing he enjoyed the most was becoming a hell of a good cowboy and horseman. He never asked for help on how to be a better cowboy, but he was always watching things closely; I had a feeling that he was really absorbing what I was all about—my voice, my manner. You could see him watching the people who really knew what they were doing."

Howard Hawks sensed Monty's aloneness, and intensity, and, even though he used it to good advantage in the film, was personally put off by it. Monty did not invite the kind of involvement—some good laughs, a few drinks, camaraderie—that Hawks expected to have with his discoveries. Monty was not about to let Hawks invade his life so thoroughly. Perhaps it was a matter of age—Hawks was now fifty—or perhaps Monty was afraid of the director's masculinity and deep perceptions of people, as he seems to have been afraid of Kazan after *The Skin of Our Teeth*. In any case, when the film finished shooting in early 1947, Monty, unsure of how good he had been, went his way, and Hawks, turned off by Monty as a man, went his. They never worked together again.

Monty would have to wait a year and a half for the release of *Red River*. Normally, the process of film editing, release, and distribution takes six months or less, but Hawks ran into difficulties with the initial cutting and that, along with a lawsuit by Howard Hughes over the ending of the film, delayed the film's opening.

Meanwhile, Monty flew to see his twin sister in Texas —Roberta (now "Ethel") was now married and living in Austin—and then went back to Manhattan. The atmosphere in the theater there had grown tense. The young actors who had gone to war were back now from that grim exercise in reality, driven by the need to change everything, including themselves. They supported acting classes all over the city, including one for advanced actors called the Actors Studio, founded in early 1947 by two ex-Group Theater potentates, Elia Kazan and Bobby Lewis. It met a few times a week at the Malin Studios, a ramshackle rehearsal building near Broadway, and was charged by the electricity of the Stanislavskian spirit. The difference now, however, lay in the do-or-die urgency with which these young men did their exercises and transformed theory into sweat. Blood and gunfire had turned them off to the niceties of the early-forties theater, and they were determined to spill their guts on Broadway. They were also horny as hell after four years of war. The smell and lure of released semen was in everything they did.

A new actor about town was generating a great deal of talk. His name was Marlon Brando, four years Monty's junior, and, interestingly, also born in Omaha. Brando rode around New York on a motorcycle, swathed himself in a leather jacket and dungarees, went to all the acting class parties and stunned the eager veterans with a bizarre temper and strange, saturnine glare. On the stage, he shuffled around and spoke in peculiar bursts of speech. The veterans gossiped with awed glee; they said that he was bisexual, that he made it with a certain well-known playwright while, with equal gusto, shacking up with the freakiest girls in town. Instead of thinking him odd, these war-matured young men, and their women, looked upon Marlon as another Walt Whitman. There wasn't an actor in town who dared make a crack about a pansy anymore; if you couldn't appreciate the joys of AC-DC living, then you just weren't grown up yet.

Monty felt semi-detached from all this new excitement —perhaps because he had not come straight from the battlefield. Yet he went through the motions of joining the Actors Studio, went to as many parties as anyone else— the "new" parties, with intense little groups arguing to the death such matters as Stella Adler's teaching methods—and donned the blue jeans and sloppy clothes. This was the new advance guard; Monty made himself join in. Despite his psychological distance, he was still, to all these intense young men, one of the two gods—Clift and Brando.

Monty met Brando for the first time shortly after returning from *Red River*. Marlon had been co-starring with Tallulah Bankhead in a pre-Broadway tryout of *The Eagle Has Two Heads*. She could not bear working with a man she considered an egotistical stud and had him fired by the time the play got to Washington, D.C. The producers contacted Monty about replacing him. Monty had seen Brando as Nels in *I Remember Mama* in 1944, and thought then that there was something special about him. He was, however, somewhat uncomfortable with the idea of Brando. Only a year before he alone had been the big, new influence, and now he had a rival. Monty had absolutely no intention of replacing Brando in *The Eagle Has Two Heads*

—his eyes were primarily on the Coast now—but, perhaps to prove to himself that he was the more desirable actor, he took the train all the way to Washington, D.C., to see the play and have the thrill of turning down the offer. On the train back to New York, he and Brando met. They talked straight through the four-hour trip, and the fragile ice was broken.

The next time they met was at a Jerome Robbins party. Brando screeched to a halt on his motorcycle in front of the Seventh Avenue apartment building and made his entrance. They kept their distance at first. Brando knew that Mira was Monty's acting coach; according to the gossip, she was taking over Monty's very life and soul. That impressed him; to Marlon such self-destruction in the name of art was derring-do. Marlon looked across the room and saw Mira sitting with her hands folded serenely. He sat next to her. "Why do you hold your hands like that?" Marlon demanded. "How should I hold them?" she answered. Marlon shrugged. Then he walked over to the record player and played a pile of drum records at top volume for the rest of the evening with his back turned to the room. People watched him and tried to pretend that they weren't watching him. Finally, Marlon walked up to Monty and asked him if he would like to go for a ride on his motorcycle. It was the big happening of the party. As they zoomed off together, Jerome Robbins half-jested to the others: "If anything happens to them, we've just lost the shining lights of the American theater."

Attempting to form a relationship, Monty and Brando would spar gently with one another, looking for a common ground, but their mutual explorations always came to a dead end. Monty found Brando too hot-headed and impetuous; Brando thought Monty too cool and predetermined. It was Dionysus versus Apollo. Monty complained that Marlon never thought things through; Brando accused Monty of having "a Mixmaster up his ass." The problem was temperament and competition, but each actor also had to admit that he had been deeply influenced by the other, a mutual embarrassment. Brando had seen Monty's unique creation of internal characterizations and had been drastically reshaped. Monty was vulnerable to Brando's indisputably superior effect on the world of the theater. To keep himself competitive, Monty felt compelled to beef up his already strained New Macho image. No wonder he and Brando found each other impossible.

Both men were listed as founding members of the Actors Studio, but Brando attended a lot more than Monty. Monty felt the original group was a fascinating one—Kevin McCarthy, Eli Wallach, Karl Malden, Maureen Stapleton, David Wayne, Tom Ewell, Eva Marie Saint, John Forsythe, Mildred Dunnock, and Herbert Berghof—and he felt close to the teachers, Lewis and Kazan, but he had reservations about what they were trying to do. Monty kept hoping the Studio would turn into a workshop that would enable him to work on scenes he would never get a chance to do elsewhere; instead, the instructors asked them to do scenes from conventional plays. The idea of the Method also turned him off. He intensely disliked tricks such as "sense-memory," which seemed to narrow Stanislavsky down to a formula of how one must produce tears and rage. Monty worked on things simply as they came up, and not from some preconceived notion of sensory experience, motivation, or technique.

During this time, he was seeing a good deal of Ann Lincoln, a small, dark-haired, beautiful actress who had appeared opposite him in *Foxhole in the Parlor.* "Annie" seemed like a cross between Judy Holliday and Margaret Sullavan, played ingenues brilliantly, and was all of eighteen when Monty started seeing her. Outgoing, hard-drinking, she had strong—and frankly-admitted—sex drives, and for a while, she and Monty had a wonderful affair. They went to all the parties, took off on spur-of-the-moment trips, and shared sexual as well as artistic closeness.

Monty admitted to Annie that he liked men, and at first it did not distress her. Pure bisexuals were rather like enviable mutants in those days. After a few years, however, the problem bore down on both of them. Annie was in love with Monty, and he felt strongly about her; but Monty's drives toward men were much stronger than those toward women. In the end, neither of them could reconcile themselves to a limited physical involvement. Annie was too strongly sexed and Monty too uncomfortable with the burden of a double life. Annie always felt she and Monty might have made it had they not been so rigid in their expectations of the sexual side of marriage.

While with Annie, Monty also resumed his relationship with his New York lover, Rick. Monty had no similar anxieties about him. Rick says, "I remember our relationship as the best I've ever had with anyone. Monty was affectionate, gentle, sensuous . . . and almost a little naive when it came to sex. I remember after he came back from Hollywood he said to me, 'You're not doing it with anyone else? I want it to be just us.' I said, a little amazed, 'What we've had was very good, but you're living in Hollywood a lot and I can't . . . I mean . . .' I was groping for words, trying to explain that I wasn't just going to sit around and not have sex with anyone else for months at a time. Then I said, 'Monty, haven't you been with anyone else yourself?' 'No,' he said, lying I was sure. And whenever the subject came up after that, he'd lie in the same sincere, vehement way. Occasionally, much later on, Monty would admit to me his outside activities.

"He was still living in two places—at his parents' and in his own apartment, the one-room walk-up off Lexington Avenue. His mother couldn't understand why he had to do that. But Monty used to tell her that he needed his privacy. My mother and father had a place in Kennebunkport, Maine, and he'd come up there with me for days at a time. We went boating a lot. We'd have sex in the boat, in the woods in the moonlight. Monty was always good sexually for me . . . He got to love my mother. He'd say to me, 'She's my real mother!' I told him he shouldn't say things like that. Monty's mother was a thoroughly possessive woman, peculiar in some ways. When she was alone with me, she'd say things like, 'I'm glad you and Monty are such good friends. I don't really like theater people.' It was a funny thing to say to the friend of a man who had been in the theater since he was fourteen."

While Monty was still working on *Red River*, he was contacted by Fred Zinnemann, a personable, quiet, German-born young man who was then making film shorts, but who wanted to break into feature films. He had directed Phyllis Thaxter in a screen test for *Thirty Seconds Over Tokyo*, and Phyllis, impressed by Zinnemann's youthful ability, thought immediately that he and Monty should get together. Shortly afterward, Lazar Wechsler, a noted Swiss producer, approached Zinnemann about directing a movie in Switzerland to do with children displaced by the war. Zinnemann says when he first saw Monty he could feel an almost palpable energy emanating from him, and he knew at once that he wanted Monty for the film. It was to be called *The Search*. Monty liked the idea, but wanted to see a script. As soon as one was ready, said Zinnemann, he would send it to him in New York.

In the spring of 1947, Monty received an outline of the script and liked it. The producer, Lazar Wechsler, was known for skillful, low-budget movies and managed to convince not only Monty, but all of the other leads—Wendell Corey, Aline MacMahon, Metropolitan Opera diva Jarmila Novotna—to work for peanuts. However, it seemed to Monty's California lawyer, Laurence Beilenson, that if he was going to receive less for this film than for *Red River*, he should only work on the film for a brief period of time. It was therefore specified in Monty's contract that he would not have to work more than six weeks on *The Search*. Monty also obtained a verbal agreement from the producer that allowed him to make changes in his own dialogue. Monty asked Mira to accompany him to Zurich so that she could look over his work. It didn't occur to Monty that the presence of a personal acting coach on a film set would be thought slightly untoward.

The film's interiors were to be shot in Zurich, and most of the exteriors in Munich, Nuremberg, Frankfort, and Würzburg. This was just after the war, and Europe was still in chaos. Zinnemann had already been in Germany for some time, making contacts with U.N.R.R.A. camps—temporary orphanages run by the U.N. for the thousands of children who were displaced from their families by the Nazi terror. Zinnemann remembers saying to groups of children: "You're going to relive what you've gone through. It will be good for others to see it. If any of you want to do it, raise your hand." During the filming, the children-volunteers needed no direction on how to look terrified. They had only to put on their concentration camp uniforms. Stanislavsky himself would have been moved by how quickly their sense memories came back to them.

The story of *The Search*, a picture "that would wring tears from a turnip" as *McCalls* said, is sheer simplicity: an ordinary G.I., Monty, encounters a dirty-faced homeless boy on a war-torn German street and brings him back to a house where he and other G.I.s are staying; the boy is hostile and fearful at first; the G.I. adopts him, makes him feel wanted, intends to bring the boy back to the States with him; but finally the boy and his wandering, searching mother are reunited in a tear-jerker ending that has never been equaled. Even Bette Davis walking up the stairs to her happy death at the conclusion of *Dark Victory* could not coax the lachrymose flood of those last few moments.

Mira and Monty arrived at the Storchen Hotel in Zurich in June of 1947. Fred Zinnemann and his wife Renée were at the Storchen too, but they had no idea that Monty had arrived with his coach. Mira, intent upon staying out of the way, holed up in her room. Renée gives an account of her first encounter with Monty. "I waited for him in the lobby; I wasn't sure what he would look like or how he would be. The lobby was full of the usual dreary European businessmen, smoking cigars and behaving in the pompous ways that self-styled prosperous men assume. The concierge, an exact twin of Adolf Hitler, threw his weight about while the bellboys, mostly in their sixties, arthritically struggled with the luggage. It was a depressing gray-brown day. Suddenly the door opened and in walked what appeared to me a knight in shining armor. He came up to me immediately and said, 'Hi! I'm Monty. I'm starving . . . let's eat.' There seemed to be no moment of strangeness between us; it was as if I had known him all of my life."

Monty was smiling and enthusiastic, but when he read the newly completed shooting script, he was outraged. The screenplay, written by non-Americans, had Monty's G.I. character, Ralph Stevenson, mouthing precious sentimental claptrap. All the idioms were wrong. Ralph sounded totally unreal. Monty had never been in the Army, but he had known enough soldiers, and played enough on the stage, to realize that the scriptwriters had never met one. Immediately, he and Mira started to reshape Ralph. They made him irritable, jumpy, responsive to the orphan's cranky moods with crankiness of his own; after all, he wasn't some sort of social worker. Unconsciously, Monty put a lot of Kevin into the knockabout way Ralph talked, for somehow Kevin always seemed the epitome of what was normal and American.

Then he asked Renée to meet him. Fred Zinnemann was away from Zurich, and in her husband's absence, she was afraid to tell Monty what she really thought, but in her opinion, "he had taken a rather pedantic, stilted script and made it come alive." He and Mira had not only changed Ralph's lines, but some of the other characters' as well. They had rewritten a good half of the movie.

It was completely nervy of them, and of course Lazar Wechsler and his screenwriter detonated at the very idea of this total nobody making such sweeping dialogue demands. Registered letters started arriving from Wechsler. He could not tolerate this! He raged at Monty and Monty raged back, with poor Fred Zinnemann acting as the confused go-between. One can imagine Zinnemann's distress at this unlikely problem on his first film assignment. In the end, Monty got his way. He simply pulled out a copy of his contract and showed it to Zinnemann, who then told Wechsler that Monty had the right to walk out of the picture after six weeks and that Monty said that was exactly what he would do if his changes weren't made. Wechsler, with all of the location shooting, and the slow work with the children, could not possibly wrap the picture up in six weeks. Monty won his first big battle with a producer; Wechsler gritted his teeth; Fred Zinnemann felt relief.

Through the course of three months' filming in Switzerland and Germany, Monty's personality remained insouciant. He was gorgeous and happy, and he attracted people to him. He suffered none of the lingering depressions of *Red River*, nor did he have to learn everything as he went along. In the evenings he played his scenes with Mira so that by the time he went in front of the camera he was totally in character.

What really made the picture was the relationship, on-and-off-camera, between Monty and the little blond Czech boy, Ivan Jandl, who played the orphan, Karel. It would be wrong to say that Monty simply loved children; the fact is, he treated them as real people. He would go for walks with Ivan, and bring him presents. He did the same with six-year-old Timi Zinnemann. It never seemed like Monty, the adult, playing father or big brother. He treated them like friends. By the time they got in front of the camera, Monty and Ivan seemed so close it almost seemed that the camera was intruding. Zinnemann particularly remembers one of the final scenes in the film, in which Monty finds Ivan after the boy has been tormented by memories of his mother and runs away. The cameras were set up by the side of a gray-blue, flowing river; the sky was shimmering. Monty talked with Ivan quietly for a while, with the help of Ivan's translator, and then the two lapsed into a kind of silence before the scene began. At this point, Ivan must be told that his mother is dead; he then turns toward Monty for the affection he desperately needs. Written by Monty himself, paced in jerky, awkward pauses, the scene plays as if, truly, the man and the boy were groping toward some kind of resolution for their intimacy. Zinnemann was overcome by its brilliance.

The only clash between Monty and Fred Zinnemann during the filming concerned the presence of Mira Rostova on the set. Mira would actually coach Monty just before his scenes were shot; right after each take he would look over to her and she would either give a little nod of approval, or shake her head "no," to indicate that Monty must request a new take. For weeks, Zinnemann said nothing to Monty about Mira's undermining his authority, but eventually he did ask Monty to have her leave the set. Mira, almost as sensitive as Monty, was ready to leave at once, but Monty would not let her. She went back to hiding in her room and coached Monty privately. Her daily presence during the filming was the key to Monty's good spirits and sense of authority. The Zinnemanns, however, could not have known that she was Monty's support. They saw only a talented, good-natured young man, with a solid ego; they never saw the means he used to achieve that effect.

Monty's friendship with the Zinnemanns became sealed after Monty saved Timi and Renée's life during a boating accident. The three of them went sailing one afternoon on Lake Zurich; Monty was the only one who knew anything about boats. The day was deceptively beautiful, and so warm, that Monty, when the boat reached the middle of the lake, decided to take a dip. As he jumped over the side, the force of his dive threw the boat away from him; at the same time a sudden gust of wind clutched the boat and took it off at great speed. He yelled at the top of his lungs, "Come about!" which Renée could not do. Monty, unconcerned about his own perilous float in the rough waves, grew panicky about the fate of the boat; at any second, the wind could overturn it. Monty had to think fast in the deep water. He knew that Timi could not swim, but reasoned if he could get the boy to jump overboard and hang onto the rope, he could become a human anchor. Monty screamed again, "Tell Timi to hang onto the rope and jump in the water!" Timi overcame his fears and jumped in, while Monty, in spectacular control of the situation, continued to bolster Timi with loud though calm instructions. The boat slowed down. Renée was able to bring it about enough for Monty to swim to it and take the helm. Monty became the hero that afternoon. It was quite a sight: Monty, with his trim physique and exquisite face, taming a berserk sailing boat in the middle of Lake Zurich.

Monty had such unique, innate masculinity that his obsession with acquiring exaggerated machismo was really superfluous. During the scene with Ivan Jandl on the river bank, Monty ad-libbed: "Don't cry, dear." He asked Zinnemann to scrap that take and wouldn't explain why, but he wrote to Rick in New York that if that scene were printed, the audience was sure to think him homosexual for having said "dear" to a boy. He was concerned about how he used his hands; he would ask friends on numerous occasions if he was using them in an effeminate way. Yet Monty's sensitivity pitted against his equal terror of giving himself away created the sensitive, ambivalent masculinity of his screen presence which was to magnetize millions.

The character which Fred Zinnemann filmed in *The Search* consisted of an amalgamation of intense fears and deep perceptions. The character was not a put-on; Monty had by now become that character.

That was the fascination for others, but for Monty himself, the terrible danger.

CHAPTER FOUR

Idol

IT was like living in an asylum. They broke through the door next to the laundromat and, shrieking, stampeded up five flights of stairs. They pounded on Monty's door, buzzed Monty's bell in desperate, unrelenting rhythms that drove the neighbors nuts. The phone rang night and day, even after Monty obtained an unlisted number. They pursued him on the street with autograph books. As soon as he walked into a café, they shrieked: "Monty! It's Monty Clift! It's Monty!" Bobby-soxers, creatures with just-sprouting breasts, encircled him, paced him. They were not quite children, not quite adults. They sprang out of nowhere.

Monty knew that he would lose his privacy when he began making films. In a moment of uncanny precognition, he told Fred Zinnemann, just after the premiere of *The Search*, that he would never be able to sit with him again in public without being hounded by strangers.

What Monty did not foresee was the speed and magnitude of his own prophecy's fulfillment. Bobby-soxers were a new phenomenon in America. The nation had never before been made so aware of the nature, social habits, and power of teenagers. The post-war prosperity gave them money to spend, made them hard to control. The boys yelled, "Hubba, hubba," and the girls collected records, pored over fan magazines, ran around in screeching cliques, and adopted their own movie idols. How strange it was that as their very first, they would pick a super-serious young man who was light years away from the reality of their own flighty world. In neither *Red River* nor *The Search* was Monty romantically cast. He had no love scenes in either film.

What was it in him that sent young girls into romantic convulsions?

In her book, *Aphrodite at Mid-Century*—a unique look at the generation of the late forties and early fifties—author Caryl Rivers tells of millions of boys and girls facing a new, sexually permissive society. The demands of a freer sexual outlook made many teenagers, especially girls, long for escape into sexless romance. Miss Rivers writes, "I was not alone. All the girls in the eighth grade fell in love with Montgomery Clift in *Red River*. His face had the perfection of a fragile porcelain vase; his beauty was so sensual, and at the same time so vulnerable, it was almost blinding. I think every girl who saw him in the quiet dark of a movie theater of a Saturday afternoon fell in love with Montgomery Clift, his dark eyes like the deep water of a cavern pool, holding promise of worlds of tenderness; the straight, perfect blade of a nose that should have been the work of some sculptor the equal of Michelangelo. . . . At the same time I was in love with Montgomery Clift, I found the growing awareness of how people 'did it' pretty revolting: all that touching and pinching and groping about . . . With me and Montgomery, it wasn't that way at all. Love with him would be long, languourous sighs, pressing close against his manly chest and telling each other all those secrets we had never told anybody, and gazing eyeball-to-eyeball, and he wouldn't think of putting his hand on my thigh."

The promise in Monty's screen image of a nature which transcended coarse love-making can be traced back to the days of *There Shall Be No Night*, when his unthreatening eyes and gentlemanly manner attracted the entire company to him. Then, at the age of twenty, Monty was aristocratic, distant; now, in his screen debut, the neutral eyes, blown up, became "deep water" and his gentlemanly manner became, through deliberate personality metamorphoses, "sensual," "romantic." The girls who drank him in needed to see no love-making to fall in love.

Monty's was instantaneous stardom. *The Search* was released in March 1948. The film's reluctant backer, MGM, expected the Wechsler effort to be another of his prestigious box-office failures which, at best, might get some European film festival award. Consequently eyebrows went up everywhere when *The Search* not only won a special Oscar, but a Best Actor nomination for the film's unknown

73

lead (along with Lew Ayres, Dan Dailey, Clifton Webb and Laurence Olivier—who got it for *Hamlet*). MGM immediately put *The Search* into expensive, nationwide distribution. Magazines and newspapers ran big picture stories on the film. Monty's name started cropping up in the fan magazines, enormous box-office stimulants in those days.

The moguls rushed to their telephones. Calls from every major studio came into MCA, which had absorbed the Leland Hayward office and Monty along with it. They'd accept a freelancer; they'd accede to his demands. Did he want his choice of scripts? That was all right. Directors, too? Good. This was an absolute first. Only a few years before, a big star like Bette Davis had fought the Crusades all over again in order to be free of the seven-year studio deal. Only established stars like Olivia de Havilland could freelance with impunity. Now here was Mr. Nobody reducing moguls to beggars. They needed him badly to replace the non-idols like Van Johnson and the worn-outs like John Garfield, who then dominated the screen. The moguls smelled the faint aroma of teen-bait. And big, big money.

Paramount, one of the more liberal studios, gave Monty the best offer and he accepted. It was for three films only, starting with *The Heiress*, at a fee of $150,000 apiece. He could turn down any script, any director. He would not be committed to any sort of publicity duties, although informally he agreed to help publicize his films. At any time, he and the studio could terminate the agreement.

The deal was bruited about in the trade papers. Hollywood was shocked that an actor could acquire more power than even Gable after the release of a single film. It was as if some beggar off the street had been dubbed a knight. It was the death knell of the producers and the moguls, and the birth of Actor Power.

Monty had been working on *The Heiress* for a month when, in July 1948, his first film, *Red River,* hit the theaters. If the reaction to *The Search* was terrific, the reaction to *Red River* was monumental. Critics deemed Hawks' film the best cattle-drive epic ever made; they talked about Monty so much they often seemed to forget that John Wayne was also in the film. Words like "instinctive," "sympathetic," "vulnerable," and "natural," cropped up again and again. *Time* magazine, in a special profile, called him an actor of "high promise . . . who plays the

74

thorny young man with a fresh blend of toughness and charm." *Look* gave him its Achievement Award and called him the "most promising star on the Hollywood horizon." *Cosmopolitan* gave him a citation for the best male starring performance of the month. *Life* put him on its cover. Bobby-soxers bombarded the fan magazines with adoring letters. He won a *Motion Picture Herald* poll as "star of tomorrow." *Photoplay* noted that six times more letters came about him than about any other actor. Fan clubs erupted all over the country.

Paramount, already anticipating the frenzy, politely asked Monty to cooperate with a build-up campaign and he acquiesced. He went from one photographic sitting to another, occasionally borrowing a jacket or a tie from a bystander because he now owned a minimal wardrobe. Writers from fan magazines came to see him in a dinky one-room apartment in a shabby hotel. They looked at his quarters, his bare clothes closet, and jumped to conclusions. He was, they said in dozens of pieces, a guy who was down to earth and so involved with his acting that he walked around in rags and lived in a hovel. It was terrific copy. Monty egged it on. He certainly did not intend to tell them the "true story of his life," which, could he have articulated it, would have made better copy for a psychiatric journal than a movie magazine. He gave them an elaborate construct, an honest picture, not of himself, but of the sloppy, bohemian World War II veterans filling New York's acting classes. He let his shirt tails hang out, put his feet up on chairs, called the interviewers "dear," talked about being "ordinary," a "second-class wolf" with women, "boring." He was just so "natural" and awkward, the stories said, that he hardly knew how to express himself. A few years before, Monty had been one of the most articulate, best-dressed young men in New York—aloofly genteel.

The image was powerful, as interesting to read about as to see, and it was Monty's own creation. How ironic it would be that a whole new generation of awkward, shoulder-shrugging actors would be formed by this well-bred, upper-class young man who was simply covering up for himself.

It was Olivia de Havilland's idea to take Ruth and Augustus Goetz' Broadway play, *The Heiress*—based on Henry James' *Washington Square*—and turn it into a multi-million dollar film vehicle for herself. She agreed on William Wyler as the director, who in turn hired Sir Ralph Richardson to play the father (Dr. Sloper), and Monty, to play the suitor (Morris Townsend). Wyler told the playwrights, who were doing the screenplay as well, that Catherine and Dr. Sloper were fine as delineated in the play, but that Monty's part had to be revamped. "In the novel," says Wyler, "you're not quite sure what Morris Townsend is: Is he a golddigger or not? In the play, he came in the house and looked around at how much things were worth. It was so obvious he was after her money. I wanted Monty to play the love scenes with such sincerity that when he doesn't show up for the rendezvous with Olivia, people are surprised."

Monty played his love scenes with de Havilland exactly as Willy wanted. He was so effective, in fact, that after the film's release, he, de Havilland, and the studio were deluged with mail from young girls in shock that plain Catherine could have let gorgeous Monty pound vainly on her door. But, as de Havilland says, "Her choice is the only possible one for an intelligent woman. She sees how false he is and she could never respect him, or herself if she sold out to him."

Wyler had a great deal of trouble getting Monty to look right at the start of the film. His stance wasn't correct for the period. His awkward walk and slight slouch were so totally inappropriate Wyler had to give him special instructions. Then there was trouble with his attire. Monty had showed up on the set wearing a jacket full of holes, a pair of blue jeans, and a T-shirt—his mandatory "bum" uniform—and managed to keep some sense of it, even under the elegant, fastidious costumes he had to wear. Wyler also tried putting a moustache and sideburns on Monty, but kept taking them off. He never was satisfied with the way Monty looked as a young gentleman of mid-nineteenth-century New York. The awkward walk was still there. Monty, sensibly, refused to part with his new image.

The Heiress was a dreadfully serious drawing room drama, totally dependent upon the subtleties of performance by the three leads. They all felt the pressure in their own ways. Monty, whom Wyler recalls only as being "charming and very pleasant," said to him, "Please don't bawl me out in front of the crew." Willy was taken aback by his naiveté. He said, "I don't bawl out actors. I might

76

correct something." Whenever he wasn't required on the set, Monty would closet himself in his dressing room with Mira. She was there as Monty's coach. For several years now, inspired by her association with Bobby Lewis and her success in working with Monty, Mira had been teaching actors privately or in small groups. The fact that she would drop them all and run to Monty only served to increase her reputation in theater circles and bring her more students. All of Monty's actor friends went to her: Kevin, Billy, Maureen Stapleton.

On the set of *The Heiress*, Monty lapsed into a super-serious pose and would talk to no one but her. Vanessa Brown, who played Moriah the maid, remembers that there was much gossip about Monty; they would wonder what was going on in that dressing room and why he would never come out. Columnists came on the set, but Monty refused to see them. Once Army Archerd managed to get to Monty. Monty knew the columnist had been questioning Vanessa Brown, and at his first question, Monty answered loudly, "Why, I would have thought that Vanessa would have filled you in on that already." Then he turned toward her with a fiendish gleam in his eye.

Sir Ralph Richardson performed brilliantly, but very competitively. He attempted to steal scenes from de Havilland as he would have on the London stage, by making peculiar gestures with his hands to call attention to himself. Cameraman Leo Tover solved the problem, however, by cropping the extraneous, theatrical body movements, while Richardson thought he was being photographed full figure. This was Wyler's conspiracy; he thought Richardson might have been offended if he criticized his acting.

De Havilland felt hemmed in by both Richardson and Monty. On the one hand, Richardson played London-stage tomfoolery with her, while on the other, Monty concentrated so hard on his own performance he forgot he had a partner. Monty rehearsed so thoroughly with Mira that by the time he got in front of the cameras, de Havilland might just as well have been a rehearsal stand-in. "Monty was painstaking and I liked that about him," she says, "but I had a sense that Monty was thinking almost entirely of himself and leaving me out of the scene. It was difficult for me to adapt to playing that way. But my having to adapt to him, and not his adapting to me, was really part of my character, so in the end it worked. But there was something else also . . . well, something in Monty that just stood apart from the proceedings."

Meanwhile, Herman Citron was begging Monty to move to Hollywood. "Sometimes you get your best offers at parties," Citron told him; "but you've got to live here to go to them." Monty was not impressed. New York, not Hollywood, was his life. "Does a factory worker live in the factory?" he said. He could be quite snide about the hypocrisy of Hollywood star-living, and once told Hedda Hopper, "Why don't you leave Hollywood and move to the world?" Such comments did not make Monty popular, but gave Paramount's publicity people a new angle for the press—*Montgomery Clift, Hollywood Rebel.*

Actually, Monty disliked parties as a rule; he preferred either little dinners or small intellectual groups, like Salka Viertel's in Santa Monica. Monty used to go there with Mira to socialize with Hollywood's most talented and subversive brains. George Tabori remembers: "Salka was the Mother Courage of Santa Monica, and the center of all the Great Exiles, like Thomas Mann, Brecht, Aldous Huxley. The Chaplins were regulars, and so was Garbo, who came on a white horse for breakfast. Salka was a marvelous bigmouth, then in her late fifties, and Monty was a bit in love with her. I suppose he had a mother complex like the rest of us. One night I saw him crawling across the living room floor, drunk, and reciting Yeats all the way to her feet, which he kissed." Kevin McCarthy was in Hollywood at the time, too, and also part of Salka's circle. He remembers that, at the time, Monty's version of being "drunk" was a few glasses of wine and a bit of *bravura.*

When the Communist blacklisting started in the fifties, the laughter at Salka's stopped. The careers of some of Monty's friends, like Annie Lincoln, were wrecked. What little group-socializing Monty did in Hollywood ceased.

Even before the completion of *The Heiress*, Billy Wilder had an idea for Monty's second Paramount film. He wanted to do a story about an aging silent screen star and a starving writer turned gigolo called *Sunset Boulevard.* Monty wanted to see the script, and Wilder killed himself to get him fifty pages of the completed screenplay. Monty loved it, told Herman Citron to give Wilder the go-ahead, and approved the novel co-casting of Gloria Swanson. It was announced in all the trade papers.

Both Wilder and Citron wanted Monty to stay in Hollywood for conferences on *Sunset Boulevard,* but as soon as he finished *The Heiress,* Monty flew to Switzerland to do some skiing and a little thinking. Something was preying on his mind. Finally he called Herman and told him. He could not go through with *Sunset Boulevard.* Citron couldn't believe his ears. *Why on earth not?* Monty explained apologetically that he had had trouble playing love scenes with an "older woman," and his artistic conscience wouldn't permit him to repeat the mistake. "Well, don't expect me to tell that to Billy Wilder," Citron roared. "You made a promise and the guy's counting on you." Paramount was counting on him, too. Finally, Citron said, "Okay. Drop out of the picture, but you come back to Hollywood and explain to Billy in person why you won't do the film." What Monty told Wilder was that his audience would never accept him making love to a woman thirty-five years his senior—a slightly different explanation from the one he had given to Citron. The real reason was that Monty didn't like the mother-loving implications that fans would sense in his image. He was already being deluged with letters from women who weren't quite sure whether they wanted to go to bed with him or wean him. *Sunset Boulevard* was too close to home.

Paramount, enraged, canceled his contract, but Monty shrugged it off and flew back to Europe. Fred Zinnemann was then in Israel with Stewart Stern, a young screenwriter, looking for a story for a new film. With great excitement, Monty joined them. Monty had never been in such a dangerous place before. Palestine had recently been partitioned; the angry Arabs and determined Israelis were fighting in spurts. The three of them spent a good deal of time in Jerusalem, and Arabs would jump on the crenelated wall dividing the two sectors and fire on anything that moved in the Jewish quarter. Big sheets of burlap had been set up to curtain off the streets nearest the wall, but the Arabs shot through blind. Monty was thrilled by the danger, the beautifully stalwart *palmach*—the elite of the young Israeli Army—and the sense of immediacy in a new country's painful birth. Monty and his two friends were forever in the coffee houses, soaking up atmosphere. Euphorically, Monty would approch soldiers, many of whom spoke English, and strike up long conversations. Sometimes he would tell Fred and Stewart that he was going off with some of the men, and he would be gone for days. The men of the *palmach* didn't know much about American movie stars, but it soon got around that Monty was famous in his own country. The Jewish soldiers found the idea of an American movie star in a combat zone fascinating. When Monty returned to rendezvous with Fred and Stewart, he shot out stories like a tommy gun, mimicking the mannerisms and hearty masculinity of the Israelis with great charm.

Stewart Stern remembers a night in Galilee when "Fred and Monty stayed on one kibbutz, which was under direct Syrian observation, and I went in a jeep to another, so that we could have different experiences. We had dinner in Monty's kibbutz. The meat they served had been hanging out in the sun for a long time, but out of courtesy we ate it. I didn't feel particularly well that night while I stood on guard with several of the soldiers. Dawn was just breaking. Suddenly I saw this shape reeling across the stones in front of us. The guard with me came alert and cocked his rifle, but as it got a little lighter there was something awfully familiar about the shape. I told the guard that I didn't think it was an Arab. It was Monty. He was so sick from whatever it was he had eaten that he had just lunged out of wherever he was and was contorting amidst the stones. He was convulsing; I thought he would die!

"He was still a gray silhouette, quite far away. I called to him, and he didn't answer, and I ran out there. I remember grabbing his head, because he was thrashing around so, and looking in his eyes . . . and suddenly there was recognition. It was weird; neither of us ever forgot that moment; it became the reference in whatever slight relationship we had. It was one of the most moving moments I've ever experienced. There was something so naked in Monty's expression, so vulnerable and so hurt. It was the physical pain, but also the jolt of recognizing somebody and trusting.

"Monty had always been my hero. I admired him so much that I wouldn't allow myself to get close to him before this happened. Now I suddenly felt trusted. After I held his head with both my hands, he grew docile and came back to the line, out of range of the Arab's observation. At any moment they might have shot him while he was out there."

Monty returned from Israel to another sort of war. The bobby-soxers usually besieged his apartment en masse after school, and it was his habit to let them into his apartment for a few minutes of ritual autograph signing, a few squeals of delight, and a bit of mock sincerity on his part. He also kept up endless interviews, even sent writers to the Mc-Carthys' apartment downtown for more exaggerated talk about how "gawddamned natural" he was.

Monty seemed to adore all the attention being paid him. He was quite jolly the night he went on a live radio show and a slightly embarrassed emcee suddenly found himself faced with an audience jammed with popeyed teenaged girls. "Please," begged the poor man, "we're going to be on live radio. Don't scream when Mr. Clift walks out on the stage." Monty loved to play fan-bait jokes for his friends. Typically, he would go into a dimly lit café and sit in a corner; he would be recognized of course, on the way in. Someone would scream: "Monty Clift's in here!", and Monty would falsetto his voice and shout, "Jesus, I just saw him go out the door." A band of girls would flock out of the café.

Monty still went up to Kennebunkport with Rick. They would go to the movies, or take girls out to dinner. Monty made a big deal out of attempting to remain anonymous—always in vain, naturally, which was part of the kick. Says Rick, "We'd make up a fictitious name for him, and Monty got such a charge out of suddenly being recognized in the middle of the evening. One of the girls would look at him a long time and then say, 'You're not So-and-So! You're Montgomery Clift!' And Monty's eyes would light up."

Then things began to go wrong. It was odd that the time Monty should have been at his happiest was the time the strangeness started. Only a few people saw it at first, but, like rippling circles in a pool, more and more of Monty's friends became aware. No one imagined, however, that it would become a permanent condition, or that it was anything more than a natural, temporary over-reaction to the fans, the loss of privacy, the interminable magazine pieces, the staggering overnight success.

Billy LeMassena was the first to notice. Monty had never touched a drop of liquor at dinner, and it was quite a surprise when he began ordering martinis. At first, Billy thought it wonderful that Monty had loosened up so. They would get sloshed, laugh a lot and whoop it up even before they got to the restaurant. But Monty started carrying it too far. He began howling at the waiters and pushing his food away. The food would splatter on the floor; Monty would goon around, making dreadful noises. Soon the laughter stopped. The scenes became terrible nightmares.

He would tell Billy about Israel, and about the Jews, and about how they were going to save the world. Jews were better than everyone else! He would rant about Lew Wasserman, head of MCA, as an example of those superior Jews who would lead them all to glory. He said he despised his parents because they were bigots who hated all the people in the world who were good and kind but different from them. Billy listened in amazement. Six years before, he and Monty had talked about the importance of never compromising honesty. Monty had always been intrigued by ethics and the need to fight such social injustices as bigotry, but Billy had never heard this fanatical tone before. It was hysterical. Billy told Monty that it was just a part of his parents' Wasp heritage and Monty should understand that; it didn't make them evil people. But Monty would insist: They *were* evil.

Says Billy, "Monty would have a few drinks and the shit would hit the fan. It was terrible, just hopeless. He would call them all of these names. He would have a tantrum on the floor. And he would swear. He would say, 'Mother, you really are a cunt.' We'd never heard Monty use such words! You'd want to die. The Clifts were just heartbroken. They couldn't understand, none of us could, what had caused it."

For a long time Ethel and Bill refused to accept what was happening. Ethel would try making a little joke of it when Monty came to the apartment. She would say, "Monty, what new thing are you going to accuse me of today?" The Clifts tried to be on their best behavior when Monty came, and watched what they said, but occasionally something would slip and Monty would go off like a bomb.

Bill was deeply distressed over these meetings with Monty. It wasn't only the temper and the name-calling that hurt; Bill feared this sudden drunkenness would destroy Monty's career. He knew from Billy that these performances were not just at the Clifts'. Bill was smart enough to sense an aura of self-destruction. He also knew that his other son, Brooks, was having marriage and career problems, yet never once did Bill acknowledge that he himself might have been partly to blame for it all. He just kept complaining that he didn't understand what was happening to Monty.

If Bill had thought about it, there was another element to Monty's anger, as well. Bill was enraged when Monty moved out of his parents' apartment. It wasn't right; it showed ingratitude. *Look* at all they had done for him. He wanted to hurt his son, and he did, excruciatingly. He sent him a bill for his education.

It took several years, but Monty paid back every cent in that itemized bill, and forever after bore a deep grudge. He never forgave them. Brooks, too, became bitter. He said, in a recent letter to Fitzroy Davis, that his parents never forgave either him or Monty for leaving home when they did.

The Clifts saw less and less of Monty. They kept calling him, asking him to come over, always hoping that things would settle down, but Monty answered them with abuse. Finally, the Clifts asked Billy to intercede, but matters got worse.

Alcoholism can begin in a variety of ways. It is uncommon for a man or woman to start guzzling in great quantities without some history of social drinking or some great shock that sets off the drinking mechanism like a burglar alarm. Monty had not been a social drinker; he was so careful about his health that he had even refused to take up smoking. If there was any immediate shock, it could only have been the shock of success. His basic approach toward life had always been cerebral, intellectual. True, he was high-strung and could experience bouts of depression, but they had never before resulted in serious acts of self-destruction.

What is significant is that this first extended alcoholic binge seems to have been directly triggered by problems with his parents. When Monty left for London in April, the alcoholic symptoms vanished as quickly as they had appeared.

Monty spent two weeks in London en route to Berlin to star in *The Big Lift*. To his delight and astonishment, he discovered he was an even bigger star in England than in the United States. Upon attempting to enter his room at Claridge's, he found the door blocked by such a large pile of letters from British fans that he had to force it open with both hands. One enterprising London columnist was so curious about the new star he actually asked Monty to open his bags for him, so he could report on what kind of underwear Monty wore, the color of his socks, the number of trousers, and other items of stupefying interest. Monty dutifully made the rounds of all the London movie magazines, saw a play almost every night and chatted with his fans on the street. He also had dinner with the actor he most admired, Laurence Olivier.

The Big Lift was not an acting vehicle. Directed by George Seaton, it was intended as simply another militaristic pro-America propaganda effort, a semi-documentary film about the airlift to Berlin during the Russian blockade of the city. The main interest lay in all the exciting aircraft doings, and the real-life Air Force men being photographed under harrying conditions. Monty knew the kind of picture it was, but longed to go into another war zone. He loved soldiers.

Before agreeing to do the film, however, he made a point of bringing Mira Rostova to Seaton's house in Hollywood and explaining that he had to have her on the set. This was the first time Monty had ever negotiated for Mira's presence. Monty knew Seaton was so hot to have him that he was sure to agree. In Berlin, however, Mira's signals to Monty began to unnerve Seaton. It was when the cameraman said, "She's directing your picture! Do you want that?" that Seaton finally broke. All his promises went out the window. He demanded that Mira leave the set. Monty answered that if she left, he left, too. Seaton capitulated. Shortly after that, however, just before a crucial scene was to be shot, his wife "just happened" to ask Mira to go to lunch with her. "I told Monty," says Mira, "that I wanted to leave Berlin right away. How could I stay, with everyone against me like that? But Monty wouldn't let me. It was ironic, because this was the first time Monty had ever formally introduced me to a director and the first time that I had been treated with such hostility."

Seaton was later credited with having made the random comment, "Well, if you cast Monty Clift in a picture, you'll have to add $150,000 to the budget. . . . He listens to his coach and will slow up the picture that much." The remark became a common item of Hollywood gossip. Such talk did Monty a great deal of harm and was untrue. In *The Big Lift*—as noted by the director of photography, Charles G. Clarke—technical problems created the added expense, not Mira or Monty. But the remark stood.

Mira began to balk at her growing reputation as Monty's Svengali. Fred Zinnemann, who felt her "hold" on Monty was unhealthy, expresses a common Hollywood feeling: "Mira Rostova reduced Monty to a state of uncertainty. She was bad for his work." The feeling was enlarged by the fact that Monty often became paralyzingly devoted to detail—which hand to put out to open a door, how to enter a room. The question was whether these obsessions were a product of Monty's fears, or of Mira's preoccupations. Mira says, "Everyone thought that I had some sort of hold on Monty. The truth was that he did follow almost all of my suggestions, but only because we were of one mind on what mattered in acting."

That summer of 1949, Monty had to rush through the final scenes of *The Big Lift* in order to get back to Hollywood. George Stevens' *A Place in the Sun* was due to go into production—and it would become one of Monty's most powerful cinematic achievements.

Stevens had a good reputation in Holywood, but he did not yet have the distinction or the power of a William Wyler. Before the war, he had done comedies and light social satires like *Penny Serenade* and *Gunga Din*, but nothing of any great seriousness or social import. The war changed Stevens' outlook vastly; for several years he had been looking for a story that would convey the tragic spirit of post-World War II America. He settled on Dreiser's *An American Tragedy*, a novel about a poor, social-climbing young man whose confused ideas about the importance of class and wealth lead him to the murder of his pregnant girlfriend and the electric chair. The only trouble was that George Stevens' own company, Paramount, had already made a version of the Dreiser book in 1931, and the picture had been a dismal failure. At first Paramount turned Stevens down flat, but he made an impassioned plea to the head of the studio, Henry Ginsberg. The new movie would be updated; it would have a strong appeal to youth. The young would see themselves in the dilemma of the characters, tempted by material riches, grasping for chimerical guises. With some teenage idol like Montgomery Clift in the main role, they would break the box office. Ginsberg was sold.

Interestingly, Monty had just read *An American Tragedy*. Rick had sent it with a note to say he would be terrific as the young man if a movie was ever made. Monty wrote back from Zurich to say that he would jump at the chance. It was as if fate had planned to bring them together. Just before Monty left to film *The Big Lift,* he told Rick he had just read the script, George Stevens wanted him, and, oh yes, who the hell was Elizabeth Taylor?

Elizabeth Taylor was then, at the age of seventeen, one of the most beautiful women in Hollywood. Her picture had already been on the cover of *Time* magazine. She was a star.

On her first day on the set, she appeared at the Paramount commissary and a kind of awed hush shot through the room. Elizabeth, usually accompanied by her mother and a "welfare" worker (a mandatory chaperone for teenage film actresses), had seldom been seen in public before. Her face, with large, electric eyes, was breathtaking; her young body perfectly formed. Directors and stars stopped eating and stared while she, her mother, and her agent headed for a side room. They finally settled at a table next to one occupied by a group of writers, at which Billy Wilder presided. During the hush, Wilder looked right at luscious Elizabeth and said, so everyone could hear: "How the hell did *she* ever get into movies!"

Taylor had been cast as the wealthy society girl for whom Monty kills his pregnant girlfriend. Although she was the most photogenic actress in her age group, her performances to date had been filled with child-actress clichés. MGM kept her playing America's darling, role after role —her most demanding role previously had been as Spencer Tracy's daughter in *Father of the Bride*. Stevens took a big chance in casting her in a principal dramatic role, but, as Stevens knew, there was guaranteed box office in casting both Monty and Elizabeth. They could not fail to be a major teenage draw.

For the part of the pregnant girl, Stevens chose a most unlikely performer: a highly temperamental young woman who usually played gaudy sexpots in grade B movies like *What A Woman!, Sailor's Holiday,* and *Tonight and Every Night*. She went by the stage name of Shelley Winters. The way she originally attracted Stevens' attention is legend.

She got Norman Mailer to write the director a note, saying she was interested in the part of Alice Tripp in *A Place in the Sun*. Stevens thought the very idea of Universal's cheapie glamour girl playing a Plain Jane idiotic, but out of curiosity, consented to meet her at the Hollywood Athletic Club. When he arrived, he could not find her, but after a while he noticed a shy, retiring little creature in a housedress sitting, as if terrified, some distance from him. It was Shelley Winters playing Alice Tripp, and rather well. He told her she was hired—provided she would do a screen test. She said she would, but she never did. Every time she was to show up, she would suddenly get sick. Stevens was furious at her for playing games with him. He finally decided to sign her without a test, but all of Stevens' confidants knew that, between them, the Punic Wars had begun.

George Stevens was also in conflict with himself over *A Place in the Sun*. By the time principal photography began in early fall, 1949, he had done a complete about-face in his original concept of the film. Perhaps, with a budget of two and a half million dollars—a lot of money for the sort of film he was making—and Paramount's fears over another commercial failure, Stevens decided to throw social commentary out the window in favor of success insurance. Now he wanted a compelling love story, with little to do with Dreiser's book except bare plot and some adherence to characterization. Instead of a young man pathetically misguided by the "American dream," Monty's character was now a romantic hero who must choose between a sorry nobody who nags him unmercifully and a beautiful, beguiling girl who loves him and just happens to be wealthy.

Stevens' defection haunted him, but he made up for it by devoting himself to creating extraordinary cinematic effects, in order to elevate what had become, in script form, a simple romance. He slaved to discover new ways of rendering conventional scenes, and to devise special cuts, camera angles, and symbolic devices. He was determined to have his performers not only tell the story, but also involve the audience empathetically.

Although Monty had not yet met Elizabeth Taylor, Paramount decided to plant the seeds of an off-screen romance by having Monty ask her to the premiere of *The Heiress*. Monty resisted until the last minute. First he said he didn't have a tux. Then he said he didn't have any money. What

87

if he had to take her out for a hamburger after the premiere? However, when Monty finally saw Elizabeth standing in the doorway of her house, a miracle of a girl, all his stubbornness vanished. His face radiated with flashing, boyish smiles.

Elizabeth had already caught a brief glimpse of Monty in George Stevens' office. She had heard he was a Method actor. All actors who attended the Actors Studio in New York were thought to be Method actors, extremely serious, and disdainful of movie stars. At the time, Elizabeth, a highly insecure older adolescent, thought of herself as a dumbbell with an attractive face. She had a mother and a legal chaperone. Monty was so advanced that he traveled with an acting coach! She was completely taken with the idea of Monty before she ever met him.

They stepped out of the limousine in front of the theater, and immediately attracted a crowd. An Associated Press photographer snapped a photo of Elizabeth adjusting Monty's tie; the shot of the two happy, single lovelies traveled all over the country. During *The Heiress,* Monty squirmed and fidgeted in absolute horror at what he saw on the screen. Elizabeth watched as Monty slipped down farther and farther, almost sliding off his seat. She was impressed. Such seriousness, she thought to herself.

That night, on a crazy impulse, he started calling her "Bessie" because, as he explained, he hated the idea of calling her by her movie-star name. The nickname stuck. All of Monty's friends thenceforth would talk about "Bessie."

The shooting of *A Place in the Sun* began in a tense atmosphere. Months of preparation and overwrought expectations filled the first few days with semi-hysteria. Stevens commanded Monty to keep Mira out of his way. It made Monty edgy and distrustful. The first sequence was to be Monty and Elizabeth making love by the side of a lake, and then splashing around in the water. Unfortunately, Lake Tahoe was freezing, and the scene was supposedly summer. It was so cold Stevens had to hose off snow patches to simulate the look of warm weather. Monty and Elizabeth were to throw off their clothes and run into the lake in bathing suits, but Monty said nothing doing. He had never exposed his body and wasn't about to now. Stevens backed down and rewrote the scene so that only Elizabeth would undress and then come back to throw water on Monty.

Stevens showed destructive impatience with everyone, especially insecure Elizabeth on that first day. He called for innumerable takes of her splashing in the ice-cold water, with extreme close-ups. Between each take, he would go stone silent with her, in essence telling her that she was garbage compared with Monty. Finally, in the scene where the two lovers are supposed to fall laughingly onto the grass, he ordered Monty to drop Elizabeth from a full-standing position. Monty did not realize he was carrying out Stevens' punishment. Sara Taylor, Elizabeth's mother, had already told him Elizabeth was menstruating and that any falls or exhausting activity would make her cramps worse. She had watched as Stevens told her daughter to run, take after take, through freezing water, but now this was really the last straw. She took Elizabeth back to the hotel and would not allow her to resume work for three days.

The rushes, however, proved extraordinary. The close-up camera caught a marvelous texture between Monty and Elizabeth, wonderful eye-work, a vulnerable yet definite involvement. Stevens' pressuring of Elizabeth plus the natural attraction Monty and Elizabeth felt for one another had created an unclichéd romantic fire. The close-ups worked so well he added more of them all through the film. He instructed the cameraman to come in tighter on their lips and pores and eyebrows than any cameraman had ever done before.

With some reservations, Monty and Elizabeth put up with Stevens' badgering—he was, after all, making them look exceptionally appealing on film—but Shelley Winters revolted. Stevens forced her to display a coarseness and vulgarity so profound that every other director in Hollywood demanded, afterward, that she play her parts the same way. As one of Miss Winters' friends observes, "Stevens was the first director to show Shelley that there was something in her that would make every man in America want to strangle her." He made her so unattractive, she finally stopped talking to Stevens altogether—which, of course, delighted him.

Elizabeth, at seventeen, reacted to Monty just like millions of other girls her own age. Like them, she longed for a benign sexual involvement with a man who was mature but vulnerable, masculine but sensitive, who had a thinly disguised need for mothering. Monty was all of those things—and, in her eyes an intellectual, besides. She was embarrassed when Monty told her he had been longing to appear in *An American Tragedy* ever since he had read the book. Elizabeth hadn't read it. She didn't know who Stanislavsky was. It was to be Elizabeth's life story that she would always be attracted to men who had something more than she: brains and talent (Monty), money (Nicky Hilton), social *savoir faire* (Michael Wilding), chutzpah (Mike Todd), theater training (Richard Burton), stability (John Warner).

She became passionately involved with Monty. Although she wanted to go to nightclubs and do all the things that top starlets did, she was satisfied to have dinner with him in little, out-of-the-way restaurants. She wrote schoolgirlish "I love you! I love you!" letters that testify to her fairly immature state of mind. Some of them actually proposed marriage. Monty turned all the letters over to Rick, with vivid descriptions of how mad Elizabeth was for him. Giving those letters to his male lover was, unmistakably, a self-congratulatory gesture, and a cruel, if unconscious, mockery of the beautiful young girl who had written them.

It was as if he thought her love to be simply a great accomplishment, rather than something in which he was personally involved. At dinner, he would go on about how excited he was that Elizabeth was interested in him: "I wonder how she could even talk to me."

Although Elizabeth surely wanted it, they did not make it to the bedroom. It was probably one of the deepest disappointments in Elizabeth's life at that time, and the possible reason she rushed into marriage with Nicky Hilton, whom she had just met. She became hurtfully aware that Monty was homosexual. As she was later to relate:

"For three days Monty played the ardent male with me and we became so close. But just as he'd overcome all of his inhibitions about making love, he would suddenly turn up on the set with some obvious young man that he had picked up. All I could do was sit by helplessly and watch as he threw this in my face. Then the young man would be gone, and Monty would act as if he were trying to make something up to me, affectionate all over again. I felt he was trying to fight it, but I didn't know what I was supposed to do. Was I supposed to say, 'Monty, everything is all right. We can be the same as before—I understand'? I thought he wanted me to play *Tea and Sympathy* with him.

It happened a couple of times. Finally I just said to him, 'Look, Monty, I'm always here for you—for whatever you want.' "

It was that sudden bolt of understanding and maturity in Elizabeth which bound Monty in friendship to her for life.

Monty seemed to have a need to "confess" to young women, as if somehow, in burdening them with his sexual conflicts, he could release himself from his inhibitions and be free to love more honestly.

Screenwriter Ivan Moffat calls what Elizabeth brought to Monty, on- and off-camera, "a thrust of physicality or sexual emotion, a convexity," while Monty played "with concavity, as if he was receiving the mothering tentacles of the world. As George Stevens watched their relationship grow, he began to direct them into a similar on-screen relationship. He inserted bits of dialogue for her: "What's the matter, George?" "Do you love me, George?" "You seem so strange, so deep, so far away, as though you were holding something back." In the filming of that extraordinary love scene, which would send teen hearts surging and pumping, Stevens had her say as the camera came in extremely tight, "Tell mama . . . tell mama all." It was Stevens' way of exploiting Monty's image as a man in search of a mother. During that scene, Elizabeth's mouth is slightly open, Monty's body hunched and his cheeks drawn. It is a thoroughly devastating cinematic moment, and one of the finest pieces of romantic acting Monty had ever done.

In *A Place in the Sun*, however, Monty achieved much, much more than simply the heights of romantic performance. With George Stevens' sometimes gentle, sometimes abrasive help, he reached a passive intensity uncommon for men on the screen. His awkward mannerisms, hesitations, and air of painful vulnerability would translate into a screen image so profound that, upon the film's release, he would become far more than just a "teenage idol"—he would be the most important young star in the movie industry.

Soon after completing *A Place in the Sun*, Monty and Kevin decided to write a screenplay. Rewriting bad passages had always been one of Monty's greatest joys, and since he and Kevin shared a disdain for the way most movies were written, it seemed natural for the two of them to show Hollywood how to do a screenplay. No movie had ever been made of Monty's stage hit *You Touched Me!*, and all they had to do was write the screenplay, then they could produce, direct, and star in it themselves!

For six months, they scribbled furiously, Kevin on writing pads, Monty on the backs of used envelopes, matchbook covers, paper bags, little notebooks—whatever was handy. He drove Kevin crazy with his meticulousness, questioning the veracity of every word, rewriting his own material so often that for every line he used, he crossed out fifteen. Finally, the work was finished, and with beaming pride they showed it to Donald Windham who, with Tennessee Williams, had co-authored the original play. "It was awful," says Windham. "The manuscript was as thick as an unabridged dictionary and full of lines like 'Would you like to stroke my pussy?' "

Nevertheless, they forged ahead, determined to get it produced. They sent it to Lew Wasserman to find a movie company (during the ensuing months, every studio would reject it), and that summer began scouting a locale. They decided on a New England setting, and partly as a home base, rented a house in Truro, on Cape Cod, from Kevin's sister, writer Mary McCarthy. It was there that Kevin and Augusta began to worry about Monty's state of mind.

Kevin had become aware of Monty's drinking but, like Billy, thought Monty was finally just "loosening up." In Truro, however, peculiar things began happening. One day Kevin and Augusta found Monty, drunk, cutting a steak on the living room floor. Another night, as they were getting ready for bed, they suddenly heard Monty thrashing about outside the house, and then a series of noises: Monty throwing the trash into his Buick Century, starting up the car, crashing into something, restarting the car, driving to the dump, dumping the trash, then screeching back to the house. Monty would suddenly begin to eat his food with his hands. He would collapse onto the floor as if he had blacked out for a few moments. Monty had only recently taken up smoking; the McCarthys saw strange cigarette burns hidden on the backs of their delicate white wooden mantelpieces.

Mary McCarthy saw some of this, too, and when Kevin and Augusta came to her for advice said she felt that Monty might be suffering from hebephrenic schizophrenia (or just hebephrenia), a form of schizophrenia which usually attacks older adolescents but can also strike adults, in which the victim reverts to childhood behavior. Augusta and Kevin told Monty, as tactfully as they could, that perhaps he should see a psychiatrist. Instead of shutting them out, Monty said, in a grateful tone of voice, "I'll do it. I must do it."

Rick, too, began to notice strange things. One time, Monty came up to stay with Rick and his family in Kennebunkport. They were still sleeping in separate bedrooms to keep up a front. Rick's brother happened to be there at the same time, and one night Monty became quite drunk, and in front of Rick's brother, who knew nothing of their relationship, kept telling Rick over and over, that he loved him. Rick looked at his brother in absolute terror that the cover had been blown, but the brother thought Monty was just putting on some stupid little scene, repeating dialogue from a film script, or whatever nutty things actors do. While Monty shouted, "I love you! You know I love your brother!" the two brothers dragged Monty down to the ocean and gave him a good dunking to shut him up.

There was, of course, liquor involved, and Kevin knew that Monty took strong analgesics for the periodic colitis and intestinal pains that he suffered; it doesn't take a genius to suspect that combining them with liquor in great quantities can bring hidden personality traits to the surface. Although he didn't know what pills Monty was taking, he could tell that the liquor alone wasn't enough to justify such personality distortion. He suspected that Monty's partial understanding of his behavior was itself part of what was troubling Monty. "Monty got a glimpse of his mental condition. When my sister said that it was probably hebephrenic schizophrenia, she inadvertently had gotten hold of the truth. I think Monty already knew about that truth."

It was an eerie rerun of Monty's childhood. That childhood contained cracks, poor buttressing, incompletions—and, like a house falling in on its poorly constructed basement, Monty, under the mounting pressures of independent adulthood and the attempt to acquire a new *persona*, was caving in on himself. Before, there had always been Ethel to keep the house from falling. Ironically, and perhaps unwittingly, she had arranged the design of her support so that any ultimate rejection of her would force the house to crumble.

About that time, Monty began seeing a psychiatrist,

confiding the details to Mira, but to no one else. The McCarthys must never know, he insisted, because "it's the lie of my life." He chose a prestigious, expensive psychiatrist by the name of William V. Silverberg, who had offices at 315 Central Park West. Fifty-three years of age, Dr. Silverberg had roots all the way back to Sigmund Freud himself through an early disciple of Freud's, Dr. Franz Alexander, with whom Silverberg had taken his training analysis in 1928. Later, after earning many outstanding credentials, Silverberg broke with Freud and became part of what we would now call the liberal Behaviorist School, which follows a set of theories that have been debated for decades. He espoused concepts such as "effective aggression," which he once defined as "the ability to achieve what one wishes to achieve regardless of obstacles." According to Dr. Ruth Fox, a New York psychiatrist who took her training analysis with Dr. Silverberg and who has for many years specialized in the treatment of alcoholics, Dr. Silverberg did not believe that rigorous analysis of childhood-based root problems was necessary, or even desirable, in dealing with neurotic disorders that made the patient's life unhappy. He believed that if one could convince the patient to live differently, then the stage would be set for a "cure."

Monty was like an excited kid about seeing the doctor. This wonderful man was going to help him. They talked every day about Monty's "not living well" and "not being as aggressive as one should be" as a young man. Monty turned down every film offer in order to see him, and continued to do so for the next two years. In an attempt to put some regulation into his life, he gave up his forty-dollar-a-month walk-up for an expensive duplex apartment at 209 East 61st Street, which he kept oddly bare, never quite bringing himself to decorate it properly. He hired a cook to prepare seven separate meals, wrap them, and store them in the freezer for him to defrost daily and eat whenever he wished. It was as if he were trying to counteract the storm of disruption within him, by erecting an environmental fortress.

But he did not get better. Indeed, as the months progressed, the drinking got worse. People would try to be supportive and tell him, "You can pull yourself together again." Kevin remembers once saying to him at a party, " 'You've gone so far in the direction of control, and self-possession, and definition . . . You're just sort of fatigued with it and you've gone in the other direction awhile.' You see, it seemed that it never occurred to him to drop this very studied approach to life and work, to just say, 'What happens if I go to work tomorrow and do that scene— just to see what's in *me?*' He said he wanted to explore what hell was like, and then come back. He talked a lot about Dostoyevsky's idea of darkness. Maybe this was *ex post facto,* a rationalization of the way he was going. Or maybe he truly did want to investigate the depths of human despair. But he never came back."

After he rented the duplex, Monty took on a "live-in" lover by the name of Dino. He was Italian-born, around Monty's age, an unemployed airline pilot married to a stewardess, and worked as a waiter in a small Italian restaurant. At the time, Monty was friendly with writer Truman Capote who, with some of Monty's other friends, knew about Dino. "He was an absolute moron," says Capote. "It was quite a mystery to me what Monty saw in him. Monty would travel with him everywhere." Suddenly, many young men like Dino were hanging around, and the ones Monty seemed most interested in were those who were the trashiest. "Perhaps," Mira speculates, "Monty had been brought up among such cultivated people that he now felt he had to rebel. Or maybe he needed people around who would not question his habits."

The new lover did not help Monty's drinking habits. Dr. Silverberg asked Dr. Ruth Fox to see him since he was having no success with the drinking, and the day of the appointment Monty walked into her waiting room and promptly passed out on the floor. Dr. Fox knew simply talking to Monty would do absolutely no good now, and immediately put him into the Regent Hospital for four days to dry him out. Unfortunately, since she sensed there might also be a drug problem, she dared not order one of the normal drying-out techniques, which is to use certain drugs to produce the same strong psychomotor effects as alcohol. For Monty, it was straight cold turkey.

She attempted to talk with him after the drying-out and make him understand the problem of alcoholism, but as Dr. Fox recalls, Monty wasn't at all interested in going to Alcoholics Anonymous; he *wanted* to drink. The only time it scared him was when he suddenly found he was unable to function—as when he passed out in her office—or when the drinking made him sick all day. She gave him Antabuse, a drug that makes the user violently ill if he consumes the smallest amount of alcohol. Monty made jokes about it, and would disappear for a month, until he came back so sick he had to be hospitalized again. Monty never did give her a chance to help. It wasn't a cure he wanted; it was a better tolerance for the liquor.

It is difficult to pin down exactly when Monty began to mix heavy drug-taking with his drinking. Most likely he had already begun taking "downs" (either barbiturate- or opiate-based) with liquor in the period that followed *A Place in the Sun*—the sudden blacking-out episodes would strongly indicate that. Bob Ardrey witnessed one such incident. Monty had heard that Thornton Wilder's sister, Isabel, was due to arrive in New York from France by ship. He wanted to surprise her at the pier, and so made elaborate plans with Bob Ardrey to meet her at eight-thirty that night. At seven o'clock, they ate a big dinner at Monty's, accompanied by only a few glasses of wine, but twice Monty excused himself to go into the john. When they finally arrived at the pier, Monty suddenly stumbled and fell like a dead weight. It seemed suspiciously unnatural, but Monty seemed to recover all right. By this time, they had missed Isabel by an hour, so they headed back toward the Gotham Hotel, where Bob was then living, and decided to have a drink.

The bartender took one look at Monty and said, "Coca-Cola for him."

"Listen," Bob protested, "we've been together all night and I know he hasn't been drinking."

"I'm sorry," insisted the bartender, "but he gets Coke."

"Fuck you!" cursed Bob, and took Monty the hell out of there. What he hadn't realized was that it was not a drunk the bartender was refusing to serve. Bob Ardrey, like so many others in those days, knew little about drugs and their effects.

Then, on the sidewalk, Monty fell again, this time completely prostrate. His eyes were weirdly half-closed. Bob helped him to his feet and said, "I think I'd better take you home."

"Yes, thanks," mumbled Monty, only half-conscious.

When they got back, Monty, groggy and incoherent, had to crawl up the stairs on his hands and knees, and Bob had to carry him to the couch. Bob just couldn't understand it; he had been with Monty all evening and Monty hadn't been drinking at all. Bewildered and even slightly frightened at the sight of self-controlled Monty Clift in this state, he finally decided to let him sleep it off, and went home himself. But he never forgot the incident and it continued to prey on his mind.

Monty also told Rick at this time that he was using drugs, and that he and Libby would get high together at Treetops. Libby's seventeen-year-old son, Christopher, had just been killed in a mountain-climbing accident in California, and she was deeply depressed.

Monty was not a ubiquitous drunk. He revealed his condition only to some of his friends. It was a holdover from his childhood, the calculating way he had of telling one person one bit of information, someone else another; of showing some his drunken, drugged state, others only a thoughtful, well-integrated personality. He was able to do this by carefully partitioning his friends. At the duplex apartment, he would hold little talk groups, which now included new Hollywood friends like Greta Garbo, and people from the Actors Studio like Karl Malden. With them, he displayed decorum and propriety. To others, old friends like the McCarthys, Mira, Billy, Ned—and a new friend from Hollywood, now living in New York, Roddy McDowall—he revealed a personality that was brittle and breaking. Prestigious writers were godlike to Monty, and so there was almost a cry for help implied in his attempts to reveal aspects of his condition to people like Ardrey and Wilder. Such solitary men, however, were the last people willing or able to aid Monty. Thornton Wilder, who told people he thought Monty incredibly handsome and delightful, used to meet with him frequently; but as soon as Wilder smelled smoke, he ran, without even looking at the blaze. He dropped out of Monty's life completely.

In March 1951, Monty received his second Academy Award nomination, for *A Place in the Sun*. Marlon Brando was also nominated for *A Streetcar Named Desire*, but Humphrey Bogart won it for *The African Queen*. It was at that time that Monty saw a young actor by the name of James Dean perform at the Actors Studio. James Dean was still a total nobody. Dean had spotted Monty at the Studio a few times, and ached to meet him, but every time Dean's name was mentioned, Monty got fidgety and irrationally defensive. No, Monty absolutely did not want to meet him—especially anyone whose style or image in any way approached his own. Monty never did say what he thought of Dean's acting at the Studio.

By the summer of 1952, Monty was ready to get back to work. Every director in Hollywood wanted a crack at him, despite the damaging rumors they had heard about the frustrating interference of his acting coach, and Alfred Hitchcock won out, with *I Confess*, based on Paul Anthelme's play about a priest who is charged with murder after the murderer has confessed the crime to him in the confessional.

Olivia de Havilland was also being considered for a part, and one night she had dinner with Hitch and Monty to discuss the movie. Olivia remembers: "At Hitch's that evening, Monty was so different from the reserved person with whom I had worked on *The Heiress*. I felt he wasn't fully himself. I think Hitch was rather puzzled too. Monty was extremely nice and attentive to me that night—flatteringly, alarmingly attentive! There seemed to be something hyperintense and overexcited about him, as if he were under the influence of some form of stimulant. It seemed to me his eyes had a different look, his pupils somewhat dilated. Monty was a slow and hesitant talker, but this night he talked fast. I said to myself that either his reaction to alcohol is quite unique, or it's something else. He offered to drive me home that night, and if I hadn't had my own car, I would still have said no."

She did not find *I Confess* suitable for her (it wasn't), and Anne Baxter finally signed for the part.

I Confess took less than two months to film in Quebec and Hollywood. Hitchcock was counting on the free use of various Catholic churches in Quebec to shoot the most important scenes, but after the local diocese read George Tabori's finished script, which included the shocking event of a priest being executed for murder, all facilities were denied. Instead of remaining stalwart and seeking a different location, Hitch called Tabori back to rewrite the ending and to soften the persecutory scenes. Tabori says, "I felt betrayed. I walked out in the middle of a story conference with the excuse of having to take a leak, went straight to the airport, to New York City, and never came back. Hitchcock still gets purple in the face when he hears my name." Another screenwriter, William Archibald, was called in. Since the core of the film had involved the Christ-like persecution of the innocent priest by his own people, Archibald had to replace that epicenter with a great deal of subplotting, involving irrelevant romantic melodrama and sentimentality. It was a mess.

Every day, Hitchcock arrived on the set with detailed instructions for the shooting of every frame of the movie. It is well known that he used his actors as pawns for his own special effects and he simply couldn't understand the fanatical intensity of a Monty. He complained constantly about "all that preparation." At the beginning of the film, Monty insisted on changing the color of his eyes by wearing special brown contact lenses, because the priest's eyes were described as brown, and his were blue. But this was a black and white film! Over and over, Hitch had to stop and explain to Monty why, at the end of a certain take, he had to look up at a church, or suddenly turn around. He wasn't used to having to explain to his actors that he intended to edit in a shot of a clanging bell or some other such event. Monty needed to understand everything holistically. In the end, his performance was a great feat of concentration, all the more powerful because of the inherent dullness of the script.

Monty drank continually throughout the shooting of *I Confess*, though never on the set. Mira became alarmed. Always before, Monty had spent his evenings quietly with her, but now he was running around to bars, getting plastered, mingling with rough trade—even provoking fistfights. He seemed to be trying to follow Silverberg's advice, to become more aggressive.

As best she could, Mira tried to find out from Monty why he had changed so. It always seemed to come back to Silverberg. Monty insisted on using a code when they discussed the psychiatrist in public, because Monty was paranoid about reporters overhearing; they had to refer to him as "Victor," his middle name. It seems Monty would describe his crazy behavior to "Victor" in New York, and Silverberg would tell Monty that this behavior was good, because it meant that Monty was reliving a carefree childhood that he had never had. Mira tried to convince Monty not to take Silverberg's advice as gospel. No, Monty said, he agreed with Silverberg. He did not have enough control over his own life. He lacked aggressiveness. He should learn to live more freely. If he wanted to hang around trashy people, he should do it. Over and over, Mira tried to talk Monty out of this new prescription for living. Monty would listen to her, then his attention would drift away.

Meanwhile, Vittorio De Sica wanted Monty for a new film, which would be backed and distributed in America by David O. Selznick. It was to be another neo-realistic art film, similar to De Sica's *The Bicycle Thief*, which Monty greatly admired, and would be called *Stazione Termini*. Production would begin in Rome as soon as *I Confess* finished. At their first meeting, they discovered that De Sica couldn't speak English very well, and Monty had completely lost his Italian, so the two of them conferred in a funny broken French. The director suggested that, because the two of them were having such difficulty speaking with each other, De Sica could use an Italian stand-in actor for Monty, direct him in his native tongue, then have Monty observe him, and copy. It was an absurd idea!

When Monty left for Rome, he did not take Mira. Instead, he took Dino. It was the first time since *The Search* that Monty had not asked Mira to accompany him. Dino carried Monty's luggage, looked after him, admired his stardom, and never made much of a fuss about his drinking. He was also a fickle opportunist, and soon began cheating on his famous lover.

Stazione Termini, based on an original story by Cesare Zavattini, was to be a film about two people, an Italian named Giovanni, and an American housewife on vacation in Rome named Mary. They have a brief tryst and must then go through the agony of parting in a Rome railway station, surrounded by the helter-skelter of troubled humanity rushing to meet trains. These other desperate people would bring the central love story into perspective and show how inconsequential it was in relation to the whole human condition. Naturally, De Sica's neo-realistic style did not admit such distractions as Hollywood close-up shots and the "star treatment."

David O. Selznick assured De Sica that *Stazione Termini* would be backed as a non-commercial art film, and that no Hollywood-type pressures would be brought to bear. Perhaps he actually believed it, but after he forced De Sica into casting his wife, Jennifer Jones, as the American woman, and then came to Rome to personally oversee the direction of the film, all promises went out the window. The filming, along with De Sica's hopes, turned into a charade.

Selznick had reached the end of his career in Hollywood and could not accept retirement gracefully. Because of the difference in their ages, his marriage to Jennifer Jones had become nothing more than a father-daughter arrangement —with Miss Jones, because of her religious upbringing, unwilling to seek a divorce. Selznick saw the De Sica film as a new chance not only to influence Hollywood again, but to guide his wife's career.

The entire film was to take place at night in the railway station, so shooting began at midnight and ended at five or six in the morning. De Sica's English was too poor to enable him to comprehend the difficulties in the dialogue, which had been worked on by such writers as Carson McCullers, Paul Gallico, and finally Truman Capote, but still sounded hopelessly sentimental. It was a case of too many cooks. Selznick would sit up all night in a lounge of the Stazione Termini writing forty-page memos on the daily rushes, insisting that there weren't enough close-ups of Jennifer, or that she didn't look elegant enough, or that her nose was too shiny. He would rewrite Capote's dialogue, sending the revisions to De Sica either just before or after the scene was shot. He would say that American audiences wanted lush romance, and De Sica wasn't supplying it. Vittorio, who desperately needed his sleep after shooting all night, spent his days trying to decipher the memos and meeting with Selznick. The memos were in English, and after a while they all became a blur to the exhausted director. He began to think that they were veiled legal threats and hired a lawyer to interpret them for him.

"In the end everybody blew his top," says Wolfgang Reinhardt, the assistant producer. "We were running into the Christmas traffic at the station, and the engine drivers complained that as they drove there were too many floodlights. The station manager told us that he could no longer assure the company security from the crowds of people. We never saw the light of day. The workers got irritable. No day went by without someone having a hysterical fit. The worst happened during the great love scene between Monty and Jennifer. It had been rewritten two or three hundred times. The scene got so tense that nobody was allowed on the set except the cameramen and principals. It was just awful! As soon as the actors did it, Selznick would have it rewritten, translated into Italian so that Zavattini, who couldn't read a word of English, could approve it, and then given to the actors to perform again. Finally Jennifer threw off her shoes and stockings and ran out into the street. Selznick ran after her, and she was so hysterical she slapped him across his glasses. They broke, and he wandered around unable to see, while we all ran after Jennifer, because she was still thrashing through the people on the street, while the technicians pretended not to notice what was happening."

Truman Capote did his best to mediate. He recalls: "Jennifer got some sort of crush on Monty, and believe it or not she didn't realize that Monty really liked fellows. When she found out she got so upset, she went into the portable dressing room and stuffed a mink jacket down the portable toilet."

Capote spent a lot of time with Monty and Dino, and recalls that Monty was drinking a lot. "I suppose there was some sort of romantic problem between them." Wolfgang Reinhardt did more than suppose. "Monty was extremely upset over Dino, and there was some kind of competition going on between Monty and Truman. It was the one personal problem that I knew Monty was having." In the end, Monty got rid of Dino.

Selznick had no control over the European editing or distribution of *Stazione Termini,* and, with Zavattini's original dialogue, it ran over two hours, and became quite successful as another fine example of De Sica *neorealismo.* For the American release, however, Selznick stupidly chopped the film up, removed most of the important subplots, and inserted huge close-ups of Monty and Jennifer all the way through. It was retitled *Indiscretion of an American Wife* (which Selznick insisted was a "commercial" title, despite studio objections), trimmed to a running time of sixty-three minutes—so short that Columbia had to preface it with a juke-box filler featuring Patti Page. Both Monty and Jennifer came out looking silly. Fortunately for Monty, Selznick spent a year cutting the film before its release in 1954, and by that time Monty had reached the height of his fame and was fairly invulnerable.

Monty's very next film, in fact, brought him to a zenith

which could have established him for the rest of his life as the most sought-after actor in the English-speaking world. Why, at the age of thirty-two, he chose to fall from that height is the puzzle of Monty's life.

CHAPTER FIVE

Demons

IT was no mere accident that Monty was chosen to play Robert E. Lee Prewitt, the greatest role of his career. An irresistible chain of events led to the matching of actor and part.

From Here to Eternity by James Jones was perhaps the single most important novel to come from the returning veterans in the early fifties, with the possible exception of *The Naked and the Dead*. Harry Cohn, Columbia Pictures' Ivan the Terrible, bought it for $82,000, despite the obvious difficulties of converting a novel about barracks life, full of sadism, sex, and four-letter words, into a strong screenplay at a time of fairly mild movies.

For several years, Cohn burnt up a small militia of writers, including James Jones himself, in an effort to keep the book's color and impact intact, but only Hollywood newcomer Dan Taradash's treatment satisfied him. Taradash insisted on Fred Zinnemann as director. Zinnemann was already gaining a reputation for pictures dealing with undercurrents of suppressed human emotions in taut action situations, such as *The Search, The Men,* and *High Noon* (as yet unreleased). After much protesting, Cohn agreed to Zinnemann, but insisted that either Aldo Ray or John Derek, new Columbia stars, play the key role of Prewitt.

Meanwhile, back in New York City, Monty attended a crucial party thrown by literary pundit Vance Bourjaily. The atmosphere was heady with writers. Most of them, including Norman Mailer and James Jones, had never met Monty before, and, as Jones says, "Mailer and I and all the others at the party were all impressed by him. He

104

seemed like such a sensitive, perceptive guy. Instead of being a self-centered, cocky kind of movie star, he played it very low-keyed. All of us felt that he was more like us, an artist rather than a typical movie star."

Monty flattered the egos of Jones and Mailer by being obviously worshipful of them; they, in turn, were so thrilled by this star who thought that *they* were the stars, that they practically kidnapped him from Bourjaily's, took him down to the corner bar, then "sat on the sidewalk just bullshitting."

Jones said to Monty, "Gee, it's too bad you're not playing Prewitt. I think you could do it beautifully."

Monty said, "I'd like to play it."

"Hell, they already chose John Derek to play it. He'll be awful. You ought to write them a letter or get your agent to do it."

"I couldn't do that," said Monty. "If I did that and they knew I wanted the part, they wouldn't give it to me just on general principle."

So Jones himself wrote a letter to the producer, Buddy Adler. Adler loved the idea. He spoke to Fred Zinnemann. Zinnemann loved the idea. "In the book there is a line about Prewitt being a deceptively slender man, and I knew right away that was Monty," says Zinnemann. Part of their attraction for one another, and ease in working together, had always been their striking similarity of spirit. Both were quiet, stubborn men who put a high value on their professional integrity. Cohn's objections only made Zinnemann more adamant. He announced that he absolutely could not do the film without Montgomery Clift.

Cohn said absolutely no; Prewitt was supposed to be a boxer and Monty looked too frail. Finally, after much sparring, they came up with a compromise: Zinnemann would at least screentest Cohn's stars, John Derek and Aldo Ray. Of course the tests showed the competition to be nowhere near Monty in suitability. Tyrannical Cohn was forced to give in to his director and producer, but would later pay them back for their independence by terrorizing the production in Honolulu.

From then on, events moved swiftly. Monty received the screenplay, loved it, gave MCA the go-ahead, and was the very first actor signed—for $150,000. It was all clean and quick.

Monty knew from the outset that *From Here to Eternity*

was special: something about the tightness of the script, the realism, the perfect Shakespearean balance between vivid character types and prototypes. Prewitt was almost Monty's exact psychological double, yet one who lived in a totally different world. Monty was struck by Prewitt's stubborn energy. He spent weeks delving into the script, plumbing motivations, working at Klein's gym to get his body in shape.

Weeks before the start of shooting, he flew out to Tucson, Arizona, to huddle with James Jones about the character of Prewitt. During those four days of intense discussions, Jones sensed Monty studying him, especially his mannerisms. Jones, like Mailer, had had his psyche partly molded by the Army, and was totally involved with military, masculine mannerisms. Monty was awed by Jones the writer and Jones the military man. At the premiere of *From Here to Eternity,* someone at Scribner's exclaimed to Jones' editor, "He's copying Jim! Look how he moved his shoulders and how he moves his head on his neck to one side." Later, Jones realized what Monty had really been doing during those four days of Prewitt-discussions.

Jones also spent time trying to show Monty how to throw a left jab so that it snapped from the elbow. Monty simply couldn't get the hang of it.

In Hollywood, Monty's marathon preparation continued. The script required that Prewitt have technical proficiency as both a boxer and a bugler, and, naturally, Monty wanted trumpet lessons so that he would look convincing. The studio got him the best—Manny Klein, a well-known trumpeter. Monty wore him out. He insisted on being taught how to read bugle sheet music, and on having all the fingering, breathing, and pauses indicated next to the notes. By the end of the first week, Monty's playing was enthusiastic but ear-splittingly off-key. Six o'clock in the morning would find distraught residents of Monty's hotel pounding on his door or calling the desk to beg for peace.

Monty was thoroughly delighted with his own "proficiency." One night Fred Zinnemann and Dan Taradash dropped by to see him in his tenth floor suite overlooking Hollywood Boulevard. Monty had had a few, but wasn't especially cockeyed drunk. He opened the window, picked up his new bugle, and blew something terribly discordant out into the peaceful night. He was wild with happiness that he could make such a sound. Fred and Dan got Monty away from the window.

Monty also took boxing lessons from an ex-fighter named Mushy Calahan for the big fight scene, and told him, "I want to look like Sugar Ray Robinson." It was the least successful of his pre-film preparations. He never really learned how to throw a punch properly. At least in that department, Aldo Ray would have been one up on him.

After waking everybody up with his bugling at 6 A.M., Monty would practice marching like a soldier and then jog around the Hollywood High School athletic field. "He worked so hard at all of this," says Renée Zinnemann, "that he was almost all worn out by the time they started shooting."

It was entirely deliberate on his part, his own way of achieving total identification with a character who must appear physically and spiritually debilitated by the inhumanity of barracks life. But if Monty was to scourge himself for the sake of creating *another* reality, he was also compelled to plumb the depth of his own reality with increasing intensity.

Mira stood by helplessly as she watched Monty court disaster. He had gotten into the habit of drinking in the afternoon and then driving around Hollywood at reckless speeds. She never knew how drunk he was before he got behind the wheel. These drunken drag races were hideous. Before her eyes, the sensitive young man turned into Mr. Hyde, careening at frightening speeds. Mira could feel the chill of something beautiful turning demonic: "I was becoming afraid of the way he was behaving. I felt that his driving was getting dangerous—not so much for me, but for him. When we were together and he was in that condition, I knew that I couldn't say anything. Monty would only have gotten angry. He was becoming so unpredictable."

At the time, Monty was friendly with Merv Griffin, who was then unknown. Mira remembers one afternoon Monty had promised to pick them up in his rented car and drive them all back to the hotel. He came screeching to a halt in front of them, from a furious speed thirty or forty miles above the speed limit, obviously soused. Monty told them to hop in. Mira hesitated. Griffin good-naturedly suggested that Monty let him take the wheel. Monty wouldn't hear of it. He kept shouting at them in angry, abusive language.

107

Griffin kept trying to change Monty's mind. Suddenly, Monty put his foot on the accelerator and took off. Hours later, he finally showed up again, in the same hostile mood as before. During those weeks in Hollywood, he often treated Mira like that.

When Monty sobered, the two of them would sit and talk, with Monty again quietly respectful of Mira's sensitivity and concern. It was only then that she communicated her fears to him. Would he consider maybe not seeing "Victor" so often, and perhaps consult with another psychiatrist? Monty contritely listened to Mira's gentle exhortations. He told her he knew that something was wrong, but he didn't know what. He didn't know if she was right about Silverberg. It was always a touchy subject.

Monty had begun reevaluating his whole relationship with Mira. Dr. Silverberg wanted him to "stand up" to her and drop her; Mira wanted him to drop Silverberg. It was really a dispute over who would get Monty, and he was torn between his need for her and his growing anxiety that her presence would weaken him as a man. He asked Fred Zinnemann if it was all right for Mira to come on the set after they began production, and, of course, Monty already knew what Zinnemann's answer would be. It was such a devious way to get rid of her. Mira returned to New York before principal photography began.

Shortly after she left, Monty called her long distance. "I want you to go to see Dr. Silverberg," he said, but gave no reason, simply saying that he wanted Mira and his psychiatrist to get to know one another. Perhaps the opponents could talk it out and reach some sort of truce on the question of whose advice Monty was to take. Mira did call Dr. Silverberg at his office. As soon as he heard her name, however, he grew hostile. He was much too busy to see her and said that, in any case, it would be unethical for him to discuss his client with her. As Mira struggled to make the doctor understand that Monty was in great danger, Dr. Silverberg countered abrasively with: "What drinking? I don't know what you're talking about," and "What dangerous driving?" Mira was unable to make the doctor admit that anything she said had validity, and his tone consistently put her off. It was clear that he was not about to let *anyone* interfere with his relationship with Monty. Mira sensed a tremendous selfishness and destructiveness, and became more convinced than ever that she had to get Monty away from him.

Mira's temporary "replacement" in Hollywood was a young actor by the name of Jack Larson. Jack was then playing Jimmy Olson on the popular *Superman* television series, and he really had that "Gosh, Superman!" quality about him, which was tremendously appealing. Monty had met him the year before, during the filming of *I Confess*, and their friendship developed into a close one lasting for years. Right now, Monty needed Jack to do for him what Mira had done. A week before filming, Zinnemann did an unusual thing: he had the entire cast rehearse the film from first scene to last. There would be no other rehearsals, just shooting. During that week, Monty would say Prew's lines this way or that way to Jack, and Jack would contribute nothing more daring than, "Yeah, that sounds good"—but that was all Monty needed, someone to listen, to act as a sounding board. In a way he had outgrown those dressing-room discussions with Mira about inter-relationships and "choices." He was quite capable now of analyzing his material himself.

From Here to Eternity was brilliantly cast. Through a stroke of uncommon inspiration, Dan Taradash and Fred Zinnemann agreed to convert Deborah Kerr from her old British "duchess" roles to that of the sexpot, Karen, Captain Holmes' promiscuous wife who had slept with more enlisted men than she could count. ("I feel naked without my tiara," she said to unit publicist Walter Shenson as they took the cheesecake photos.) Burt Lancaster supplied the obligatory beefcake, as the tough but sympathetic Sergeant, Milt Warden.

Lancaster was not Monty's sort of man or actor. For one thing, Lancaster was very vain. Jack Larson tells this story. Monty had just arrived at the studio for the start of filming and was still in the process of meeting all the actors. He hadn't shaken hands with Lancaster yet, and was on one of the set telephones, when he suddenly spotted Lancaster walking over to him. Monty was always particular about the amenities at the beginning of any film, and was anxious that Lancaster would not think him rude, so he tried to catch his eye to give him a look that said, "Oh, God, I wish this phone call would end." But Lancaster would not look him in the eye. Instead, while Monty stood with one arm akimbo, Lancaster's eyes roamed his slender body, taking in every inch of Monty's torso with burning interest. Monty later told Larson that he realized instantly that Lancaster, far from making an unexpected pass, was sizing up the competition. During the course of the film, Monty and Lancaster were polite, but found no common ground for friendship.

Donna Reed was Harry Cohn's choice for Lorene, the young prostitute with whom Prew falls in love. She remembers that Monty was extremely nervous and apparently troubled. "I could feel the enormous struggle he went through to perform . . . he looked distressed all the time."

On the very first day of actual filming, she became aware of Monty's extraordinary uphill effort. They were to meet at the New Congress Club, the film's euphemistic translation for what in Jones' book was a whore-house. Monty and Frank Sinatra (as Prew's pal, Maggio) were supposed to arrive drunk and out of breath. "We were ready to roll and suddenly they couldn't find Monty! They looked all over the set—but no Monty. It was a harried fifteen minutes . . . calls went out all over the place. Then Monty ran in—out of breath. He had left the lot to run around the block to prepare himself."

Miss Reed had never played opposite anyone quite like Monty. At the studio, he was intense and brooding, almost incommunicado, but in their scenes, she could feel Monty transfusing the energy of every word and gesture into her body, his climb upward pulling her to a level of exposure in front of the cameras which she would never have achieved ordinarily. "It was a shock. No actor ever affected me that way. I was just stunned. After our scenes, I'd go home and our work would push me into myself. Our scenes would be on my mind all evening."

Monty showed no friendliness at the studio, he was much too bound up, but every night he would call her at home. The calls were long, rambling and extremely cheerful, almost as if he were out to show her the other side of himself. He talked about their scenes. Would this work? Would that be a better way of doing it? He had always used Mira to toss ideas to, but now he was learning to reach out to others. It was what Silverberg had wanted him to do.

Monty's drinking was beginning to affect his work on the set, the first time it had ever happened on a film. James Jones was present at the shooting of one sequence. Monty was soused. At first it seemed that he was just being playful, but when he began losing control and running around, Zinnemann realized that there wasn't going to be any scene. Sinatra also realized it and took Monty to his dressing room. Sinatra, by now, had developed an incredible power over Monty—no one had realized exactly how much power until this incident.

Jones went to Zinnemann and asked him what was wrong with Monty. They had gotten drunk together in the evenings, but never raving drunk like this.

"Yes, Monty's drunk," Zinnemann told Jones, "but I think the problem is more emotional. It's exhaustion, too. He's completely worn out from the way he's been working himself." Zinnemann put the emphasis on Monty's dedication rather than on a specific problem in his psyche. But certainly this was no longer the soberly wholesome young man Zinnemann had worked with on *The Search*.

After three-quarters of an hour, Monty and Frank came back, ready to shoot the scene.

To onlookers, like Fred Zinnemann, the change seemed brought about by Sinatra, whom Monty worshipped during the filming as a small boy loves a baseball hero. He had never gotten close to anyone like Sinatra before. Sinatra was a lovable daredevil; vulnerable inside, but a hard-drinking, noisy, brash, self-protective soldier of fortune on the outside. Physically, he was like Monty, but in all other respects he was different. The product of a lower-class New Jersey Italian family, Frank had learned to be a street-fighter in every sense. He knew how to turn depression into drunken fun, how to fight it out with misfortune and win. Monty—at heart still the little prince of a boy who had been protected from the grit of life and jailed in a prison of wealth and a mother's idea of refinement—was fascinated with such an obvious winner. And Sinatra was a singer! Singing, good singing like his, was to Monty almost a supernatural accomplishment. He could hardly put two notes together himself.

Even their circumstances on the film indicated how vast the gulf was between them. Monty, at the pinnacle of his career, was handed the coveted part of Prewitt like a birthday gift. Sinatra had to beg for Maggio. No one had wanted Sinatra around anymore. His vocal cords had hemorrhaged, killing his singing voice, as well as his film and nightclub career. The bad publicity which he attracted during his courtship and marriage to Ava Gardner had turned much of the industry against him. The last straw was when MCA, the biggest agency in the business, dropped him cold. He owed the government $100,008 in back taxes and didn't have the money. When he heard about *From Here to Eternity*, he thought himself perfect for the role of Maggio and sent Harry Cohn message after message asking to be considered for the part. But what had Sinatra done in films besides sing and dance with Gene Kelly? Harry Cohn, who could display a surprising humanity at times, agreed to let Sinatra test, even though Eli Wallach had practically been signed for the part. At his own expense, Sinatra flew from Nairobi, Africa—where Ava Gardner was filming *Mogambo* with Clark Gable— to meet with Harry Cohn. The test was good and Sinatra told Cohn that he would pay *him* if he would let Sinatra play Maggio. Cohn was moved, but told Sinatra that Zinnemann had all but demanded Wallach. Sinatra flew back to Nairobi, and a marriage which was entering its terminal stages. Weeks later, he was notified that Wallach had turned down the part because of a previous commitment to Elia Kazan to play in the Broadway production of *Camino Real*. Sinatra would be signed—for a paltry $8,000, less than ten percent of what Monty and Burt were being paid.

But his long shot had paid off. Through sheer guts he was now turning misfortune into a brilliant career. Monty longed to be like that—to be able to steer his own life, to fight failure with a laugh and a slug from a whiskey glass.

The attraction was entirely mutual. Every instinct in Sinatra told him that Monty was an actor's actor. *From Here to Eternity* was to be Sinatra's debut as a *real* actor, and Monty was a symbol of that sort of accomplishment. He was able to achieve a oneness with Monty, onscreen and off, that would have been impossible without the symbiotic effects of a loving friendship. In a matter of weeks, Sinatra had to rid himself of all the hoofing and songs of his previous musical films, and bear down into the character of the stubborn and victimized Maggio. Monty was always there, guiding, showing him how to get rid of the extraneous. Interestingly, the film would win best-supporting Oscars for Donna Reed and Frank Sinatra— both as a direct result of Monty's influence.

After two weeks in Hollywood, the cast flew to Honolulu for exteriors. In Honolulu, Monty and Sinatra continued their emotional communications in the only way their characters and backgrounds would allow them, through the common denominator of liquor. They drank up a hell of a rousing storm during their three weeks among the leis and floodlights, and everyone connected with *Eternity* seemed, in turn, amused, shocked, titillated, and frightened for the safety of the film by their day and night carousing. There was what seemed to be a nightly ritual. At 10 P.M., the two of them would have a bottle in Sinatra's room, and Sinatra would decide that it was time to call Ava in Nairobi to see if things could be settled between them. The telephone lines between Honolulu and Nairobi were, in those days, shaky at best, and it often took him an hour of dickering with the Honolulu and Nairobi operators to get through to Ava's location. Monty would have a drink, and then Sinatra would have a drink, and after all that Sinatra would usually be told that Ava was out for the evening. They would both moan and pour themselves some more of the good stuff. Members of the cast would pass the open door: "Did he get through yet?" Then Sinatra, saddened by his failure, would lead his sympathetic friend out the door, away from the hotel, and into the wilds of brightly lit, bawdy, tuneful Honolulu for a sloshing good time. Monty had never been so happy. They drank almost competitively, each trying to outdo the other in consumption. But it appeared obvious to everyone who the leader was in these forays. Fred and Renée Zinnemann had never seen Monty like this; they had thought him practically a teetotaler. Sinatra got blamed for leading the innocent astray but, in fact, Sinatra had done no such thing. The lamb had already left the fold. For the first time, Monty was drinking openly for everyone to see.

The atmosphere of the Hawaiian location was brittle and filled with personality problems. The difficulty was that the script was *too* good. Bitter quarrels came about because it was clear that *From Here to Eternity* was to be a hit, and everyone wanted to make sure that his own interests were protected in the final print. Cohn himself came to Honolulu to supervise the production. That only increased tensions. As the days went by, the rushes were seen and edited on the spot—Cohn had decided that *Eternity* was so hot he wanted it in the theaters by August, three months away! Studio and newspaper people stormed the location. "Millions of people seemed to be buzzing around us," says Fred Zinnemann. "Word gets out fast."

Burt Lancaster worried about everything: his physique, the camera angles, the script. During breaks in filming he would go off by himself to jog and do push-ups and sit-ups. He wasn't happy about his lines, and kept arguing about changes in a script that everyone had already agreed was perfect. He led Zinnemann, an extraordinarily even-tempered man, into verbal brawls on and off the set, and finally provoked him, uncharacteristically, into telling Lancaster to go screw himself .

Sinatra, too, was causing trouble. He was a man of moods. "He was wonderful to work with," says Zinnemann, "about ninety percent of the time." The other ten, he could be quite loud and objectionable. In one scene, Maggio is drunk and Prew is worried that he might be caught by the MPs. Monty and Sinatra had rehearsed it standing up, but just before the shooting, Sinatra decided that it felt more natural sitting down. Zinnemann didn't like the idea, but Sinatra persisted—quite objectionably. Monty, who was sober for a change, decided to follow the script, as Zinnemann wanted, and remained standing. Sinatra slapped Monty. They were such good friends that Sinatra knew he could get away with it, though by now everyone was going bananas watching this silliness. Zinnemann placated Sinatra by agreeing to the sitting position, but then producer Buddy Adler called Harry Cohn at the Royal Hawaiian Hotel, where he was dining with General O'Daniel—in charge of the entire Pacific Air Force. The whole dinner party came roaring onto the set in an Air Force limousine. Cohn, still in his white dinner jacket, slammed the limousine door behind him and strode up to them. How did actors dare tell the director what to do? Why wasn't the director following the script? He then threatened to shut the picture down if things weren't done his way. Embarrassed, Zinnemann told Cohn he would go back to the scene as written. Minutes later Cohn was off into the night with his Pacific Air Force entourage.

Monty worked desperately to find all the right things for Prew, to make him perfect. Every member of the cast was impressed by his total involvement. His tension during filming was almost palpable. Before takes, a haunted look appeared in his eyes, and one could sense his fear that maybe *now* it would all collapse in front of the cameras, that he wouldn't find it. He looked less and less confident as the film progressed. As Mira had sensed for several years, the fear was growing that suddenly it would all go away.

Because of the fear, not despite it, Monty was able to utilize his assets to the fullest. He was even able to compensate, with Zinnemann's help, for his greatest liability, his tendency to punch like a girl. Zinnemann put in a double for the long shots, but in the close shots Monty took attention away from his fists by showing awesome reluctance with his face and crouching body. The way he finally played the scene, the audience believes that Prew is fighting peculiarly because he is still tormented by the memory of having once blinded a man with his fists. None of the film's critics picked up the technical weakness.

Monty refused a stunt man stand-in for his death scene. Zinnemann gave Monty some instructions, but no one knew how the scene would come across, until the cameras rolled and Monty ran across the field. On take one, a shot was indicated and Monty just tipped over, like a rigid, inanimate toy-soldier, head-first into a ditch; there was a weird thud. "It was so real, shudders went through me," says Renée Zinnemann; "For all I knew, Monty could have been lying there all smashed up from the fall." Deborah Kerr remembers, "After he fell, it wouldn't have surprised me if they said, 'Monty's dead.'"

Monty was able to achieve all this perfection while continuing to drink up a tornado with Sinatra. However, the sheer physical pressure and tension on his body and nervous system was becoming just too much by the end of three weeks on location.

Dan Taradash had been intensely proud of the death scene he had written for Maggio, and with good reason. Every line had been honed down to the barest minimum, every word calculated to create one of the most moving scenes in the film. Three events were to happen simultaneously: Maggio was to die in Prewitt's arms and wordlessly show that he had loved Prew most of all; Milt Warden (Lancaster) was to come to understand the difference between what is truly human and worthwhile and what is barbaric; and Prew was to be spotlighted as the only man left capable of love in an oppressive environment.

It was to be shot the night before the whole company

115

was scheduled to leave Honolulu, and the scene had to be in the can that night. Monty and Frank showed up drunk —and then Monty passed out. Zinnemann was horror-stricken; there was no way the scene could be postponed. Sinatra grabbed Monty, slapped him on the face, shook him. It was almost an hour before Monty began to come out of it. Zinnemann was shaken, fretting, breathing hard. He couldn't understand why Monty was letting him down this way.

Finally, Sinatra got Monty half-sober and they began the scene. First, Sinatra stumbles onto the road, a bloody mess from being victimized in the stockade by Fatso (Ernest Borgnine), and dies in Monty's arms. Then Monty is supposed to watch them place Maggio's body, face up, on the back of a truck, and say: "See his head don't bump." Monty couldn't concentrate to say it properly. Zinnemann had him do it over, but at 2 A.M., hours after the shooting should have ended, he called it a night. During the rushes, he shook his head and decided to cut the last part of the take. It was the first time Fred Zinnemann had been made aware that drinking would interfere with Monty's work.

He may have also suspected that Monty was becoming a bonafide alcoholic. Alcoholics have work troubles because they drink beyond their bodily tolerance. Sinatra, on the other hand, had no problems with the death scene because he was merely a heavy drinker who kept within his toler-ance while he worked.

The Maggio death scene and the scene James Jones wit-nessed in Hollywood are crucial in Monty's life; they mark a turning point in a career that had been going brilliantly up-ward. Now the demons would start to visibly rip Monty apart.

Monty still hadn't seen *Eternity* when it opened at the Capitol Theatre in New York on August 5, 1953, to ex-travagant kudos. Every paper in town went crazy over the movie. Critics racked their brains trying to find *something* wrong: It seemed perfect. Burt Lancaster and Frank Sinatra got a lot of ink, but it was Monty's terrifying screen impact which was uppermost in the reviews. "Montgomery Clift adds another sensitive portrait to an already imposing gallery with his portrayal of Prewitt," said the *Times.* The *Saturday Review:* "Montgomery Clift reveals again his un-canny ability to lend eloquence to an incoherent personal-ity. His eyes, his gestures unfailingly suggest the nuances

Well-bred, Chattanooga-born William Brooks Clift was Edward Montgomery's father. Bill's absence from the family until the boy was 13 had much to do with Monty's later problems.

At the age of 14 Monty appeared in his first Broadway play, *Fly Away Home* (1935), a pleasant comedy. Monty and Joan Thompkins played Thomas Mitchell's mischievous children. Everyone who worked with little Monty thought him an absolute charmer. (Credit: Vandamm Collection)

Above: Monty was the boy with the good manners, Prince Peter, and
Jackie Kelk played his antagonist, ruffian Prince Rudolph, in the
Cole Porter musical, *Jubilee* (late 1935). The boys were also at odds
offstage and so were their mothers. (Credit: Vandamm Collection)
Below: Monty turned 18 in his fourth play, *Dame Nature*, a comedy
about a young man (Monty) who suddenly discovers that he is to be
a father but doesn't know how it happened.

At left is Morgan James, who used to take his aristocratic Monty to a burlesque house in Newark, New Jersey. Mrs. Clift didn't know. At right: Forrest Orr. (Credit: Courtesy, Morgan James)

Right: Monty at 20 used to go to Janet Cohn's place in Pound Ridge, Westchester, where he met writers like Thornton Wilder and Robert Ardrey. To get away from his mother, he rented a barn across the street from Janet's—but Mrs. Clift came up anyway. (Credit all 3 photos: Janet Cohn)

During the war years, Monty appeared in one splendid role after another, and gained for himself an enviable reputation as an up-and-coming matinee idol. Top left: In 1940 he began a two year run with the Lunts in Sherwood's *There Shall Be No Night*. Alfred was the greatest single influence on Monty's later acting style. Bottom left: In 1944 he appeared opposite Cornelia Otis Skinner and Dennis King in Lillian Hellman's *The Searching Wind*. Monty had the short but pivotal role of the wounded young man returning from the war.

Below: The following year, Monty's quiet, brooding technique in Tennessee Williams' and Donald Windham's *You Touched Me!* became obligatory study for every other young Broadway hopeful. Below: At left are Catherine Willard and Edmund Gwenn, and smoldering at right is Marianne Stewart, the sexually suppressed girl who is awakened by Monty's serene physicality. (Credit all 3 photos: Vandamm Collection)

While Monty's first film, *Red River*, was still being edited, he went to Zurich in 1947 to appear as the star of Fred Zinnemann's *The Search*. Monty was the G.I., Ivan Jandl was the orphan boy he adopts, and Wendell Corey was a fellow soldier. Zinnemann (hand on windshield) was taken with Monty's charming liveliness, but had no idea that Mira Rostova, Monty's acting coach—hidden in a Zurich hotel—was the glue that was holding up Monty's enthusiasm. During *Red River*'s shooting Monty had suffered bouts of depression. (Loew's Inc.)

How could the shorter, trim Monty stand up to the Duke in the greatest cattle-drive movie ever made, *Red River*? Howard Hawks thought he could. He showed Monty how to stare a hole into Wayne and convince the audience that he was physically and psychologically more impressive. (United Artists)

Young girls, who now squealed at the first appearance of Monty in a darkened movie theater, thought Olivia deHavilland dreadfully cruel and stupid to reject their delicious Montgomery Clift at the end of *The Heiress*, his third film. Olivia received voluminous protesting mail from his admirers. (Paramount)

After the release of *The Search* and *Red River* in 1948, and *The Heiress* in 1949, Monty became the nation's number one teen idol. Photos of "casual", "ordinary", "one suit" Monty Clift appeared in every fan and slick magazine, which ran stories that helped Monty perpetuate a series of lies about his personality, character, and sexuality. The Barbizon School of Modeling voted him "America's Most Eligible Bachelor of 1949," presenting him with a scroll—one of many typical idol votes, polls, plaques, icons and the like. (Credit both photos UPI)

Monty, with acting coach Mira Rostova (left) and best-friend Kevin McCarthy's wife, Augusta Dabney.

Impeccably photogenic Montgomery Clift, and Paul Douglas, in a scene from *The Big Lift*, released in 1950. Director George Seaton became paranoid about the presence of Mira on the set and insisted she leave; then Monty threatened to leave if she did, and Seaton capitulated.

Monty adored children. Somehow they always sensed this and came to him. At left is Cornell Borchers, his romantic interest in *The Big Lift*. (Credit: UPI)

Facing page:
The day after the premiere of *The Heiress*, all the newspapers in the country ran this service photo of a beaming 17 year-old Elizabeth Taylor and her famous escort. They weren't pretending. Quite early during the filming of *A Place In The Sun* Elizabeth fell in love with Monty—their convincing love scenes were the result. Monty could not love her back sexually. (Credit: UPI, Paramount)

Both men and women succumbed to the ecstacy of this image belonging to the 30 year-old.

With Augusta Dabney and Alberto Moravia in Rome, February of 1950, right after *A Place In The Sun* was finished. Monty was travelling through Europe with the Kevin McCarthys. (Credit: Kevin McCarthy)

A rare glimpse of Monty pulling one of his many dangerous hanging pranks. Coming back to New York with the McCarthys on the Queen Elizabeth, Monty feigned impatience with the slowness of the trip and swung his body over the topdeck rail. He was pretending to walk home on the waters of the Atlantic, with just one hand keeping him from an icy death. Kevin rushed to a lower deck to take the photo. (Credit: Kevin McCarthy)

After their return to New York, Monty and Kevin went up to North Brooksville, Maine, looking for a location for their screenplay collaboration of *You Touched Me!* (At right is Martin Swenson, Kevin's college roommate.) It was around this time that Monty began suffering a hebephrenic-like breakdown: eating food off floors, momentary blackouts, sudden childish behavior, drunkenness, dreadful scenes in restaurants, cursing at his parents. (Credit: Courtesy, Kevin McCarthy)

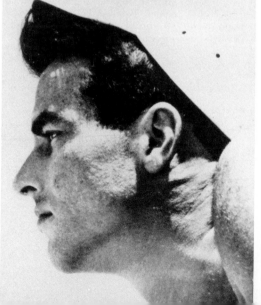

Photos taken by Monty's lover Rick on beaches and boats in Maine and Long Island. A bisexual, Monty had had a two-year affair with a small, dark-haired actress named Annie Lincoln, while seeing Rick. Now, during this tormented period (the early fifties) Monty was mixing drugs and liquor, and untypically treating his sexual partners abusively.

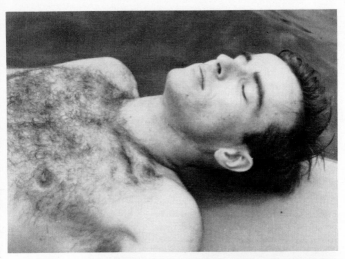

Monty came to Las Vegas to watch Tallulah Bankhead's performance at a posh Strip club, while he was making Hitchcock's *I Confess* in 1952. He had appeared with her once, in *The Skin of Our Teeth* (1942), and was then put off by her aggressive sexuality, but was only amused by it now. With Monty are, at left, Lucille Ball and Desi Arnaz, and, at his right, Marlene Dietrich. (Credit: UPI)

One of Vittorio de Sica's passionate "art" shots in the dreadful *Indiscretion of An American Wife*. Jennifer Jones had a crush on Monty during the Rome filming and was furious when she found out she had a male rival, a young Italian. Monty acted at night and drank by day. Mira Rostova was absent. (Columbia)

of feeling that the script writer dare not let him speak." "Clift's version of Prewitt is both taut and sensitive," said Otis Guernsey of the *Herald Tribune*. Even *Films in Review*, whose editor, Henry Hart, had a personal loathing for Monty, said, in a review by Robert Kass, that "Clift is perfectly cast as a man who is a shock absorber for the insensitivity around him."

It was one of those rare occurrences in cinematic history where critics and moviegoers seem in unanimous agreement. The first release of *From Here to Eternity* grossed Columbia $19,000,000—on a total outlay of $2,000,000. New York's Capitol Theatre had to keep its doors open day and night to accommodate *Eternity*-crazed patrons.

Months later, Monty was nominated for Best Actor. He was convinced—justifiably so—that he would get the Oscar. His performance was, without question, the best of 1953.

He was now at the peak of his star power. Lew Wasserman sent him script after script; producers begged to offer him any salary he wanted, pieces of the action, anything. It was apparent now that Monty's presence in any film, whatever the quality, was a guarantee not only of box-office, but prestige. It wasn't often that a young, romantic leading man could keep the girls *and* the critics happy. He was in a class by himself. No other young actor projected that awesome quality of stubborn independence and introverted intensity coupled with romantic vulnerability. Brando, after a great screen success as Stanley Kowalski in *Streetcar* in 1951, spent the next three years in vastly less impressive roles. On the ladder of prestige and popularity, he was many steps below Monty. There was a sort of pecking order for film casting at that time. Roles that had been considered tailor-made for a young "Method actor" —the misnomer often applied to both Monty and Marlon— were first offered to Monty, and then, if he declined, to Brando.

That was the case with *On the Waterfront*. Monty was sent the Elia Kazan-Budd Schulberg screenplay shortly after he finished *Eternity*. Sam Spiegel was to produce it for Harry Cohn. Monty thought the writing bad and sent the script back to Wasserman with a polite rejection note: too corny, overblown. Harry Cohn, who wanted to tie *Waterfront* in with the success of *From Here to Eternity*, next offered it to Frank Sinatra, but at the last stage of

117

negotiation changed his mind and Sinatra sued. Then Brando got it; the rest is history.

Monty sat around his apartment reading the deluge of scripts and returned them all. Nothing was right. He had no intention of returning to Hollywood for something less than exceptional. *On the Waterfront* was certainly not "exceptional." *East of Eden* was certainly not "exceptional." Nor were countless others that many established actors would have given at least one limb to do. At the height of his success, the point at which most ambitious, self-realizing actors—like Frank Sinatra—would have ridden the crest of the wave, Monty chose another course.

He spent a great deal of time in his semi-furnished duplex—moping around, sleeping late in his black-curtained coffin of a bedroom, drinking in the daytime, drinking at night, making daily trips to Dr. Silverberg's office.

Monty had always been high-strung and filled with a bouncy, nervous energy. That had been one of the special things about him: an incredible enthusiasm tempered with intelligence and restraint. Above all, there had been absolute sincerity. But this was a new Monty, a most disturbed and disturbing Monty. The youth seemed faded; the sincerity tampered with. The high-strung enthusiasm had turned to perpetual anxiety, as though Monty were encased in a shell of nerves that kept him an unwilling prisoner.

Everyone saw it—Mira, Kevin and Augusta, Rick, Libby, Billy, Ned: all of the old crowd. Things bothered him. He would sit with Bill or Rick and complain that he was being used. He never knew what people wanted from him anymore. They didn't want to meet a man; they wanted to meet a movie star. He found himself mouthing words that he once would have found intolerable and Hollywood-phony.

He was annoyed and terrified by fans. He had once been so full of fun when the girls rushed up to him with their autograph books and their shrieks: "Oh, Monty Clift!" Now his face became a perplexed mask. They would sometimes sit for eight hours straight in front of his door on East Sixty-first Street waiting for a glimpse of their idol, but their idol had turned into a frightened figure running past them and up the stairs.

He stayed bottled up in the theater world, occasionally going to theater parties, but always winding up alone on a couch or in a chair, nursing a drink and peering with distrusting eyes at the confusion of faces around him. The host or hostess would suddenly spot him running out the door and into the night.

Strange, cloistered Monty: like that boy he had been when Mrs. Clift possessed his soul. James Jones, remembering the sloshing good times they had had together, made the mistake of calling him at the townhouse. Monty sounded distant, and Jones was instantly sorry that he had called. He was about to say a quick good-bye when Monty, without enthusiasm, asked him to come to the house. Jones asked if he could bring a girl. "Monty said it was okay. When we got there, he was all alone, and the curtains were drawn. He came out in a robe, looking a little funny with that stooped posture of his. It was very dark and he turned on a few lights and made us a drink. We talked for a while, but I felt that I was imposing because he was so quiet. We left and I never called him again." Jones had the feeling that Monty was offended by Jim's very physical presence— by his brightness, which belonged in the sunlight rather than in that brooding darkness, which it insulted.

He would spend his time alone or in the company of a few trusted friends. The year and a half of celebrity-courtship—when Garbo and Dietrich would come to parties at the duplex—was past history. He was often with Mira, discussing things that he wanted to do in the theater. It was as if he were talking about a holy temple to which he was at last returning. He had been reading plays. He wanted to do something with Mira and Kevin: something that was all their own—a special play that the three of them would fashion and polish and expose like a rare jewel. He wanted, at last, to create art.

He came a lot to the new acting group which Bobby Lewis had formed in January 1953. Lewis was disgruntled with the effect that his one-time brainchild, the Actors Studio (now led single-handedly by Lee Strasberg), was having upon actors. He wanted to give actors a chance to extend themselves by working on whole plays, not just disconnected scenes. Mira was Bobby's assistant, and they would work with Kevin McCarthy, Maureen Stapleton, Kim Stanley, John Fiedler, among others, on whole productions. Monty never worked in the actual scenes, but sat on the sidelines and offered criticism at the end of the play when the floor would be open for discussion. His comments were incisive but diplomatic. "It was wonderful having him there," says John Fiedler. *"From Here to Eternity* was playing in all the theaters and there was Montgomery Clift. I think, to a degree, we were all intimidated by his presence because he was such a big star. But I remember what he said to us was always very alert and helpful."

Kevin and Augustus had moved to Dobbs Ferry that year, so Bobby's classes were a good excuse for Kevin, Monty, and Mira to get together to discuss what new play the three of them would do. The choice was an important one for all of them: *The Sea Gull*. Lewis had once tried to direct them in scenes from the awesome Chekhov play years before, when Monty came to classes at the Actors Studio, and Monty had at that time walked out on Lewis' "production" over an interpretation dispute. *The Sea Gull* was a gnawing, unfinished thing for the three of them.

They were going to start from scratch. No outside director would influence them. No outside translator would get between them and Chekhov. Mira would translate from the original and Kevin and Monty would help fashion the script.

At first, Monty was terribly enthusiastic. Through innumerable meetings and phone calls, they engaged in the sort of endless intellectual discussion of "choices," character inter-relationships and words that Monty cherished even more than the acting process itself. He seemed totally caught up in the intensity of the work. Then suddenly, about halfway through, Monty just stopped showing up. When Mira called the duplex, Monty would sound drunk. He'd come next time, he said, but when next time rolled around, there was no Monty. She would ring the bell—but no one would answer. "I used to think about Monty in there," says Mira. "I could see in my mind those steep steps leading to Monty's bedroom, and I knew that sometimes he could hardly walk. I had this fear that maybe he'd fall."

Then Monty appeared again, sober and just as excited as ever, as if nothing had happened. He was determined to arrange for a production immediately. "But we weren't ready," says Mira. "We were hardly through with the translation. We hadn't planned our work carefully. And Monty had missed at least half the meetings." Monty, without waiting for Mira to agree, zoomed ahead with plans for a spring production.

As far back as 1945, Monty and Norris Houghton had discussed putting together a play with Monty in a lead role for Houghton's new group, Theatre Inc., the granddaddy of all the non-profit theater companies which were to follow. Monty never forgot that original urge, and at his request, Kevin McCarthy called Houghton, who, along with T. Edward Hambleton, had just founded the Phoenix Theatre. They had started off with an outstanding season: Hume Cronyn and Jessica Tandy in *Madam Will You Walk?*, Robert Ryan in *Coriolanus,* and *The Golden Apple.* Naturally, when Kevin called, Houghton's ears perked up. What better topper for the Phoenix's first season than to offer Montgomery Clift?

He called Monty directly. Monty told him that he, Kevin and Mira had already prepared their own version of *The Sea Gull,* and that Thornton Wilder was acting as script advisor, Kevin would play Trigorin, and it was absolutely necessary that Mira Rostova play the part of the nineteen-year-old Nina. Monty kept stressing Mira's great talent. "She's the Laurette Taylor of our generation," he said, with emotion in his voice. "I've become very dependent upon her in my performances." Monty was obsessed with the subject of Mira's greatness; he said he positively would not appear as Konstantin without Mira as Nina—even though Houghton raised no objections. He would have cast Bugs Bunny as Nina to get Monty in the play.

Norris Houghton recalls, "Monty brought Mira Rostova to the Coffee House Club on Forty-fifth Street one afternoon. I liked her. She looked right—a quiet, small, blackbird of a woman—although she was too old. At the time Mira was more like forty, when she should have been twenty. During the whole meeting Monty was nervous and very anxious that Mira and I like one another. She was rather introverted, like Monty, and the atmosphere was heavy. He was so enthusiastic about her that the idea of auditions never came up. He wanted her, and I was anxious to have Monty. He was a superstar."

Early on, it was decided that Houghton himself would direct the play—or perhaps "supervise" would be a better word for what he wound up doing. He got the message loud and clear that it was *their* play and *their* production and no tampering was allowed. Since the arrangement seemed like a good one for his theater, he went along with it, and plans went forward for four weeks of rehearsals in April and a six-week run in May. Judith Evelyn was to play Madam Arkadina; Maureen Stapleton, Masha; Sam Jaffe,

Sorin; Will Geer, Shamraev; June Walker, Polina; George Voskovec, Dr. Dorn; and Karl Light would double as Yakov and assistant stage manager. With the exception of Evelyn, all the casting choices were Monty's.

Houghton already knew *The Sea Gull* well. He had been around Chekhov performances and rehearsals for years. Still, he had no inkling of what Monty had in mind when he spoke of the "special idea" that he, Mira, and Kevin had of the play. The way Monty spoke of it, it was a private interpretation, very different from anything that had ever been done before. Houghton made visits to the duplex with the express purpose of trying to fathom this personal feeling so that he could communicate it to the rest of the cast, but every time he came, Monty would have a bottle of brandy and would get Houghton drinking too. The conversations were so rambling and vague that, to this day, Houghton can't remember a single point that Monty made. Much of the time, Monty would be on the phone talking long distance with Elizabeth Taylor or Frank Sinatra. By the time Houghton was ready to leave, all he would be absolutely sure of was that Monty had demolished a bottle, and that he had had too much himself. He rationalized that perhaps Monty was simply nervous about his comeback in the theater.

This was to be Mira Rostova's New York debut—and what a stellar debut, to appear on stage in the company of so many greats. She now had a hefty reputation as a somewhat eccentric acting coach who inspired either fierce praise or avid rebuke, and should have been working hard, but instead she spent much of her time fretting about Monty. She was perfectly aware that, aside from the drinking, the codeine and Ritalin pills and all the other painkillers and mood changers he had been taking, Monty had graduated to the harder stuff—Demerol, amphetamines, barbiturates. She sensed something awful happening.

She stepped up her campaign against Dr. Silverberg. She could only guess at the damage he might be doing. Sometimes, when she offered Monty a ride to Silverberg's office on Central Park West, Monty would be absolutely stoned, and Mira would be sure that Silverberg would have to admit the truth of Monty's condition. But Monty never said that they had ever discussed drinking. At other times, Mira would meet Monty after sessions with Silverberg, and Monty would be irrational, whereas hours before he had been soberly lucid. She would say something, and Monty would shout back, completely out of context, "I don't know! Leave me alone! Don't bother me!" Those outbursts evidently took place after Monty and Victor had discussed *Mira's* "destructive" effect.

"In retrospect," says Mira, "I think I should have done even more to stop him from seeing that doctor. I should have tricked him and brought him to another psychiatrist. I should have done something. But what? Every time I brought up the subject Monty would get angry with me."

As soon as the papers announced *The Sea Gull,* lines of people several blocks long formed in front of the Phoenix's ticket office on Second Avenue. The name of Montgomery Clift was instant box-office magic. Monty could have done random readings from Old English poems and those lines would have been just as long. It certainly wasn't Chekhov that attracted them in such numbers.

Before rehearsals, Monty gave a party at his duplex as a sort of initial get-together for the cast. There was electricity in the air—not only because they were about to embark upon an exciting venture, but because they were going to do it with Montgomery Clift. The members of the cast who hadn't met Monty before looked him over carefully—respectfully, but voraciously. What was this superstar really like up close? George Voskovec was shocked that he looked so much older than even in his most recent film. He was "unkempt, pale, and there was a greenishness in his face."

"He struck me as being a tortured creature. I said to myself, 'Oh boy! Oh boy! There's a tragedy there.' I saw a fear, a terror, in him. I felt that he didn't know where he was standing—whether he was a man or wasn't a man. This was not a hypocrite—he was outgoing and tender—there was something he was trying to hide and show at the same time. I saw the furies riding him."

Whenever Monty was in the company of more than just a few people, as at that get-together, he became hyped-up. It was just as though—as George Voskovec notes—Monty were trying to tell you something and not tell you something simultaneously. The effect was strangely mechanical. Monty had always been high-strung and nervous, but now those qualities seemed artificially induced.

On March 25, 1954, only days prior to the first rehearsals of *The Sea Gull,* the Academy Awards were televised from Hollywood. Monty was nervous the whole day.

The top three contenders for Best Actor were Monty, Burt Lancaster, and William Holden (for *Stalag 17*). Everyone had told Monty that he would get the Oscar—he simply *had* to. No one had beat his performance as Prewitt that year and this was his third time around as a nominee. Monty wasn't one to worship prizes, but he was a movie star now and, much as he loathed to admit it, he wanted the Oscar: the prize that meant Total Approval. Forty-three million people watched that night as *From Here to Eternity* walked off with all the Oscars—*almost* all: Best Picture, Best Director (Fred Zinnemann), Best Screenplay (Dan Taradash), Best Black and White Cinematography (Burnett Guffey), Best Film Editing (William Lyon), Best Sound (Columbia), Best Supporting Actor (Frank Sinatra), and Best Supporting Actress (Donna Reed).

But William Holden got the Oscar for Best Actor.

Monty was depressed. He wasn't at the Pantages Theatre to hear Fred Zinnemann tell a circle of reporters, "I couldn't have gotten this without Monty."

It seemed terribly unfair to Monty and all of his friends. And it was. What had happened was a simple problem in mathematics. *From Here to Eternity* drew more votes for Best Actor than any other film, but since so many members voted for Burt Lancaster as well as Montgomery Clift, the votes canceled each other out, leaving William Holden the winner. It was just rotten luck.

That same night Monty called Renée Zinnemann. He sighed a lot and made despairing noises. It was more a conversation of guttural sounds than of words. The next day Renée bought Monty a miniature gold trumpet and had it mounted like an Oscar. He was deeply moved. "This means more to me," said Monty, "than ten Oscars." He kept the gold bugle with him as long as he lived.

Monty was fragile enough to have gone into a long, major depression over the loss of the Oscar, but *The Sea Gull* distracted him.

He became excessively dependent upon Mira again. He would only take significant direction from her, and then always out of earshot of the others. He rehearsed his major scenes with her only, in private. If Norris Houghton had something to say to either of them, or even to Kevin, he couldn't do it in front of the others. The cast, demoralized, began to refer to Monty, Mira, and Kevin as "the Unholy Three." No one knew who was really in charge.

T. Edward Hambleton's office got a barrage of complaints from the actors and their agents about these non-rehearsals. There was never any discussion of character, and even the staging was a non-directed affair. Says John Fiedler, "There was a kind of gentlemen's agreement about the blocking. It was sort of 'Well, if you want to do that, I'll do this.' "

As preview time approached, continual little battles erupted among the actors, and a sense of panic developed. Judith Evelyn and Kevin practically had a brawl onstage one afternoon about what he thought was Judith's tendency to overplay her scenes. The Unholy Three had decided that Judith was pedestrian for developing a performance before the sense of the play had been worked out. Judith was resentful because they hadn't even attempted to convey to the cast what that sense was; she certainly was not going to wait until opening night to develop her role. She had given a superficial insincerity to Madam Arkadina—which indeed did fit the character—but Mira, who was still struggling with her role, felt overshadowed. Judith would explode when Mira gave her notes, and quickly became a backstage villainess among those who were closest to the Unholy Three.

The panic was understandable: Everybody who was anybody in New York theater was coming to see the play. On opening night, all their reputations would be on the chopping block—and the ax loomed larger every day the rehearsals' chaos continued.

One key scene between Monty and Mira was not even unveiled to the company until the very last week of rehearsals. Everyone waited tensely. Houghton was stunned. They were practically whispering their lines. Houghton dared to suggest that they speak up in order to be heard by the audience. They replied, in so many words, that that was superficial directing. It became apparent that Monty was trying to keep his own voice down to the level of Mira's tiny pin-voice, and the effect was that of two people in a sort of onstage cocoon—so much wrapped up in each other that the audience would have to lip-read to understand.

In that crucial scene, Konstantin has a line that makes the audience aware that he has decided to take his own life. During the "unveiling," Monty said that line upstage, his back to the audience; he spoke the words so softly that he couldn't be heard past the third row.

Houghton said: "Monty, this is almost the turning point in the whole play, and I think you've got to play this down front. The audience has got to see what's happening to you."

"Oh, I couldn't do that," said Monty. "This is too personal a moment. I couldn't share that with anybody."

Monty was questing for that "special thing" that Mira wanted. Everyone remembers a sense of awe at how totally Monty was caught up in the character. He *was* Konstantin. The character had that some sensitivity, that same defenselessness toward all the demons of this world, the same sort of love of facing all the pain for the sake of truth.

Konstantin, the true artist, is a masochistic victim of love entanglements with women who tend to have a mesmerizing hold on him, and who only pretend to be artists themselves. His mother, who dangles maternal love in front of him like the donkey's carrot, is a fake; her "art," egocentricity. Nina, who thinks mere recognition is art, is also false.

Many in the group thought it uncanny how similar in behavior Konstantin and Monty were—especially in the way they related to Mira. It is difficult to believe that Monty, with his unique intelligence, did not also see the parallels.

By now, Monty knew everything was wrong. An hour before the dress rehearsal, he stalked off after exchanging nasty words with some of the actresses, and could only be lured back to the stage by Lehman Engel, who, responding to an emergency call, walked him around the block and calmed him down.

In desperation, Monty had Arthur Miller come to see the previews. Miller sat through the first performance.

"We could feel waves of hatred coming from the audience during that performance," says Maureen Stapleton. During the intermission, friends and relatives of the cast could hear people practically yelling that they didn't know *what* was going on onstage. After they had virtually stormed out of the theater at the end of the play, Houghton asked Arthur Miller if he had any notes for the cast.

Miller stood up, an awesome six-foot-three figure. He glanced down at a piece of paper and then up at the stage, where the actors all stood limply.

"Yes," he said. "My first note is the audience can't hear." He paused. "My second note is the audience can't hear."

He paused again. "My one hundred and fiftieth note is the audience can't hear."

He was marvelous. He stood in front of the poor actors and made a devastating postmortem ("Monty, don't be such a dumb tramp. You have to stand up straight, stop slouching around, and behave like a gentleman."). It was like fresh air being blown into the theater. For the first time, someone with real muscle was telling the Unholy Three off, taking charge and bringing real concepts into a production that had been a mere whim, a flight of half-baked imagination.

For three days, Miller talked constantly, giving a virtual seminar on Chekhov and *The Sea Gull*. He explained motivations, and gave practical explanations for each bit of action. There was no mystery about *The Sea Gull*, he said; it was a play about a bunch of people who—because of selfishness, self-protectiveness, fears, and illusions about the role of art in life—are cannibalizing one another. Like hungry children clamoring for food, the performers shot questions at him. People like Maureen Stapleton, who hadn't had the vaguest notion of what her character was about (once, during rehearsals, Houghton had asked her why she was moving about so much in a scene, and she had said, "It's hard to hit a moving target, Norry!"), came away delighted and illuminated. Mira, it turned out, was not speaking in a pin-voice because she was trying to suggest something internal; it was simply that she wasn't used to projecting her voice, after so many years of being away from the theater.

It looked like *The Sea Gull* would be whipped into some sort of shape after all, but with only three days before opening night, could Miller perform a miracle?

Opening night, May 11, 1954. A star-studded premiere. The residents around the Phoenix Theatre at Second Avenue and Twelfth Street had never seen so many famous people in their neighborhood. Marlon Brando, Marlene Dietrich, Patricia Neal, Richard Harris, Fred Zinnemann, Mike Nichols, Anthony Perkins, and a host of others crowded into the theater; critics from every major paper in town lined the aisles. It was the theater event of the season.

Jitters ran through the company. Weeks before, Maureen Stapleton had taken Judith Evelyn to lunch, and to calm her down told her a dirty joke, with the punchline, "In the cool of the evening, when the fucking begins, I'll be there." The story was intended to mean, "Don't worry, Judith, even though we're all not there now, on opening night we'll all be wonderful and together." Well, here it was, opening night, and Judith, standing in the wings next to Maureen, began to sing nervously under her breath: "It's the cool of the eeeeevening . . ." Maureen broke up.

The miracle didn't happen. There were eight different styles of acting, and a lot of it couldn't be heard past the fifth row—but everyone who saw the play insists there had never before been such a powerful Konstantin as Monty's. Even though Monty kept his voice down to Mira's, somehow one managed to hear every word he said. The play often tended to hobble along, but whenever Monty was onstage, his every gesture projected excitement.

The reviews in the next morning's papers were exceptionally kind to the production. While the critics pointed out the higgledy-piggledy nature of the performance, none of them condemned it, and, almost every one of them strongly advised New Yorkers to see it. Walter Kerr of the *Herald Tribune* said: "Mr. Clift does not really work any more openly, any more showily, than the others. But there is a secret, and very clear, line of emotion behind the terse facade. The actor's edgy anxiety before the performance of his adventurous play; the elusive contempt with which he tells the novelist his works are charming; the management of a difficult soliloquy in which he edits his own work— all are casual bits of playing and completely telling ones. And Mr. Clift's groundwork is firm; when the play rises to its few passages of explosive emotions—the boy's rage with his mother, his abandoned gratitude for a compliment—the performance enlarges without effort, expands into furious fire."

And Brooks Atkinson of the *New York Times* added: "Montgomery Clift's lonely, brooding Konstantin is beautifully expressed without any foolish pathology."

Mira and Kevin got the worst notices. Atkinson summed up their performances by saying, "Without a good Nina and a good Trigorin, a performance of *The Sea Gull* is imperfect. That is the situation here. Mira Rostova, as Nina, is handicapped by a heavy accent. She is further handicapped by a florid style alien to the whole spirit of Chekhov. And Kevin McCarthy's amiable, weak Trigorin has none of the worldliness or lazy corruption of the part.

These important parts are inadequately played, which is a pity."

The real critics, however, were not these reviewers, but the members of the theater world who sat in the audience. Word got out quickly that *The Sea Gull* was a bumbling, botched-up disaster.

There were moans and groans among the performers but not much overt unhappiness. Mira must have been crushed, but her demeanor did not change appreciably. Kevin was a rock. But Monty was destroyed. It didn't seem to matter that he had acquitted himself nobly in the eyes of the public and his peers. The fact that ate at him was that the play was bad; the whole project was ugly. He couldn't bear it. He shied away from Mira. He became moody. Sometimes he rushed offstage and locked himself in his dressing room. If Mira called him during the daytime, he would be drinking. "I used to wonder," she says, "whether he'd make it to the theater."

At night, after the show, he needed someone to be with him while he wallowed in self-pity. He couldn't bear to be with Mira at all, and only occasionally with Kevin; they reflected and magnified his self-loathing. He turned to Maureen Stapleton. Every night they would go to a local tavern and sit at a table. "It was the first time," says Maureen, "I ever heard anybody order a triple." She told him that it was just a play, and it would soon be over, but he refused to be consoled.

Monty's attitude toward Mira became more ambivalent than ever. With friends of hers, like Kevin and Maureen, his attitude was one of concern for her welfare. With others, he tore her apart mercilessly. He said that he was in shock about how bad she was in the play, that she was everything she had told him not to be: selfish on stage, rigid. "I only did *The Sea Gull*," he told Jack Larson, "to give Mira a career." He later told someone else that the real reason he turned against Mira was that she dared tell him, when she was told she would have to leave the set of *From Here to Eternity:* "But Monty, you *need* me to perform."

It was just like with his mother. Here, again, was that lingering, painful withdrawal from dependency on what he so wanted and didn't want at the same time: the strong woman-in-authority. And, as with his mother, the withdrawal entailed a campaign of bitter outbursts.

Monty wasn't all gloom. Occasionally he could laugh—especially toward the end of the production, when everyone had settled into a kind of fatalistic, low-keyed good humor, not unlike that of the characters they played. Bob Cromwell, one of Monty's actor friends from earlier days, came into Monty's dressing room one night and he, Kevin, and Monty good-naturedly finished off a bottle. "Maybe we can't play Chekhov," said Kevin, "but we sure as hell can drink Scotch."

The play ran for six weeks, and every performance was sold out, thanks to Monty's glamour. A Hollywood atmosphere surrounded the theater. After performances, a solid mass of bobby-soxers milled around outside. Matinee days were impossible. Autograph books waved in the air, young girls stood on tiptoes to see if Monty would show. He and some of the others had to sneak out the back way, sometimes fighting their way through girls to get to a waiting cab.

None of this amused or affected Monty. He wanted only to be left alone.

Monty no longer had involvements with women by this stage of his life. His last major attempt at a heterosexual relationship—if it was really even an "attempt"—was with Elizabeth Taylor during A Place in the Sun. After that would-be affair aborted, the only woman with whom he seems to have had a physical relationship was Libby Holman, and by now that had clearly become a Platonic friendship. They did spend weekends at her places in Maine and Connecticut, but their relationship seemed to center around mother-love and son-like dependency. Like Augusta and Kevin, Libby offered Monty a ready-made family with her two small boys, Tony and Timmy.

Monty's sex life had become wholly male-oriented, which was not disturbing in itself, but his homosexual relationships now contained the same destructiveness that was pervading every other aspect of his life.

He was becoming callous about his partners. Rick, for instance, had always been loyal and undemanding. They had seen little of each other lately, but he was still a valuable friend and partner. They would make late-night dates simply to spend the night together—since Monty often had one or two people over to the house for dinner and was still squeamish about letting his theater friends meet

130

his boyfriends. The meetings were always at Rick's place. "He was getting into the habit of never showing up and not even calling to explain," says Rick. "I wrote him a long letter telling him that I didn't understand why he was doing this to me and that I didn't care if I never saw him again. He called me up as soon as he got the letter and apologized. He just said that he had gotten drunk and forgot to call."

But there was more than just drunken forgetfulness.

That summer, Monty rented a house in Ogunquit, Maine —only a block away from one rented by Dr. William Silverberg, and near Libby's place in Kennebunkport. Monty invited Rick up for a weekend. "The night I got up there Monty was drinking and carrying on and higher than I had ever seen him before. I didn't know much about pills, but I figured he had downed something else besides liquor. We took off our clothes and went to bed. Suddenly Monty started slapping me around. He got his belt and started beating me. I was frightened. Nothing like this had ever happened before. I ran out of his bedroom into another and locked the door. Monty pounded on it. The next morning he was crying and asked me why I had locked the door on him. I told him and he said he couldn't remember a thing."

Ogunquit, in those days, was not quite Provincetown or Fire Island, but it had a quiet undertone of mixed sexualities that made it perfect for super-discreet homosexuals who wished to make contacts without appearing obvious. It wasn't touristy, and many celebrities rented summer homes there. Monty, who was so careful about not being "known," liked the environment. Since Ogunquit was a dry town, cocktail parties were given at the slightest provocation. Every night something was going on.

One day Monty saw a handsome twenty-year-old on the beach. He walked over to him and said, "You're a very beautiful boy." His name was Dickie. When Dickie realized it was Montgomery Clift who was making a play for him, he was thrilled. They made it that night, but what they had lasted barely a week. "Monty was so sadistic that I just couldn't put up with it. I only saw him at big parties and we got very drunk. When we did get it on, I'd wake up in the morning all battered and bruised. He was rough and overly dominant. He threw me around like a toothpick. When he kissed you, he kissed you so it hurt. One time, I came away with a bloody mouth. But he was so beautiful and so physical that I didn't dare object. His eyes were like green crystals. When you looked at them, it was like looking into diamonds. Sometimes they were glazed over, and I guess he was on uppers, but in those days I didn't know anything about them or their effects."

Dickie planned a party for Monty the night after they met. Monty said he would love to come but didn't want a crowd of people staring at him. Dickie assured him there would only be a handful, but after word got out, Dickie's friends called and begged to meet Monty Clift. There were almost thirty people assembled, when they heard a loud ripping sound, and there was Montgomery Clift crashing through a screen door, just like Captain Marvel. It had the effect Monty wanted—everyone was impressed. He came over, said a few hellos, then sat on the couch and retreated into himself. Coming through the screen door like that was just about all the personality Monty could muster for the crowd. After a very short time, Monty left.

Dickie says that there wasn't a thing about Monty that would lead one to suspect that he was a homosexual. At parties, his behavior was very heterosexual: he talked with the women, when he did talk, as if he wanted to go to bed with *them*, and not with another man.

"I didn't like that rough stuff in bed. I was young and I was into love and affection, not violence. I felt that he was angry at himself—and this was the way he showed it— for being in bed with a boy. He was doing it, but he wasn't going to accept it."

Monty's summer in Ogunquit should have been relaxing. He saw Victor every day, he lounged on the beach, he met people—and yet he was never calm. The change of environment seemed to have little effect on Monty's state of mind.

Monty spent a good part of that summer reading the mountain of scripts that Wasserman's office continued to send. Edith Van Cleve from the New York MCA branch also provided plays and books optioned for movies. Monty typed up meticulous lists of everything he received, dividing the tally into books, plays, and movie scripts: he would then log in the date the item was received, who the producer or director was, the terms of the offer, and later log in when the item was returned—all in separate, neat columns. Nothing he read interested him; but he loved going through the elaborate sorting process.

By the end of the summer of 1954, he was in debt to MCA for $10,000. His finances were a mess. Every penny he had put away from his movie earnings had been lost in bad investments. It also turned out that he had received three $150,000 fees from his previous films all in the same year. Since Monty hadn't bothered to set up special tax shelters as was the practice with most highly-paid Hollywood actors, he ended up paying most of the $450,000 to the government. He told Jack Larson that it was his disappointment over keeping so little of the nearly half-million dollars that kept him from jumping into another role right after *From Here to Eternity*. Whether this was true or not, Monty never had much of a head for financial matters, and, poor or not, he didn't intend to be pressured into taking another film assignment until he found that special script.

At this time, Monty told Harvey Orkin—one of those rare publicists that Monty actually liked—that he was unhappy with his present secretary, Roddy McDowall's sister, Virginia, because she could only work part-time and had a family to take care of, and didn't have enough time to keep his "affairs" in order. By "affairs," he meant not only typing up letters but taking care of Monty's whole life. Orkin knew Monty had to have someone to help him cope with an existence that was getting out of hand.

Orkin thought immediately of Marjorie Stengel, an attractive single woman in her mid-twenties. In his uncanny way, Orkin was able to sense the compatibility of Marge —a shy, literary type, who had just won a Eugene Saxton fellowship to write a novel—and the high-strung, deeply sensitive Monty.

On their first meeting, Monty asked her: "Something to eat? A drink maybe?" Marge was too shy to accept. Monty said he was going to get himself something and left her in the living room. He came out of the kitchen eating something red. From a distance, with the shades drawn, Marge thought it was a tomato or an apple. When he came closer, she was shocked. It was a piece of raw meat.

After a few weeks of booze, pills and some fairly odd behavior, Marge went back to Harvey Orkin. "This is absurd," she said. "I'm quitting. I'm a serious human being, Harvey. I'm not cut out for this kind of work." Orkin leaned forward and said: "I want your word of honor that you will stay with him for at least six months. Monty needs you and you need him."

How she could possibly need Montgomery Clift, she didn't understand, but she went back. "In my wildest dreams," she says today, "I wouldn't have imagined that I'd stay for seven years." She began to realize, very soon, that Orkin was right. She did need Monty, because he so needed her; at that point in Marge's life, Monty was exactly the sort of person to fill an emptiness.

"It certainly wasn't the money that kept me with him all those years. I was supposed to write a novel with my fellowship, and in the beginning I think I lied to myself and thought, 'Well, here's a perfect opportunity to write a novel about an actor. I'll learn all about this actor.' But that wasn't it at all. I became deeply attached to Monty. He needed someone to get him through each day."

Marge became all sorts of people to Monty: secretary, nursemaid, confidante, even wife, in the sense of a hostess. She sat with him and listened to his troubles with infinite patience. She often came to the dinner parties. She answered the telephone and typed his correspondence, and if, now and then, Monty grew careless and spilled orange juice all over a stack of letters that she had spent a day or two preparing, she patiently redid them without a word of rebuke. And at night, if he had no plans, she couldn't bear to leave him alone with his liquor. She would stay and sit through dinner with him and leave only when she felt he would be fine for the rest of the night.

After a while there was no one as close to Monty as Marge—not even Libby—because Marge was there all of the time, looking after Monty, making sure that his depressions didn't get out of hand, or if they did, that he would at least survive that night, or that day, or that week.

Marge admits that she had more than fondness for Monty. "But I never loved him romantically. I didn't have a crush on him. My God, if that had been the case, I wouldn't have been able to stay as long as I did. But I think in every other way it was true love for me. I can't speak for Monty. I think he felt a lot for me, too."

Monty isolated himself more and more with a little family of people, each of whom filled a certain need in his life. As his drinking and use of pills got worse, he became more selective than ever before in his choice of "family" members. To simply call them friends would be to mis-name their true function which, stripped of all niceties, was to take care of Monty. They were not there to stop him from drinking. They were there to hold his hand, be sympathetic, watch his drinking, and supply him with the security he needed to go on with his life. It was a meticu-lous setup that Monty arranged with incredible lucidity and logic, almost like a man designing his own perfect sanitar-ium. Without it, Monty would have gone under very quickly.

Monty's little "family" dinners were a phenomenon. Libby, Roddy McDowall and Marge were the regulars; there were perhaps two or three other old friends, like Kevin and Augusta, along with a few relative newcomers, like Arthur Miller, Maureen Stapleton, or Truman Capote: people who were already somewhat used to Monty's habits —for one had to be used to them to be able to stand the ritual.

The scenario, most of which was supplied by Marge Stengel and Maureen Stapleton, went something like this. Monty would greet his guests, while his cook, Elizabeth Guenster, prepared dinner. He might show some of his new guests around the duplex, of which he was terribly proud. There would be a record playing on the new stereo. Elizabeth would signal from the kitchen that dinner was ready. It was difficult at this time to tell how much liquor Monty had already consumed, but he would still seem sober. He would sit down at the table with the others and finish a second or third drink. Then he would go to the bathroom, and come back much more wobbly than before. Suddenly, Monty would start to slur his words. He would say something about having to put on a new record, and get up and walk across the room. Then he would fall on his face. There would be a thud and heads would turn in his direction: No one would budge. The regulars knew he wanted to be left where he was. The conversation would simply continue as if nothing had happened. After half an hour or so, Monty would get up off the floor and head up to his sealed-off, hell-black bedroom. The dinner guests would simply continue on their own.

There were variations on the basic theme. He might not keel over at all. He might make it back to the table and begin to play with his food, or the food on the plates of others, tearing at it or throwing it around. Or he might

135

have drunk so much that he was already asleep in his "coffin" by the time his guests arrived. In that case, one of the regulars would conduct the evening without him and everyone would understand.

Or there might be slight differences in the essential choreography. Instead of walking toward the record player, Monty might head toward the couch and pass out there—preferably, for Monty's purposes, on the floor in front of the couch instead of on the soft couch itself, since he had an infant's primordial love of keeling onto floors instead of man-made objects.

It was always the same reversion to the state of childhood, the "hebephrenic schizophrenia" surfacing in front of the necessary audience. His repertoire included: hands on food, body and face on the floor, crawling, going to sleep in front of "grown-ups"—yet there are indications that he was aware of what he was doing, controlled its effect, and was still able to bounce back to lucidity. Stewart Stern, who had gone to Israel with Monty and Fred Zinnemann, once came over to one of these dinners. This was his last night in town, and he was anxious to see Monty again. When he got to the house, he was told that Monty hadn't made it. Refusing to accept that, he ran up to Monty's bedroom. He somehow managed to find Monty in the voidlike blackness and shook him. Monty came awake and they had a long, pleasant conversation at a time when he was supposedly dead to the world.

Unless one were a regular family member, Monty's sudden blackouts would seem incomprehensible. As most of the regulars knew, however, the part of the ritual which included the obligatory trip to the bathroom was when Monty took a downer, usually Demerol. The synergistic effect of the drug and the alcohol put Monty out. No pill "accident" could happen that often. Monty knew everything about pills, and how to mix them with alcohol for the right effect. He intended to pass out when he did.

For the longest time, Kevin and Augusta did not realize what was happening. They ascribed "Monty's blackouts" to some sort of physical ailment or emotional instability. For them, it was still all part of Monty's boyishness and his understandable need to relive a stilted childhood. Yet even they couldn't help feeling that what was happening was serious. At times, Kevin would take Monty aside and tell him directly that it was time to pull himself together.

136

Monty would reply, "Absolutely. You're right. Thank you, thank you, Kevin. Thank you for your interest. Thank you for being my friend, because it takes a friend to tell you." Monty would sound amazed, as if he truly had no idea how bad his behavior was becoming, and would tell Kevin to just wait, that the next time they got together he would be completely sober. The next time Kevin would see Monty, it was as if the conversation had never happened.

But Kevin had his own career to worry about. After *The Sea Gull,* it occurred to him that working with Monty was hurting him as an actor. While Monty came out fairly unscathed, it was widely felt that Kevin's Trigorin was outrageously boring and mishandled, and that Monty had cast him in the play simply out of friendship.

Some important agent in California had told Kevin that it was just assumed that Monty had added his name to the authorial credits of *You Touched Me!* as a favor. And then there was that other rumor, about which Kevin had been totally in the dark.

"I'll never forget the conversation," he recalled. It was in Henry Hathaway's office at Twentieth Century-Fox on Fifth Avenue. I went up to see him about doing a part in a film, and suddenly he said: 'People are talking about you. They're saying that you're shacking up with your buddy, Monty Clift.' I said: 'Jesus! Where did that come from?' He said: 'I don't know where it came from, but you've got to listen to it.' He meant that literally, that Monty and I were a little too close, that there was a hint of a homosexual relationship. Nothing could have been farther from the truth." Hathaway said, "Lose that guy . . . he's killing your career."

There were incidents of a different nature, as well. The McCarthys were in a play together at the Bucks County Playhouse, and Monty drove up to see them. After the play, he offered to drive them back to Manhattan. Kevin wasn't aware of Monty's new driving habits. On the highway going back, Monty's foot kept pressing the accelerator until the speedometer was practically off the dial—120 miles per hour! Kevin distinctly remembers that Monty was "sober." The passengers held their breath. At that speed, anything could happen. Still, Monty wasn't satisfied. He came alarmingly close to cars passing on the opposite side of the highway, almost clipping them, as if it were a grim prank. By the end of the ride, everyone was completely shaken. What was Monty trying to prove? Kevin wondered.

Soon after, Monty came to see them in Dobbs Ferry. Their daughter, Mary, was a year and a half old. Monty was playing with her in his arms when Kevin suddenly saw him put one hand out to grab onto the refrigerator. The other hand couldn't hold the infant and she started to tumble. Kevin lurched forward and caught her just before her head hit the stone floor. Then Monty "blacked out," keeling over onto the floor himself. After Monty left, Kevin and his wife had a serious talk. They called Monty, and in the nicest way they could, explained that, for the welfare of their children, it would be better if he didn't come out to see them again. Although Monty never mentioned it to Kevin, he never forgave him.

Although Kevin and Augusta still came to Monty's house for dinner, they deliberately began seeing less of him. Kevin had no small opinion about his own talents, but a poor opinion of the opportunities that had come his way. By 1955, his most important leading-man film role had been in *The Invasion of the Body Snatchers,* and it struck him that he had become, in the eyes of others, one of those lesser lights that heavyweight movie stars normally have around them. That, and the helplessness he felt about Monty's increasing behavior problem, made Kevin virtually end his best-friend status with Monty in 1955.

Billy LeMassena came occasionally, but not often. He felt uncomfortable because he knew so few of the people that Monty had over, and Monty wasn't anxious to keep around the friends he had made in his late adolescence.

Ned Smith also paid infrequent visits. He had always felt out of place among Monty's theatrical crowd, but saw Monty out of force of habit. He thought Monty's condition repulsive. Eventually, Ned stopped coming altogether. "I walked out of Monty Clift's life in 1955 when I found myself confronted with a dope addict. I left his house one day and I said to myself, 'All right, well, I guess that's the end of it!' "

There were many dropouts and few newcomers. But if there was any steadfast, loyal friend, during this time— apart from Libby Holman and Marge—it was Roddy Mc-

Dowall. He worshipped Monty as a performer and as a human being. Monty was to him what Alfred Lunt and Olivier were to Monty: Roddy's professional idol. He would do anything that Monty asked: run errands, take pictures, talk to reporters for him, come to the house day or night.

During the two and a half years that Monty stayed away from films, Roddy's career was non-existent. A year or so later, he would have a Broadway success and do endless live television shows, but now he was down. Roddy had nothing to do, so every day he would come over and sunbathe on the roof, or he would look for chores to do around the house. Although Roddy was not a person in whom Monty could confide all his anguish, he nevertheless offered Monty a rare, unquestioning friendship. For all Roddy's loyalty, however, Monty could pay him back with cruelty. He would often let Roddy know there was a dinner party afoot, then not invite him. It was as if Monty were testing him to find out just how steadfast he was.

There were other cruelties as well, but the outcome was always the same. Roddy never showed even a glimmer of bitterness or the least slackening of enthusiasm for their friendship. If indeed this was a long, drawn-out "test," Roddy passed it. He was the only member of Monty's "family" to remain close to Monty until the day he died.

Monty continued the interminable process of reading plays, movie scripts and optioned novels. Edith Van Cleve, from MCA, would call and tell Marge Stengel that Monty absolutely *had* to read this new play she was sending over, or this new movie script. Marge would tell her, apologetically, that Monty only read material from "the top of the pile" and that even if Shakespeare were alive and a play of his were sent over, it would still be placed on the bottom. Edith was instructed to tell all producers that Monty wasn't interested in money; if he liked something he would do it for any price.

One hundred and sixty-three movie offers were returned to MCA, and Monty was still borrowing thousands from them to live on. Was it to be a movie for $150,000 or a play for $100 a week? The answer did not lie in logic, or even in an instinctive quest for artistic truth—as Monty would have everyone believe. Monty was simply afraid to spend any more of his life's blood for so little in return.

139

The "return" was always the same: hard work, the mere appearance of achievement, and then anxiety and depression. What he told others, however, was that he felt he had erred in spending so many years in the movies when he should have been on Broadway building a carer like Alfred Lunt's. Now it seemed nearly impossible for him to return to Broadway. He had a reputation to uphold; he could appear only in something extraordinary. He felt shoddy and commercial for having done nothing but films since 1946, and spoke as if the only thing troubling him was that he was so removed now from the creation of real Art; his stardom and romantic image were all so unimportant to him.

Of course, when Maureen Stapleton gave him the opportunity to do John Millington Synge's play *The Tinker's Wedding,* he said she was crazy. Stapleton said, "What do you mean? It's a beautiful play." To which he replied, "Yeah. But I can't play a blind old beggar."

It appears that his romantic image was slightly important to him after all.

By the summer of 1955, the list of Monty's rejections included Tennessee Williams' *Cat on a Hot Tin Roof,* which made Paul Newman the "new Montgomery Clift"; *Desirée,* Dan Taradash's screenplay, which went to Brando; *Friendly Persuasion,* which became a Gary Cooper vehicle; *Not as a Stranger,* the Robert Mitchum success; *Suddenly;* Audrey Hepburn and Mel Ferrer's *War and Peace; On the Waterfront,* which got Brando the Oscar in 1955; and *East of Eden,* another step in the manic legend of James Dean.

That summer, Monty tentatively agreed to return to films in D.H. Lawrence's *Sons and Lovers,* and got together with Thornton Wilder on his new play, *A Life in the Sun.* It was to be tried out at the Edinburgh Festival and open on August 22, with Irene Worth opposite Monty. Two weeks before the opening, Monty asked Wilder to make drastic changes in his part. No one, be he actor or God, gets Thornton Wilder to make drastic changes in a new play. Monty not only walked out of that play, but *Sons and Lovers* as well. He flew to Florence, where Libby was vacationing, and, just for the hell of it threw an expensive party for the maids and barmen at her hotel.

Monty didn't want to work and he didn't want to not

work. It was quite a choice. He could either work and be unhappy or not work and be unhappy.

In the end, economics and Elizabeth Taylor made the choice for him.

CHAPTER SIX

Smash-up

IN 1956, Monty signed for the lead in *Raintree County*, because it meant the chance to work with Elizabeth again, and because he was in such great debt to MCA that he simply had to take this film. It was to be the first in a three-picture deal with MGM.

Monty liked the book; it was a kind of pathological *Gone With the Wind* filled with sensitive, crumbling characters who were searching for "truth," instead of just plain old happiness like Scarlett and Rhett. Monty felt, however, and Elizabeth agreed, that somehow the screenplay didn't quite capture the novel. "The script is just good enough," Monty would say in his qualifying way— as if to justify his taking this film over so many superior ones offered to him during the previous two years. He sprawled the 1,066-page Ross Lockridge novel and two copies of Millard Kaufman's screenplay on his desk, and like a devoted Bob Cratchit, with meticulous glare and tensely held pencil, he went from one to the other, taking dialogue from the book and enlarging or substituting for Kaufman's dialogue.

Two months before actual filming began, Monty flew out to the Coast. He had always traveled with a lot of pills, but this time he packed a whole trunk full of them. From this point on, Monty never traveled without it.

In Hollywood, he rented a small, dark house near Pickfair, hired a car and a chauffeur/part-time butler named Florian—Monty's driving habits were even beginning to frighten Monty—then called up Dr. Rexford Kennamer. Rex Kennamer was then, as he remains today, the physician most widely associated with Hollywood stars. *Everyone* went to him, not only because he was an excellent doctor, but because he was also a trusted confident. With his easy Southern charm, he mingled well at parties, and was able to help the most disparate personalities find friendship. A famous star would often ask Kennamer to take him to dinner with another famous star that he was dying to meet but too shy to call.

They liked each other right away, particularly as Kennamer was responsive and sympathetic to Monty's chatterbox interest in anything medical. "For some reason many actors have an interest in medical things," he says, "but with Monty, it seemed to be an extraordinary preoccupation." It would not be long before Kennamer would play an important part in one of the most devastating events in Monty's life.

A week after arriving in Hollywood, Monty met with Jack Larson. Jack had only recently been with him in New York, and was surprised to see how nervous and unkempt he had become. His eyes had lost that translucent quality, his hair was thinning; his face seemed many years older; he slouched a lot; his walk lacked confidence. And there was that nervousness.

But Monty was with Elizabeth! No one had the effect on him that Elizabeth had. She was more than just a friend and an ex-romance: she was like a devoted sister. Working with her, spending evenings at the house she and Michael Wilding had near the very top of Benedict Canyon, was what Monty was looking forward to, not the film. He could have taken a dozen other pictures, with superior screenplays, but he accepted *Raintree* because Elizabeth had specifically asked for him as co-star.

She was now a big MGM star, box-office, but in the six years since *A Place in the Sun,* she had only done one role with any range and depth—and even that was on a loan-out to Warner Brothers for *Giant.* She needed Monty's fanatical work involvement as a model—and she knew it.

Naturally she had seen the big change in Monty, but she was "family" and Monty was free to indulge in "hebephrenic" behavior in front of her—eating off other people's plates, being rude to dinner guests, getting excessively drunk and incoherent. "Elizabeth saw it, but she never talked about it much with me," says Michael Wilding. "She didn't like speaking of Monty behind his back; she was much too protective of him. And she loved him and wanted what was best for him, and I think she felt that telling Monty to stop, or any kind of criticism, was not going to pull him out of whatever doldrums he was in." Apparently she didn't know about the pills. Like many others, she and Wilding assumed it was simply liquor.

For Monty, the relationship was better than any pill. He became enthusiastic and laughed a lot. He went to the house every other day. On weekends, she, Monty, and Michael Wilding would go for excursions and have a great time. However, beneath the surface laughter, there always seemed to be a lingering depression. Not even Elizabeth's presence could cure that. Sometimes, when the three of them were together, Monty would drift off into remoteness. Elizabeth would speak with him privately and, eventually, Monty might come out of it. Wilding never felt "left out" at these times. "I was happy that she had such a dear friend, and I knew how important he was to her. I never felt in the least that they were too close or anything like that."

From its very beginning, *Raintree County* had a history of trouble. The first novel by Ross Lockridge, a thirty-three-year-old English teacher from Bloomington, Indiana, it became a big best-seller in 1947 and instantly skyrocketed its author to fame. Metro-Goldwyn-Mayer bought the movie rights for $150,000; plans for the movie were announced—and then, in March 1948, unable to cope with his new success, Lockridge killed himself. Then, when Dore Schary, head of the studio, read the disappointing screen versions that had been attempted, he decided the book would be impossibly expensive to convert to a satisfying film and shelved it.

Seven years later, he changed his mind. A new screenwriter at MGM, Millard Kaufman, had run screaming to the head of Metro's story department, Ken McKenna, about a film from which he had just been removed. "While I yelled and ventilated, Ken looked around his office, which was as big as a small motel, and lined with bookcases, and pulled out the fattest book on the shelf . . . just to keep me quiet. He said Metro would pay me while I read it and that I should not come to the studio but stay home while I read. He just wanted me to cool off. When I opened the damn thing, I started reading and couldn't put it down. Three days later I came back to Ken and said, 'Ken, I want to do it.' He said, 'Do what?' He had no idea what the hell he had given me."

Kaufman's final shooting script of *Raintree* was 206 pages, or about three and a half hours of film. Schary liked it, thought of William Wyler as director, then Richard Brooks, and finally settled on Edward Dmytryk. It was a curious choice. Dmytryk had done some fine action films, including *The Caine Mutiny* in 1953, but essentially he was not a director of films dealing with complex characterizations or that needed strong directorial interpretation. Why Schary was willing to give him this particular film—not only tricky directorially, but one of the most highly budgeted MGM films in years—remains a mystery.

The choice of producer was also odd. A virtual unknown by the name of David Lewis had met Lil Schary, Dore's sister, onboard the *Queen Mary*. David Lewis told Lil Schary that *Raintree County* was his favorite book, and "One morning," says Millard Kaufman, "I came to the studio and I heard that David Lewis was the producer of *Raintree County*. Nobody knew who the hell he was."

Raintree County, a simple story told with complicated historical trappings, was intially budgeted at $5,300,000 and scheduled for two months in Hollywood and two months in each of three locations: Natchez, Mississippi; Reelfoot, Tennessee; and Danville, Kentucky. The screenplay offered Ross Lockridge's personifications of the forces of self-realization and self-destruction. "Self-realization" is John Shawnessy, an idealistic young resident of Raintree County, Indiana; "self-destruction" is Susannah Blake, a mysterious beauty who comes up from her home in the South to trap John into marriage. The Civil War breaks out; she goes crazy and runs away with their small son; John joins the war and discovers her in an asylum; he takes her and the boy back to Raintree County, where she dies one night in a desperate attempt to find the raintree in the swamps. Throughout the story, the raintree has been a symbol of the good, the true, and the beautiful for which John looks and which his son at last finds.

As Monty saw with his considerable literary intelligence, the major problem was that of sentiment. Only the proper acting and directing could raise the script and story into more than a one-dimensional soap opera. As in *Gone With the Wind,* attention had to be riveted on the characters.

Principal photography began on April 2, 1956, on

MGM's Lot Number 3. Millard Kaufman and Edward Dmytryk watched as Monty captured John Shawnessy perfectly in the opening shots. It was the result, of course, of months of painstaking preparation by Monty. The sequence involved events surrounding graduation at Raintree County's secondary school. In a long scene with Eva Marie Saint, John's sweetheart, Monty had to be boyish and yearning, and catch the sentimental mood of the young man without making him look silly. Suddenly, thirty-five-year-old Monty became twenty again; his face, his eyes, worked constantly, saying so much more than his lines. His manner was captivating. All Eva Marie Saint had to do was follow. As Millard Kaufman reflects, "Monty knew what even Elizabeth didn't know then—but later learned—that motion picture acting isn't the art of *doing* something; it's the art of *reacting*." Monty was able to instantly shape his character and define the tone of the whole picture.

Monty and Millard Kaufman became friends. Monty would come over to his house and was always on his best behavior. Kaufman was, after all, a *recognized* writer, and therefore a Holy One. At the Kaufmans' he never displayed any of the bizarre behavior seen by others. Despite all appearances to the contrary, he was still fully aware of how others saw him, and could mold his actions according to the effect he wanted to create. He was excellent at response changes: a chameleon of the emotions. He wanted Millard to respect him, and that was the response he got. They talked about writing; Monty told Millard about his own writing ambitions.

Monty had a specific concept about the identity and the lives of writers. To his orderly intellect, certain people, like press agents and writers, were associated with an unflappable series of ideas. Writers were people who were free to guide their own lives, and they helped guide the lives of others by their work. One way for anyone to win Monty's interest was to say: "I'm trying to become a writer." More than one young person had wheedled his way into his life with that line. Because he felt that writers were super-powerful, he tried to be in control when in their company. One night, Kaufman's housekeeper had had a run-in with another car on the way down the winding hill from his house. He and Monty dashed down. They could see that the housekeeper was on the verge of hysteria. Kaufman was a little tight. It was Monty who was sober. He took charge of the situation, calmed the woman down, straightened out the whole situation, and later even drove the woman and her son home himself. Monty could relieve tensions by absorbing them into his own nervous system, and he could generate them as well by reversing the process.

Monty was mad about Mary. Mary was Millard's six-year-old daughter. He treated her like an equal—that is, he was as much an anxious child as Mary, and met her on some common level. Well after the picture ended and the relationship faded from lack of use, Monty would call from New York and ask, "May I please speak to Mary?" Monty and Mary would be on the phone for half an hour, screaming, yelling, and falling down. But Kaufman never really knew what they were talking about. All he could hear from his end were nonsense syllables. One day, many years later, Kaufman had reason to call Mrs. Clift. He was trying to explain who he was, when suddenly Mrs. Clift's voice brightened: "Oh, Mary's father!"

Millard Kaufman had a uniquely positive view of Monty because Monty wanted his respect. It was different with the rest of the *Raintree County* company. After a few weeks, the general feeling was that Monty was an oddball. There was a good deal of growing suspicion about his personal habits. At first, Monty never drank in front of people on the set, but he would come in in the mornings complaining about "headaches" and "not having slept." And then people began to notice "the gray bag." It looked liked a doctor's satchel, only a little larger. It was routine for prop men to handle actors' belongings, but Monty would allow no one near his bag.

"Everybody knew what was in it," says Eddie Woehler, the production manager. "One look at Monty's face and I could tell what he had taken. His face would be blank and his eyes open and staring. We always knew when the gray bag was coming and we all laughed about it, at least at first. Actually, no one paid the bag much mind until things started happening."

Cameraman Bob Surtees says, "It was sad. We all respected him so much in the beginning, but after a while the company seemed divided fifty-fifty in their attitude toward the gray bag. The more sophisticated felt sympathy for Monty's plight. The less sophisticated were intolerant and thought of Monty as degenerate. A lot of people like me saw the tragedy in him."

Whatever people felt about the mysterious bag and the glassy stare, almost everybody liked him anyway. He had a lost soul's craziness about him that was tremendously appealing—even when, as a result of the craziness, one wound up with a burn or a bruise. Bob Surtees recalls, "Monty was a gentle soul and very affectionate. He'd come up to you, for no reason, and put his arms around you. But then he'd also have this maddening habit of hitting you with a cigarette and burning your hand as he passed. I think he would forget that he was holding a lit cigarette. He would sometimes smoke it down so far that it would burn his fingers and he wouldn't feel it. The next day he'd say to me that he didn't know how his fingers got burned."

Monty had other odd habits, as well. He liked to put the weight of his body on people's feet, or lean on them, or throw himself on them like a big dog. It was a sign that Monty liked you, and that you were the kind of person that he wanted to depend on. He was not physical with other men on the set in an erotic sense—not even in a mock-erotic sense—so this habit was never misunderstood. Monty particularly liked the assistant director, Ridgeway ("Reggy") Callow. He would throw one of his arms around Reggy's back, slouch his full weight against him, allowing his head to go limp to one side so that it knocked against Reggy's head, and let himself be dragged in this partially supported manner for thirty feet or so. It was peculiar, but nobody minded.

Meanwhile, Michael Wilding and Elizabeth Taylor were breaking up. Monty was one of the first to learn that their troubles had reached a crisis. He was disturbed. He liked Wilding a lot: Wilding was thoroughly civilized, British, a product of the stage like himself, sensitive, and unpossessive. And Monty adored "Bessie," as he still called Elizabeth, and their two children.

At the time, there was no one closer to the two of them than Monty. Since it had become pointless talking out their problems with each other, they each turned to him. One of them would come to his house one evening, spend practically the whole night talking about the desperate situation, and then leave at four or five in the morning; the following night, the other would come and talk until the wee

148

hours. Wilding was especially agitated. His marriage to Elizabeth was coming apart at the worst possible time for him. His career was going nowhere; his chief occupation seemed to be to appear in publicity photos as the husband of a superstar. He was also in bad shape physically; a slipped disc kept him in bed for days at a time.

The problem was, simply put, that Elizabeth was no longer the shy, self-conscious young girl who broke down in tears because no one would talk to her at a party, or who was afraid to voice an opinion because others would think her ill-educated. In essence, Elizabeth had outgrown her need for a cultivated father figure like Michael Wilding, and now they had little upon which to base a relationship.

Monty spent most of those nights just listening and trying to relieve the panic that they were feeling. But he was really in no shape to give up his sleep listening to someone else's troubles.

On Saturday, May 12, Elizabeth called in the early afternoon to make sure Monty was coming to a dinner party she was holding that night. After the past few days of marital soul-searching, Monty told her that he honestly didn't think he had the strength to make it. Later she called back, obviously disappointed, and told him that a priest was going to be at the party, and that he was really unusual—the sort of priest who says "fuck"—and he had seen *I Confess*, was tremendously impressed, and was dying to meet Monty. Monty didn't care, and kept trying to get out of the dinner diplomatically, telling her that he had already dismissed Florian and he hated driving at night, but she was insistent, and Monty in the end gave in.

That evening, he drove up to the Wildings'. In the daytime, the Benedict Canyon hills are superbly gorgeous, lazy and rolling, and the wind rushes through the shrubbery in the perpetual semi-tropical weather. At night, however, the wind howls, and what is scenic and lovely by day turns into a treacherous ordeal of twisting narrow roads.

There are many houses, today, above and below the house which the Wildings lived in, but at the time there were only solitary houses here and there, most of them unfinished. The landscape was practically uninterrupted. There were no lights on the road.

It was a simple, staid dinner party. Kevin McCarthy was there, and Rock Hudson, and some others. Monty arrived quite sober, and drank only a few half-glasses of wine that evening. Sometime that night, however, Monty went to the bathroom and took "two downers." No one knew about it then, but Monty admitted later that he had taken them in the hope that they would help him sleep later on—he hadn't been able to sleep for nights. It was early, only half past midnight. Kevin announced that he was leaving; he had to make a plane the next morning. Monty came out to see him off, and began to talk in a lucid and very chipper manner about the film and Hollywood in general. For an instant, there was a surge of the old friendship between them.

Kevin was just about to take off when Monty said, "Why don't I leave, too?" He went back into the house, made hurried good-byes, and came back out to the parking area. "I don't know how the hell to get home from here," he said to Kevin, so Kevin volunteered to lead the way downhill until they reached a turn into an intersection where Monty could go on by himself.

As Kevin tells the story, "We started down the hill and all of a sudden he was coming up very fast behind me. We were approaching the first turn in the road, and it was very sharp. I didn't know why he was coming up behind me so fast. At the time I thought it was a prank, since I knew he loved to pull things like that. His lights were getting brighter and I thought he was going to hit me and I was going to go right through the house, which was on the hill just beyond the turn, and off the cliff! I turned quickly. I thought to myself, 'He'll have to put on his brakes or he'll bump right into the fence in front of the house . . . Wow! That's close. I wish he'd stop playing around.' At the next turn, I figured I had it and I wasn't going to get involved any more in the game. I was probably down the road about a hundred yards ahead of him when I saw his lights swaying erratically from side to side, like a dangling lantern, in my rear-view mirror.

"Suddenly his car just wasn't there anymore. I couldn't see it at all in my mirror. I still thought Monty was playing a game. I waited and waited for him up on the road, and then I thought that he must have gotten stuck, that he had gotten a wheel into some soft ground and was trying to get out, because I kept hearing the roar of his motor. Finally I jumped out of my car, ran back up there, and saw that he was smashed into a cliff and that the motor was still running . . . *how* I couldn't possibly have imagined. Obviously he had taken the turn too wide, or didn't

150

see it, and scraped the cliff on one side of the road; the car veered and went over onto the other side, crashing into a telephone pole, rebounded and then smashed into the cliff again. I'm sure that's why I kept seeing the lights swaying back and forth like that in the rear-view mirror. The motor was making a horrendous noise. I was afraid the car would catch fire, so I reached in and turned off the ignition. And I didn't see him. I thought, 'Holy shit! He's been thrown out of the car!'

"It was dark as hell. There was nothing. I turned my car around and shone my lights into his car and saw that he had been in the car all the time . . . under the dashboard. That's why the motor was running. Apparently his ass was squashed on the accelerator. Gas was leaking. The car could have gone up in flames. I thought he was dead. I thought he was gone. You've never seen such a mess. Blood all over the place. I didn't attempt to move him. Everything might have been broken, his neck, his back. From what I could see in the light from my car, it looked like the whole head had been pulled apart. I was frantic . . . it was horrifying. I remember thinking, 'It's all over . . . he's dead . . . the movie's over!' I was confused. I didn't want to leave him, because if a car came down the road fast it would hit Monty, and if he was alive he'd be hit again. I went across to one of those unfinished houses, just wondering if there was somebody there . . . a caretaker, a phone, or something. No one. So I just drove up the road like mad, and called, and Mike came to the door."

Kevin was shaking. "Monty's had a terrible accident. He hit a telephone pole."

"Oh, shut up, Kevin!" Wilding laughed. He thought Kevin had come back to play a sick joke.

Then he could see, after a few seconds, that Kevin was not play-acting. He was shaking so badly that his words weren't coming out properly. Elizabeth came to the door. She didn't understand what Kevin was saying at first, but then she distinctly heard: "Monty's dead. I think he's dead."

Elizabeth rushed out the door. Wilding told the others what had happened, and left them to call Rex Kennamer and the police. Elizabeth, Michael, and Rock Hudson followed Kevin's car down to the accident site and sprayed their headlights on the wrecked car.

Within the spotlighted circle of horror, Elizabeth could

just barely make out a smashed head and a body jammed into the darkness under the dashboard. Glass from the shattered windshield was everywhere. Blood gushed from Monty's head. The doors of what had once been an automobile were jammed shut.

After a struggle the men got a door open. Elizabeth crawled in, found Monty's head, and gently lifted it away from the steering wheel. His blood ran all over her dress. He was still breathing and moaning, his body trapped under the dashboard, which was now just bashed metal and hanging wires.

There was still no ambulance, no doctor, no police. Instead, a battery of photographers arrived. At the time, there was a grotesque system in Hollywood. Members of a camera club, hungry for scoop photos, hung around the police stations waiting for emergency calls, especially those involving movie stars. When they got to the accident site, there were Elizabeth Taylor, Rock Hudson, Michael Wilding—and Montgomery Clift mangled and half-dead in the wreckage. It was a bonanza. They rushed forward, but Michael, Rock, and Kevin formed a human wall around Elizabeth and Monty. Elizabeth's voice could be heard raging from inside the car: "You bastards! If you dare take one photograph of him like this, I'll never let another one of you near me again!"

The command was loud and clear. No flashbulbs went off; the crowd just stood there waiting.

Rex Kennamer was the first to arrive. The ambulance and police still hadn't come. After a lot of maneuvering, Kennamer and Rock Hudson, the biggest of the men, managed to get Monty out of the car, and Elizabeth again put his head on her lap. Kennamer did what he could about the bleeding, which was so profuse Monty was in danger of dying just from blood loss.

The men kept up their wall against the photographers, for Kennamer, Monty, and Elizabeth were now completely out in the open, easy targets. One dramatic photo of bloodied Monty would have brought any one of the photographers several thousand dollars. At last, after fifteen minutes, the police arrived.

Monty came to, but he was in shock, and Kennamer immediately gave him medication for pain. Elizabeth wiped the blood off his face, which was now a mass of fat, swelling pulp. He was, nevertheless, surprisingly clear-headed.

152

He talked to "Bessie." A tooth was hanging by a tiny bit of flesh, and he asked her to pull it out, which she did, trying not to get sick. In very clear sentences, he said, "Save it for me. I may need it later."

Then he began to panic and said, "The film . . . I've got to be at the studio . . . what about the film?" Elizabeth said, "Don't worry about the studio. We'll shoot something else."

More than half an hour passed before the ambulance arrived. The driver was terribly apologetic. He hadn't been able to find the road, he said. They got Monty into the ambulance at last, and Elizabeth went with him. As she described it: "By the time we reached the hospital, his head was so swollen that it was almost as wide as his shoulders. His eyes had disappeared. His cheeks were level with his nose." Michael followed the ambulance in his own car to Cedars of Lebanon Hospital. Elizabeth, with the help of a sedative, had held up incredibly well. She and Michael stayed at the hospital until Monty was put under heavy sedation and the doctors could assure them that there would be no brain damage.

She had been holding everything back, but on the way home she let it all out. "She felt," says Michael, "shock, anxiety, worry, depression. But I never once saw her grow hysterical or break down that evening. Elizabeth could be remarkably strong in a crisis." Nevertheless, she remembered later that the memory of all that blood made her want to vomit. In the car, she looked down and saw her beautiful dress smeared with dried blood. The smell of it was overwhelming. She would have nightmares about that.

Reports of the accident were heard on the late-news radio and television programs that night, and were bannered in the papers the next morning, along with startling UPI and Wide World photos of the wrecked car. The accident received spectacular publicity. Newsmen bombarded the hospital all day. Some reporters asked to be connected to Monty's room that very minute! Dr. Kennamer promised a statement on Monty's condition fairly soon.

On Sunday, May 13, damage to Monty's person was assessed. Monty lay in the hospital bed with a head as big and orange as a giant pumpkin. He had a severe concussion. The face was bad. There were numerous cuts, especially under the eyes; his lips had been lacerated badly, and a hole gouged right through the middle of his upper

153

lip. Whatever had caused it had also knocked out Monty's two front teeth. Under the swollen flesh of the outer head, the situation was even worse. It was as if a face had been painted on a hard-boiled egg, and then the egg dropped; cracks rippled through the facial skeleton. His jaw was broken in four separate places; the nose broken in two; one whole upper cheekbone was cracked, and the cracks ran into the sinus area.

Yet there was hardly any damage done to the rest of the torso. By some prank of fate, the accident seemed only to have gone after Monty's face.

All visitors were barred. Monty was so heavily sedated and medicated that he wouldn't have recognized anyone in any case. He was restless, and so fitful that he even sleepwalked. The night following the crash, he climbed out of his bed, walked out of his room, and down the corridor, still dead asleep. No one saw him; then there was a scream. He had sleepwalked into the room of a woman with a severe heart condition. She saw this scrawny torso and giant, science-fiction head coming toward her bed, and the fright nearly killed her. The next day, when Monty found out what he had done, he begged the nurse to go to the woman to say how sorry he was.

On May 14, MGM's press department issued an optimistic statement via the Associated Press wire service. The headline summed it up: MONTY CLIFT WON'T BE SCARRED BY CRASH. For several days the bulletins kept predicting that the film would be held up for only a few weeks at most. No mention was made of the fractures. The public impression was that Monty had just been banged up a little.

By the time Elizabeth and Michael were finally permitted to see him, the doctors had skillfully wired both his jaws together. He could only take nourishment through a straw and he couldn't talk very clearly. He was not supposed to get out of bed because movement would slow the healing process. The doctors were pumping him with cortisone, which was also bringing down the swelling. He was not depressed, but both Elizabeth and Wilding sensed that Monty didn't want to be seen in this condition.

The hospital room was full of flowers. Hank Moomjian, the second assistant director on *Raintree County*, collected money from the crew for a giant floral arrangement. Monty called Moomjian and told him through clenched teeth that the flowers were the nicest thing that could have happened to him. "I'm going to leave them on my table until they rot," said Monty. And they stayed there until they rotted.

Monty never said "don't come," but most of his friends in Hollywood sensed that he wanted to be left alone. Kevin came to see Monty about a week after the accident, and found him drinking martinis through a straw. Monty had somehow managed to get all the contraband stuff he wanted smuggled in. Judging by his blasé, uncaring attitude, he probably had gotten hold of some Demerols as well. He hated hospital rules. He wasn't supposed to walk around, because all the cracks in the facial skeleton that the doctors had so carefully pasted back together might come apart if the neck weren't poised just so, but he walked around anyway.

The studio executives, after consultation with Kennamer and the other doctors, decided to close down production on *Raintree County* for six weeks. They were told that Monty would just barely be in shape to resume work by then—if the healing went well and he took care of himself. Surprisingly, very little plastic surgery would be required. Most of the trouble was with the bone fractures and not with the surface of the face.

On May 23, Dr. Kennamer told reporters that Monty had cheekbone fractures which required "further treatment." It was another way of telling the public that the accident had been more serious than already admitted, and that work on *Raintree County* would be delayed considerably.

Yet salaries, to the tune of $50,000 per week, still had to be paid, and MGM executives thanked their lucky stars. They had taken out an insurance policy on *Raintree County* to cover just such a mishap. It was the very first time MGM had ever done it. Taking out policies to cover films against the sudden sickness or injury of stars was a practice just starting to take hold at the major studios. The insurance company finally shelled out $500,000 for production costs during Monty's convalescence.

Naturally the doctors were under intense pressure to get Monty back into shape as quickly as possible. Libby came out and was horrified. She noted the doctors and nurses rushing back and forth; the continual injections which Monty said were cortisone and other "stuff" to keep scar tissue from forming and make him heal fast; the at-

155

mosphere around the corridor and in Monty's room was slapdash and frantic. She told Monty that he looked like hell, and he needed to rest quietly for months, not just weeks, if his looks and health were to be restored. Monty was surprised. All the movie executives had been coming in and telling him: "Gee, you look so great."

After two weeks in the hospital, Monty went back home (he had moved from the small, dark house to one on Sunset Boulevard with a swimming pool and pallid, ever-blooming geraniums). Libby was around constantly and Jack Larson would visit. Monty would lie around in the sun, his head not really functioning. He drank constantly, which was forbidden because it would interfere with the healing process and was dangerous in combination with the morphine-based painkillers he was taking. He was doped up on everything—what the doctors had given him, plus the pills from his own trunk—and at night he took sleeping pills. He walked around in a perpetual stupor, which left him uninterested and uncaring. Kevin only came to the house a few times, because he couldn't bear to see him like this. "Talking to him about taking better care of himself was like talking to a blank wall. You wondered what was going to happen to him." Kevin honestly thought that Monty was trying to kill himself.

In fact, Monty was trying to squelch his discomfort by taking as much dope as he could. He was in much "hidden" pain from the concussion, from the many cracks in his head, and from the sudden snapping-back of the bones of his face into their approximate original position. One could no longer tell if it were the pain or the assault of the analgesics, morphine-based drugs, and liquor which made his nervous system rebel, and threw him into convulsions of agony.

One afternoon, Libby and Jack were eating with Monty. Monty's version of "eating" was to liquefy food in a Waring blender and drink it through a straw; or to mash softer foods, like avocados, between his tongue and the roof of his mouth. It was unpleasant to be around him when he was trying to eat. Suddenly, Monty got up from the table and disappeared. Jack went to see what was wrong. He found him in another room, standing in one spot, every part of him shaking with pain.

Libby begged Monty to come East with her to recuperate at her place, where he wouldn't have to worry about going back to work. She would have nurses look after him, and he would be at peace for months. No studio executives would be stopping by to see if the face were ready yet. "You must make up your mind," said Libby, like a determined matriarch, "not to go back to this meaningless film. Let them collect on their insurance." She tried to make Monty see that all of the supposed concern was part of the studio game, that if he went back too soon and imperiled himself, he wouldn't be appreciated any more than if he chucked the whole thing and went back with her for his own good.

Libby all but convinced Monty, but he didn't want to disappoint Lew Wasserman and made up his mind to finish *Raintree County*. Libby was beside herself. It was as if her own son had thrown her loving advice back in her face and taken the word of uncaring strangers. She left.

The six-weeks hiatus in production turned out to be more like ten. Elizabeth and Michael didn't come to see Monty much—they were preoccupied with their own problems. A hint of a separation had already been announced in the papers. Toward the end of Monty's convalescence, Elizabeth met an aggressive, burly huckster—a man with a peculiar genius for getting what he wanted—who told her, point-blank: "You're going to marry me." His name was Mike Todd. While still living with Michael and the children, Elizabeth became involved with the other man, the start of a complicated mode of living that was characteristic of what Monty, with his puritanism, hated most about movie stars. It marked the beginning of the end of Monty's closeness with Bessie.

Monty came back to work on *Raintree County* on July 23. There would be one more week of rehearsals at the studio before the whole company moved to the first location site, Natchez, Mississippi.

Monty tried his best. There is no one connected with *Raintree County* who feels that Monty at any time after the accident began to walk through his part, but the brain-circuitry simply was not working properly. Monty had to struggle more than ever to get anything from himself. He had to stay doped simply to get through the day, let alone attempt a performance in front of the cameras; and at night he needed barbiturates to counteract the intense restlessness that had built up during the day. In the morning, only amphetamines, plus painkillers, could get him into the makeup room. Of course, he was always chipper when he came to work in the morning, but then the high would turn to exhaustion and glassiness as the day wore on. No studio executive or lesser power ever made an effort to stop Monty from over-medicating himself. Perhaps they suspected this was the only way Monty could cope well enough to finish the film. And, to them, the film was all-important.

The combination of drugs and alcohol began breaking down Monty's already precarious superego: that part of him that always kept his bizarre behavior within a close circle of friends and forced him to assume a professional posture during most of his working hours. Monty now became publicly antic, sometimes with a sheer genius for spectacle, at other times with morbid and/or childish pointlessness.

On the plane headed for Natchez, Monty got bombed. He already knew that Reggy Callow was supposed to be keeping an eye on him. Monty liked Reggy, but hated the whole idea of being supervised, so he planned a sort of "get even" game. Monty and the others were supposed to change planes at New Orleans and fly on to Natchez, but when they stepped off the plane, there was a flock of reporters. Suddenly, Monty began running, like a crazy, the reporters after him, Reggy chasing behind. He ducked behind a partition, someone would spot him; he'd dash out again and hide somewhere else. People gawked in amazement to see Montgomery Clift doing a fifty-yard dash, weaving in and out of crowds. Reggy finally found him hiding out in the airport bar, celebrating his escape. The New Orleans reporters never did get their interview, but the story about the drunken chase hit the wire services. The next day, the people in Natchez were already reading about "lunatic" Montgomery Clift as the company settled in.

It was just a small Methodist town, and the sight of movie stars upset and awed the plain folk there. The story quickly got around about the buggy incident. In one scene, Monty was supposed to get into a horse-drawn buggy, followed by Elizabeth, and then drive away. A crowd of townfolk watched. The cameras rolled, Monty got in one side of the buggy and, instead of landing in his seat, fell out the other side. Dmytryk asked for a retake, and again Monty fell out the other side. People started to laugh. Monty looked up at them with a big, silly grin. He was too high to feel embarrassed. Finally, they decided to shoot from the other side. Elizabeth volunteered to get in first so that Monty couldn't fall out. The take went smoothly until Monty took the reins and hit the horse. The horse went forward and Monty went backward—right out of his seat and onto the ground. The crowd roared. Then, Dmytryk decided to do the shot in two takes. After the "cut," members of the crew got in the buggy and tied the completely oblivious Monty in. After they finished, he came off the buggy and sat in a chair; no sooner had he settled into it than he keeled over onto the floor.

Monty had begun to misjudge the amounts of drugs he was ingesting. In a more normal state of mind, he ordinarily knew just how much to take, but one day, he failed to show up on the set at all. Reggy Callow rushed over to his hotel and found Monty in a near coma from an accidental overdose of sleeping pills. In his clenched fist was the burned-out stub of a cigarette which had badly seared two of his fingers. Reggy poured coffee into him, and later that day Monty was back at work with a bandaged hand.

Photographing Monty had become a problem. There *had* been changes in his face; it was thinner, the cheekbones stuck out, the shape and slant of the nose was slightly different, and the line of the jaw was not as fine as before. But the biggest problem was what the drugs were doing to Monty's expression and eyes. "They had a dead quality," says Bob Surtees. "Thy were always slightly bloodshot and veiny. We had a hell of a time trying to compensate. All we could do was give him a little softness and photograph him so that the camera never saw two eyes at the same time. The question of what to do about Monty's face came up a lot when we saw the rushes. But Monty was never told that we were worrying." The irony of it was that *Raintree County* was being shot with MGM's new 65mm "Window of the World" process, which was supposed to give the sharpest, clearest image ever seen on a color screen.

By the time the company was ready to leave Natchez, the small Southern town was a shambles. Monty and Elizabeth holed up in their hotel every night and ate dinner in their rooms, because the streets were swarming with movie-star gawkers. The local gossip columns informed Natchez residents that Montgomery Clift and Elizabeth Taylor were probably having an affair right there in their own hotel. At six o'clock in the morning, teenagers would show up before school, hoping to get autographs, but the two of them just dashed by. Neither Monty nor Elizabeth was feeling particularly well. The public-relations people at MGM knew they were supposed to be keeping the public and the press away, yet they encouraged local officials to court them. Two official parties were thrown in honor of Monty and Elizabeth, who never showed up. The papers and fan clubs named them the "deep freeze stars" and claimed they showed "complete lack of consideration for their public."

As Monty, Elizabeth, and the rest of the company got ready to leave Natchez, three hundred teenagers milled around the runway behind a fence. Elizabeth and Monty arrived in a car three minutes before take-off and bolted for the plane. The crowd shouted, "Turn around, Liz! Let's see ya!" and began to boo Monty, who gave them an icy stare. Between boos, the crowd chanted: "Come on out . . . come on out . . ." Inside the plane, there was a conference. A few minutes later, Monty and Elizabeth came nervously down the ramp. They waved at the fans, posed for photographs, and for the first time since they arrived in Natchez gave some autographs. The incident got international coverage. London's *Daily Mail* headlined: ELIZABETH TAYLOR AND CLIFT BOOED BY ANGRY FANS—"DEEP FREEZE STARS" SNEER.

By Danville, Kentucky, the last location site, Monty had become a walking disaster zone. Wherever he went, on or off the set, he brought with him a circle of tension. As much as the crew liked him, the uncertainty of what he would do next had a disturbing effect on everyone.

Meanwhile, Dmytryk made no attempt to direct Monty, and also gave the other principals considerably less interpretive direction than they felt they needed. His method was to leave the acting to the actors and concentrate instead on directing the photographers. Millard Kaufman was extremely unhappy with the shape his screenplay was taking. "It was turning into a sentimental, sweet-ass picture, which it was never meant to be. Dmytryk let everybody work alone. It wasn't that he was afraid to direct. His problem was that he was not a very talented guy. He said to me once that location shooting was becoming very difficult, because as soon as rehearsal for a scene was over, the actors would come over to me for direction. At that point, I had a choice of saying, 'Well, that's because you're not directing the damned picture," or 'Jesus, I'm sorry . . . I'll stay out of the way,' to get the picture finished, which is what I did." Eddie Woehler says: "Dmytryk had no balls. There was no real head man. Everything was allowed to float. Actors were demanding too many changes, and Dmytryk was allowing them. If we had had somebody like George Cukor, we would have had a great picture."

With Monty and Elizabeth, however, Dmytryk was probably right not to interfere. As strung out as Monty was, he was still directing Elizabeth. In those days, Elizabeth was not the actress she later became. Her first instinct was to be lazy and fall into obvious traps. Much later, when Elizabeth talked about the part in her autobiography, she said: "Mine was a strange part because the girl was quite mad, which gave me a chance to climb up the walls and chew a lot of scenery. I thought, I'll really try to act and not just walk through it. So I enjoyed doing the film and I started to blossom a little and get confidence." Elizabeth felt that she already had the key to Susannah's character, and she used the key with a vengeance. Her Southern accent was execrable, her neurotic's demeanor overdone, and her general aura throughout that of a movie star trying to act her newly confident little heart out. Monty wanted her to abandon that confidence, expose her vulnerability and show how Susannah deteriorates.

Elizabeth would sometimes listen, sometimes not. What is interesting as we can see in the films, is that her speeches in *A Place in the Sun,* done at a time when she was much more imitative of Monty's interior way of delivering dialogue, are incomparably superior to her garish style of monologue in *Raintree County.* Nevertheless, these monologues were the only real pieces of acting Elizabeth did in the film, and the fact that she got as far with them as she did is attributable to Monty's superb direction of her.

The situation was strange. Here was the real director sitting around, while they went off somewhere for Monty to direct their scene. Then when they finally got in front of the camera, it would be Monty who couldn't get his machinery working right. The life would go out of his face. He would lapse into a listlessness that made John Shawnessy look sleepy. The result was a woozy John and a scenery-chewing Susannah.

Like anyone who took on the responsibility of being a close friend of Monty's, Elizabeth was likely to receive shocks. Once in Danville, Monty and Elizabeth both had a day off from shooting. Monty had been at Elizabeth's rented house, but she said she wanted to be alone. When Monty resisted, they had some words, and she finally ordered him out of the house.

Some time after, she decided to see how he was. Not seeing any sign of him at his house, she looked around, and in the bathroom found the glass shower-stall broken, with blood all over the place. She ran, terrified, to Millard Kaufman. Kaufman immediately called the Chief of Police, then, scared to death, drove with Elizabeth to the scene of the disaster. Late that afternoon, Monty casually walked in. It had all been his idea of a joke. Knowing that Elizabeth would eventually come, he had broken the glass, then taken a mixture of mercurochrome and methiolate and thrown it around to look like blood.

Another episode also involved the Chief of Police. Monty's nights in Danville were agony. The mixture of pills, nerves, pain, and work pressures caused him episodic, fitful sleep and nightmares. He would leave the light on in the kitchen and bathroom; otherwise, when he woke up in the middle of the night he wouldn't know where he was and would walk around and crash into walls, thinking he was in his New York apartment. During one of those fitful sleeps, he had a nightmare so terrifying that he woke up and ran stark naked into the street. A policeman spotted him and grabbed him. A call went to the Chief of Police, who in turn called Eddie Woehler—it was well after midnight. Eddie did his best to calm Monty, and got him back to bed. The next day, he made an arrangement with members of the Kentucky State Guard to stay outside Monty's house all night, and to call him if Monty made a run for it again.

Libby's original gut feeling that the studio had only been showing mock concern for Monty's welfare turned out to be correct. MGM sent a planeful of reporters to Danville to interview the entire company. The executives couldn't have been more insensitive. A number of the reporters started snooping around, asking: "What's wrong with Monty?" Most of Monty's co-workers covered for him, but there were enough eager amateur psychologists on the set to provide juicy stories about the actor who was "hellbent on self-destruction." By the time the company came back to Hollywood for the last weeks of shooting in October, the

Raintree County set had become a free-for-all, with gossip columnists, including Hedda Hopper, and photographers all over the place. No one connected with the picture seemed willing or strong enough to complain or take action.

The resulting stories portrayed Monty as pathologically disturbed. Not once did anyone speculate that his bizarre behavior was due to too many pills—pills, for the most part, that he *had* to take to finish the film.

Meanwhile, the situation between the Wildings was, to say the least, unorthodox. Not only was Elizabeth being openly courted by Mike Todd, but they practically announced their engagement while she was still living with Wilding. Monty resented Mike Todd. He was possessive, brash, showy, pushy, and uncultivated: the complete opposite of Michael Wilding. Further, Monty's finely tuned sensors told him this dynamo not only intended to marry Elizabeth, but buy her, body and soul. With Todd around, how could there be room in Bessie's life for a sensitive soul like himself?

One day, Elizabeth came to the studio with an enormous diamond Todd had given her. The scene called for a wedding band, and she said to the propwoman, "I'll turn it around so it'll just look like a wedding band." Monty only had one line in the scene, but he blew it, take after take, for hours. Finally, Elizabeth got sore and walked over to Kaufman and said, "What the Christ is going on here?" He said, "You want to finish this up fast? Call the propwoman over and in Monty's presence say that the ring that Mike gave you is uncomfortable and take the thing off and use the prop ring and see what happens." She did it, and the next time around, Monty said his one line perfectly.

The last day of the film came on Monty's birthday, October 17, and Monty threw a little party: The Zinnemanns were there, and Bob and Maydell Surtees and Jean Simmons. When the guests decided to leave, Monty became distraught and kept insisting: "Oh, don't go . . . don't go . . ." as they piled into Bob Surtee's car. Then he disappeared. By the time they got to the end of the driveway, they found out where he had gone. He was on top of the car. Surtees and Zinnemann picked him up and sat him down on the lawn. Monty got up and put his arms around each one of them, saying, "I'll never see you again."

Monty was supposed to fly back East for a long rest at Libby's, but he didn't want to leave his house and the

163

California sunshine just yet. For several weeks, he just sat in a deck chair beside the pool, his face to the sun. Jack Larson often came over and sat with him. One afternoon, Monty got up from his chair and went into the house. An hour passed; he did not return, and Jack began to worry. When he went into the house, the curtains in Monty's bedroom were drawn and, because they were black, it was too dark to see. As Jack turned to go out, he noticed the bathroom door ajar. There was Monty, kneeling on the bathroom floor, sobbing, his face buried in his hands.

After a moment's hesitation, Jack said: "Monty, are you all right?"

Monty didn't seem to hear. The sobbing continued. Knowing he could do nothing, Jack went back outside.

Some minutes later, Monty came out of the house and sat next to Jack. He reached over and gently took Jack's arm.

"I know you came to the bathroom and you saw," Monty said. "I heard you call my name. I . . . had seen . . . myself in the mirror. For the first time I really . . . *looked* . . . at my face. Jack . . ." His hand now gripped Jack's arm tightly. ". . . I still have a career in films."

It was one of the most emotional moments in Monty's life.

No one had known it. Monty had finished *Raintree County* believing, every second, that his career as an actor was over.

CHAPTER SEVEN

Aftermath

MONTY was still a beautiful man.

From the way he secluded himself after returning from California, one would have thought he was Quasimodo. True, his face *was* different. It had a kind of Welsh, bulbous look now; it would strike one as a whole rather than as a collection of incredibly dazzling parts. Before, it had been a mutant, supernatural face, devastating because each part had seemed charged with a separate life force. It was now the normally imperfect face of an attractive man. It had good angles and bad angles.

The accident had caused some of the change. It had taken away whatever fine lines were left in the chin, cheeks, and nose—especially the nose. But the greatest change by far had already occurred before the accident. During the period between *From Here to Eternity* and *Raintree County*, boozing, drugs, psychological conflict, and time itself had taken away the eerie glow and glamour.

The few people who had seen Monty regularly during that three-year period—Marge, Roddy, Libby, Kevin and Augusta, Rick—had observed the gradual change. But as far as the rest of the world was concerned, Monty's glamour had been destroyed by "the accident."

Raintree County was a loathsome three-hour bore and the critics panned it. But people flocked to the theaters. The smash-up had gotten sensational publicity. The public found the idea of being able to see the before-and-after of Monty's once-beautiful face both ghastly and fascinating. Picking out scenes which were done before the accident and after was the gruesome game that kept people from falling asleep in their seats.

Rex Kennamer says, "After Monty's face healed, the residual damage was mostly dental. Many people who went to see *Raintree County* came away saying, 'Oh, what a terrible thing happened to his face.' But that was because the Montgomery Clift they remembered was the one in *From Here to Eternity*. A great change came over him in the three years after that. I know that there were parts of *Raintree County* shot before the accident that people attribute to after the accident."

Even before the film hit the circuits, MGM had made back its original investment from just the first-run engagements. Monty's terrible crash gave MGM unusual and undeserved dividends.

For months, Monty was solitary and depressed. He told a friend that he thought himself so unattractive that sex was out of the question. Rick called several times, but Monty always made an excuse. One no longer saw young, attractive males at the duplex—though they certainly would have come if Monty had felt secure enough to send out the right signals. The Clift family was also barred. Brooks and Mrs. Clift made attempts to see Monty, but it was useless.

Monty's personal habits were not really so different now, except that he had become far more careless about maintaining his body. He never went to Klein's gym anymore. His major exercise was walking up and down the stairs of his apartment. His eating habits grew worse. He would decide that he liked a certain type of smoked fish, or raw chopped meat, or liver, and would eat nothing but that one food all day long for days. His main excitement came from pills. His body lost muscle tone and grew sluggish.

Monty inhabited his duplex as a small furry animal hibernates in the warmth of a cave during a bitter winter. There were times when he didn't leave the apartment for weeks. Monty particularly loved the indoor activity of the telephone. It gave him a way of communicating with the outside world without actually having to trek into it. He called Rex Kennamer constantly to ask things like: "My dentist wants to do a root canal on the lower molar. Do you think I should let him?" Sometimes he would call Kennamer for no other reason than to say: "I'm going to the dentist. Is that all right?"—like a small boy asking a parent for approval. Indeed, all of Monty's closest ties at the time turned out to be parental in nature. Kennamer was extremely fond of Monty, and knew full well the scope of his problem. "I'm not a psychiatrist," he says, "but I realized that Monty had severe emotional problems. Monty was health oriented and knew much more about medicine than the average person, so his abusing himself the way he did had to lie in his emotional makeup. I asked him all the time: 'Are you making progress with your psychiatrist? How often do you go?'" He never billed Monty for these endless supportive calls. "He wasn't just a patient," says Kennamer, "he was a friend."

Monty did not totally keep away from people. Rather, he had become much more suspicious and guarded about the possibilities of relationships. The past had taught him exactly the kind of rare creatures he needed to sustain his life; now his knowledge and sensitivities in this area had increased. In the vast ocean of meaningless New York faces, one blip appeared on his scope. Her name was Nancy Walker.

At the time Nancy was a comedienne on the New York stage, her husband, David Craig, an actor turned coach. Monty liked her work. Eight years before, Nancy had stumbled into a tacky, dimly lit bar on Lexington Avenue to make a phone call, and had called into the darkness: "Is there a phone here?" A voice answered: "It's in the back." On her way out, she stopped to thank the voice. He said, "Aren't you Miss Walker?" introduced himself as Montgomery Clift and asked her to join him for a drink. "I had great admiration for his work," says Nancy, "but the two of us were such shy stumblebums that we could barely talk to each other."

It wasn't until 1956 that he began his all-out campaign for friendship. Early in the year, he came backstage to congratulate her on a performance in a play, *Fallen Angels*. At the end of the year, he sent a message, through a mutual friend, that he would like Nancy and David—and their three-year-old, Miranda—to come for lunch. He came again and again to see her show, each time bringing people. Finally, he asked Nancy if she would join his group for dinner. When Monty learned that David Craig had been ill and was recuperating in St. Thomas, he began to keep her company, taking her out to dinner after the show. When David returned, Monty said: "Listen, I have a wonderful idea. Elizabeth, my cook, is marvelous. Why don't we do this at my place?"

The relationship grew, and eventually Monty wanted to include other people in the dinners, but Nancy said: "Oh, Monty, I don't know any of your friends. I'd feel awkward." Monty replied with a line so honest it was paralyzing. "Nanny," he said, "I don't have any friends. You're my only friend."

Nancy Walker says: "I've never become so close to any man except my husband. We were completely honest with one another. I told Monty things that I didn't tell David. Monty and I had a wonderful-for-us-but-odd-for-other-people relationship. Often we didn't say words. He'd say, 'Listen, do you think . . . ?' And I'd say, 'I knew you thought that.' This kind of dialogue could go on for minutes, and other people would object. We'd say, 'Oh, sorry.' Sometimes at a party, we would be so wrapped up in each other that someone once said to me, 'You and Monty make me feel intrusive.' The communication was sparse, but deep. My husband, who is one of the great men I know, was very considerate. It wasn't a threat to him because he thought we were two very rare people who could communicate."

Monty liked Nancy's no-nonsense gutsiness. She quickly discovered that Monty had surrounded himself with a small cluster of people who looked after him. Each felt that his or her presence was vitally important to Monty's survival. As Nancy got closer to Monty, she found herself rebelling from the pattern. A member of the "family" reminded her early on: "Make sure Monty eats." Nancy came back to Monty and told him unequivocally: "I'm not going to be anything but a woman friend to you. If you don't have the brains to eat—*fall down!* And when you finally have the strength to eat, call me!" She told him that she had one child, and that was enough.

Monty *adored* this kind of talk. It also opened the door to Monty's endless discussions about the people who were trying to "save" him, which he claimed he found annoying. He and Nancy used to laugh about this.

"Guess who wants to mother me?" Monty would say.

"*Ooooooooooh,*" Nancy would shriek, "please *who?* I'm so bored with this."

"*You're* bored!"

"What are you going to do?"

"Be gentle, I suppose," Monty would reply, sighing.

Nancy gave Monty a chance to laugh at himself. It was as if someone had finally given an invalid a chance to ridicule his iron lung. Her combined qualities of slapstick wit, seriousness, coarseness, sensitivity, and warmth were as therapeutic as any amount of help that he could receive from others.

Their lunches became "sessions." They would talk for hours. Monty had a scientist's fascination with intricate dilemmas. After his accident, very few people bore witness to his brilliantly analytical, almost clinically objective mind, but with Nancy he could give his intellect free sway.

"May I ask a qustion?" she said to him during one session.

Monty was taken aback. "Listen, there isn't a question in the world that you can't ask me."

"Well," she said, quasi-seriously, "I was told this afternoon that I have to treat you like a star. Could you tell me how I do that?"

Monty gagged. "What does that mean?"

"I thought *you* knew. I was told that 'one such as that' needs care."

Monty gagged again, even though the latter, in his case, was God's truth.

There came that inevitable test, which every new friend of Monty's had to undergo. Nancy relates: "We were having dinner in a little French restaurant in the forties. It was just the four of us: Monty, Roddy, David, and myself. Monty used to eat food off my plate, and I just didn't like it. I said, 'Don't do that.' And he replied, 'Oh, but I'd love your anchovy.' I said, 'Please, it makes me very nervous when people eat food off my plate, and I can't explain it to you when I'm trying to eat dinner.' So he did it a third time, and I dumped my whole plate in his lap. I got up and said, 'Now, you stupid ass, I told you not to take food off my plate and I mean it!' I said to David, 'I want money to go home. Give me cab fare.' This time Monty almost got to me, because he was crying. David said, 'Sit down, honey; it's all right.' I said, 'I told you *no*, and I want money to get home!' Later, Monty kept calling. Could he bring fried chicken over? I said, 'No, I'm not hungry.' I was really angry. What a stupid bore! I hate *children*. A grown man! *Whugh!* I said, 'Monty, you acted like a horse's ass.' Monty said, 'Oh, I'm so sorry . . .' I said, 'Okay, you're sorry. Fine. You killed dinner—you've got that on your conscience? Now get off the phone and leave me alone!' "

In 1957, Monty emerged from his cocoon to sign for another movie. It was *The Young Lions,* and his co-star was Marlon Brando.

Edward Anhalt had written the screenplay from the Irwin Shaw novel about the simultaneous lives of young recruits in Nazi Germany and the U.S. during World War II, and Edward Dmytryk was to direct. Brando was supposed to play a nice young German, Christian Diestl, who turns into a monstrous Nazi villain; Monty, Noah Ackerman, a sympathetic Jew who battles anti-Semitism in boot camp. Dean Martin was cast as Noah's slick, draft-dodging pal whose values change as a result of contact with Noah. These were the three lions, all from MCA's den.

Noah Ackerman was a fine role for Monty, yet disturbingly similar to Prewitt in *From Here to Eternity.* Noah had the same masochistic determination to buck the system as an attempt to uphold his self-respect. Monty had done it all before, but went through the usual preparations—with variations. He decided that because Noah Ackerman was an underdog, he would look not only Semitic, but *dreadfully* Semitic. He changed the shape of his nose with putty, and put wax behind his ears so they would stick out. He starved eleven pounds off a torso that was already emaciated. The slouch and other mannerisms did the rest. It was effective, but one also notes the elaborate joke Monty was pulling on the millions of people who relished his "accident looks" in *Raintree County.*

Half of the picture was to be shot in and around Paris over the summer of 1957, the other half in Hollywood. The atmosphere on the Paris set was friendly but cliquish. Brando surrounded himself with a small entourage, which included his long-time friend and acting coach Carlo Fiore. Dean Martin, with his likable, extroverted nature, would certainly have fallen into a similar group if Monty hadn't practically kinapped him.

The Young Lions was Martin's big break. He had just broken with Jerry Lewis, had starred in three not-so funny bombs, and was now barely getting by with his nightclub singing. When the role was offered to him for pin money

—$25,000—he took it and felt damned lucky. Martin was awed by the heavyweight landscape. Here were Montgomery Clift and Marlon Brando, actors so powerful and removed from the ordinary procedures of movie-making that they virtually directed themselves. Monty became, in a sense, Martin's coach, helping him with all their dramatic scenes together. He was completely taken with Martin, particularly his sense of wit. At one point, the shooting was held up for several days by rain, and a telegram came from Fox's studio head, Sid Rogell, saying, "Mr. Dmytryk, what's all this tripe about bad weather?" As the telegram was read aloud to the whole company, Monty and Martin were freezing their backsides off in an ice-cold river, buffeted by cold winds. Suddenly, there was a crash of thunder. Martin looked up, clapped his hands, and said, "Massa Sid, we're really trying." Monty was overjoyed and smitten with Martin.

Monty's attentions did become a little excessive. Very late one night, Carlo Fiore walked into a café and spotted somebody trying to hide his face. Suddenly the somebody called out and said, "Carlo, come here." It was Dean Martin. Carlo asked, "What are you doing here?" Martin replied, "Having a drink alone for the first time today." Monty wanted him all to himself.

The Anhalt script was written so that the two Americans never see the Nazi until the end of the film, so Monty and Brando had no scenes together. They probably could not have worked together if they had. Monty was methodical, always knew exactly what he wanted, and gave everything he had on the first take. If anything went wrong, technically, he would have to stop by take three or four, rest, and come back fresh. Brando, on the other hand, had to feel his way. It was typical for him to require as many as forty takes before he really knew what he was doing. He used up film as a chain-smoker uses cigarettes.

Yet they indeed admired one another and, in a peculiar way, liked one another—if only from a distance. The old days when the two of them stumbled around each other, a little irritated and awed by the threat of the other's talent and individuality, were over. They had each settled into their own worlds of accomplishment.

Before Brando received his Academy Award, he had regarded Monty as the Master Teacher, from whom the least bit of praise was manna. After *From Here to Eternity,* he often called Monty to ask him things like, "What did you think about my last picture?" Once he asked, "Did you see me in *Guys and Dolls*"? "Well," Monty said, hesitantly, "I was watching the picture, and . . . you know what I saw? . . . I saw . . . this big . . . *big* . . . BIG . . . fat-ass!" Brando had a fit. "But what did you think of my performance?" Monty said, "I don't know. I couldn't see it. Your ass got in the way." It was his way of telling Brando he had given a mediocre performance in a mediocre picture. But Brando kept calling.

Brando, as well as everyone else, knew that Monty was boozing most of the time. Brando had his demons, too. He was, according to Carlo Fiore, heavily on amphetamines and Seconals at that time. Yet, as Fiore says, what Brando took tended to "straighten him out," whereas Monty stumbled around like a drunk in front of the crew.

During the day, Monty would walk around with his eyes like pin holes, and pretend that it was just fruit juice he was drinking from his thermos. Duke Calahan, the cameraman, remembers that they used to try to get finished with Monty before lunch. By afternoon, he would start to giggle and treat the whole film as a joke. He would crouch in corners, rolled into a ball; use his hands like monkey-paws, moving them awkwardly and uncertainly, with much touching of the face, lips, and cheeks; or slink around on two legs, like a four-legged animal forced to rear up. All of this, oddly enough, became incorporated quite touchingly in the character of Noah Ackerman.

"When I first met Monty I thought he was a spastic," Carlo Fiore recalls. "His movements were so uncoordinated. He'd have a weird posture, slouched; his pelvis would be thrust forward, hands in his back pockets. He was really tied up in a knot, and if he started to move, he seemed to have to untie himself."

Dean Martin got the crew to make up a special director's chair for Monty with a picture of a spider on the back. The minute Monty saw it, he knew it was his.

Edward Dmytryk had already done one film with Monty, and was prepared this time for some of the problems he might have. Dmytryk asked Ben Chapman, the production manager, to take Monty in hand. There were to be no more chases through airports. Ben Chapman had been the production manager on *Raintree County*, and Monty was already crazy about him. "Chap" was a fifty-year-old, six-foot, 190-pound, ex-World War II fighter pilot—as burly, as Irish, and as rough as they come. When a director told him to keep an actor in line, Chap did it. Before one foot of film was shot in Paris, Chap came to Monty and said: "I'm only going to tell you this once. I don't care what you do at night, or where you go, but when seven o'clock rolls around in the morning, you're going to be on the set. 'Cause if you're not there, I'm going to make you buy a new ass. I'll just take the one you've got right off you."

Monty loved it. Of course, he had to test him. The first morning, he deliberately came out of the revolving door of the Prince deGaulle a little late. And there was Chap, big as the Jolly Green Giant, standing in front of the hotel, arms folded, burning a hole through Monty's skinny frame with his eyes. Monty waved and slipped into the limousine. The next morning, Ben was there again, and again the following morning. This time Monty didn't smile so broadly. He'd found out: Chap meant business.

Monty liked to play "oh-you-wouldn't-dare-hurt-me" games with him. He would pretend that he wasn't going to do a damn bit of work, and make Chap come racing over, scowling, threatening to give Monty a new ass. Monty would laugh and say, "Dad, you're mean to me!" One day, Chap and his wife, Tay, spotted Monty going around and around in the revolving door of the hotel, as if he were stuck. They waited, but finally the prank went on so long, Chap had to drag Monty out and give him a good scolding, which is what Monty had really wanted all along!

Tay helped keep Monty in line, too. He liked to hear her tell him that she would rip his poor little body to shreds if he did anything wrong. A typical exchange followed one of Monty's more daring escapades. He had been given three days off, but the note Chap found slipped under his door said, "See you in six weeks. Love, Monty." After much legwork, he was tracked down in Rome and escorted back by men hired by MCA. When he got off the plane, there were Ben and Tay.

Tay said to Monty, "You get your Goddamned ass over here! I'm going to give you a new asshole!"

"Mommy, now don't pick on me," said Monty, putting his hands defensively to his face.

"I'm just going to give you a new asshole, mister!" said Tay.

"Oh, Mom . . . I love you."

"Don't try to get in good with me!" said Tay. "You loused up the whole film."

Monty hugged Tay. Scenes like this made him feel extremely loved, a totally delighted child. Clearly, the refinement, suppression, and artificial restraint of his actual childhood had created a need in him for the kind of "parents" who would show they loved him by demonstrating vivid, raw emotion with him. Perhaps that is what attracted him to "rough trade" and the tongue-lashings people like Nancy Walker and the Chapmans gave him.

By the end of August, the company moved to Hollywood to finish the non-military interiors, and most of Monty's work was with Hope Lange. He took her through the usual joy and agony of scene-probing while simultaneously leaning on her for emotional support. Those who didn't understand Monty's habit of transfiguring his leading ladies into love objects and mother figures thought that there was something between them—even though she was happily married to Don Murray at the time. There *was* romance, but only in Monty's adolescent sense of the word.

Lange had never worked with Monty before but, like so many others, she quickly learned how to mother him and cope with him. During one scene, they had to sit on a couch, supposedly toasting each other with champagne. Monty spat all of the champagne in his mouth onto Lange's face and dress. For a second, she was appalled. Then she laughed, changed her dress, and did a new take as if nothing had happened.

Monty took to the screenwriter, Edward Anhalt—which is no startling revelation: Monty took to *all* writers. Anhalt liked Monty as well, and was probably the first one to discover the exact nature of the mysterious "fruit juice" in Monty's thermos. "I remember sitting in Monty's trailer, drinking some of that junk of his. 'What the hell is this stuff?' I said. He told me, 'It's a mixture of bourbon, crushed Demerol, and fruit juice.' I began to feel weird; Demerol and liquor are both depressants. Monty drank this all the time, but I don't think it affected his performance much. There were a few times when he sort of OD'd, and then he would become impossible. As I remember, he only

174

went out like that twice while I was around. They just shot around him while they poured him full of coffee."

Monty's drinking and consequent behavior stimulated widespread speculation among the crew about other eccentricities—including the rumor that he was homosexual. This was the first time that there was ever open talk around Monty on a set. The talk was not nasty, however, but oddly sympathetic and analytical. Duke Calahan says, "There was a good deal of discussion among members of the company and the consensus of opinion was that Monty was a homosexual. The theory was that when he was sober he fought it, and when drunk he submitted to it. But there was nothing overt about Monty's homosexuality. It was just something we felt." Monty didn't make passes at the crew men, study the bodies of young boys in the company amorously, or camp. It was simply that he "gave himself away"; that he couldn't help "being honest." He communicated it without words, without any conscious effort. Everybody knew—and everybody understood.

Fox had gotten Monty a cottage at the Bel-Air Hotel in Hollywood. Edward Anhalt recalls that cottage well, because at the time Anhalt had a young, attractive secretary, newly relocated from the Midwest, who broke into Monty's apartment and tried to force him to have sex with her. She had been crazy about him for years. Monty attempted to reason with her, but when she began attacking him, he finally had to call the management. She screamed and yelled when they dragged her out. Monty never mentioned the incident to anyone, but somehow the word got to Anhalt. When he brought it up, Monty only shook his head and said, "Gee, she scared the hell out of me."

Every night, Rex Kennamer used to drive up to the Bel-Air to take Monty and Marge—who had flown in from New York to take care of him—to dinner. Marge used to say to herself, "Oh, thank God!" when she heard Kennamer's car pull into the driveway. Someone else could help her with Monty for a while! The doctor tried everything he knew to keep Monty from downing so many pills and pouring so much liquor into his system, but he was a sophisticate, as well as a conscientious doctor. On Monty's birthday he took them out to dinner and presented Monty with an enormous birthday card. There was a gleam in his eye. "HAPPY BIRTHDAY, MONTY" was spelled out in pills of every size, shape, and color imaginable. Monty was ecstatic.

He knew the identity of every pill just by the color and shape and started picking them off the card like pieces of candy.

The final confrontation between the three young lions was shot, in part, in California. The rest of it had already been shot near Paris. In this sequence, Brando discovers that the Nazis had in reality been murdering 30,000 a day (Brando, against all logic, wanted himself portrayed as the only Nazi in Germany who didn't know about the atrocities until the very end of the war). As a result, he becomes completely disillusioned and wanders in the forest in a daze; meanwhile, the Americans move in. Monty and Dean Martin's company seize the nearby concentration camp and also confront the atrocities for the first time.

As the sequence ends, Monty and Dean walk outside the camp, talking about what they have seen. Suddenly, they hear a noise from a hill above. It is Brando dashing his rifle against a tree, disavowing Nazism. Dean shoots him, thinking him a hostile "Kraut," and Brando falls down the hill dead.

Dmytryk aimed at shooting the whole thing in one day. Monty was bombed. He had a long speech about people who show respect for humanity, and was to say: "You know, people like that are going to take over the whole world. There are millions of them." Then he should have gone on. Instead, Monty just fell against a tree, waving his arms and repeating wildly: "Millions!" Dmytryk wanted to finish up with Brando, so he just accepted the take.

Actually, the scene worked the way Monty did it. The audience sees him so worked up over what he has found that he becomes a little wild in the head.

All well and good. But now Brando's fall had to be filmed. As usual, he came to Dmytryk with a suggested change. Instead of just falling down the hill and dying face-down in a puddle of water, why couldn't he land on a roll of barbed wire and have one of the strands encircle and cut into his forehead like Christ's crown of thorns? It wasn't to be a death scene, but a crucifixion.

For some reason, Dmytryk seriously entertained the idea, until Monty came over to him and said, "If Marlon does that, I'm going home."

Brando immediately conceded, without ill feeling, but for some reason the whole incident got blown out of proportion when the press got hold of it. According to the endless published accounts, the story presumably is symbolic of the rivalry between Monty and Brando for top-dog status as Christ figures. Someone who was on hand supposedly said, "When Monty is in a film, nobody else plays Jesus Christ," and the quote has been used ad nauseam in almost every piece about Brando or Monty, but no one has ever found the source. Monty was annoyed at the incident, and felt Brando had totally bowdlerized his part in the film, but there was no rivalry for crosses between them. Indeed, by this point in their careers, there was no rivalry at all, except that conjured up by writers who couldn't see that they were exceedingly different, with different methods and goals.

Dmytryk suggested a stunt man for Brando's fall, but he insisted on doing it himself. The tumble was so difficult Dmytryk ordered it done in one take. Brando was to slam against the trunk of a tree, fall down the hill, and finally land, face-down, in a puddle of muddy water. He stayed that way for what must have seemed like hours. When Dmytryk yelled, "Cut," Brando picked his head up and let out a shrieking yell. The impact of hitting the tree had completely dislocated his shoulder, and his arm had been welded into a straight-up position, making him look like an Eastern fakir. Fiore was about to wrench the arm back into its socket, when Brando yelled out, "Does anybody have a drink?" There was a moment's hesitation before Monty answered: "I do." He ran to his trailer and came back with the thermos that he had been telling everybody for months contained "fruit juice." The mixture of Demerol and bourbon visibly relieved Brando's agony, but Monty stood by shamefacedly. The little charade about the fruit juice was over.

The last scenes with Monty, filmed in New York, turned out to be his most brilliant. Monty, just after having met Hope Lange at Dean's Manhattan party, volunteers to take her all the way back home to God-knows-where in Brooklyn. When he gets to her door, he makes an awkward attempt at a kiss. She slaps him, accusing him of being self-centered and opinionated, and runs into the house, leaving him shattered. He starts home, then goes back and taps on her window. He asks for directions to get home. Suddenly she is struck by the childlike hurt in his eyes. He says, in a voice that tears at the heart, "I want you to know something. I am not self-centered and I am not opinionated. I don't think I've had an opinion in my whole life." Hope again tries to explain the way home, but Monty lifts his hands to his face in that babylike way he had developed, and his eyes plead for love while he says, "This has been the most confusing evening of my whole life. I only kissed you because I wanted to impress you." Finally, she kisses him and he tells her that he loves her. It is probably one of the most tender and convincing love scenes ever captured on film. Every look, every vulnerable nuance was right.

There were those who felt, and still feel, that the accident robbed Monty of his powers. One viewing of *The Young Lions* gives them the lie.

The premiere was scheduled for early April 1958. On Saturday, March 22, only weeks before the opening, Mike Todd's plane, *The Lucky Liz*, crashed in the Zuni mountains of New Mexico en route to New York City. Elizabeth Taylor Todd became a widow. Monty flew to Chicago to attend the funeral, but Elizabeth wouldn't see him. Rex Kennamer stayed with Monty for a while, and he could see that Monty was deeply hurt. Monty waited in his hotel room all day, but no call ever came from his "best friend."

Kennamer explains: "Their friendship didn't end on a bad note; it just petered out. Elizabeth had an active life, God knows, and there just wasn't any room anymore for Monty. And with Monty, part of the relationship was that you always assumed a certain responsibility for him or you just didn't hear from him. It happened that way with many others like Elizabeth—eventually they just didn't have the time to assume the responsibility."

The star-studded premiere at the Paramount Theatre had Monty in knots. He was completely in publicist John Springer's hands that night, and it took all of Springer's efforts to get him to go. Until the very last minute, Monty kept whining, "I won't go . . . I can't go . . . I can't face it." Springer kept repeating, "But Monty, you've got to go." Monty wasn't even dressed yet. It became an ordeal. He changed his tie, and then his studs, and then his shirt about a dozen times. It was supposed to be a black-tie event, but Monty kept complaining, "I'm not the black-tie type." Springer said: "Come on now, Monty, it's just going to look affected if everyone is in black tie and you show up in a sports jacket." At last, Springer got Monty hustled into the limousine.

John Springer remembers what happened next: "After the movie, everybody came up to Monty and said, 'Oh, Jesus, it was such a great, beautiful performance and I was so thrilled,' and Monty was very pleased, because he loved his performance. Then we went on to the party at the Waldorf. Don Murray and I kept leaving to see if the papers were out with the reviews yet. When we finally got the *Times*, we found that Bosley Crowther had destroyed the movie and was particularly vicious to Monty. By this time, Monty was in seventh heaven. Everyone had told him how moved they were by his performance and he was on the crest of the wave. Don and I immediately hid the paper so that neither Monty nor Hope would see it, but Hope suspected something, and we finally told her. 'Okay, it's a bad review in the *Times*, and Crowther was particularly nasty to Monty.' Her eyes filled with tears. From that point on, we were determined to protect Monty. People came up with the paper, and we'd say, 'Put it away!' Or they'd start to say, 'Gee, it wasn't that awful . . .' and we'd gesture frantically for them to stop. Monty said, 'Shouldn't the papers be out by now?' By now, the *News* review was out, and it was great, but the *Times* was always the most important one. Around four A.M. we left the party and went to Reubens, on Fifty-eighth Street. Monty would say, 'Gee, there must be a paper around here somewhere!' And one of us would say, 'Oh, my God, there's so and so. There's Maureen Stapleton! Maureen . . . !' Anything to distract Monty. He had to go to the john, and Don and I jumped up to go with him and try to prevent him from seeing the mound of papers that were on the way. But Monty saw them. He read the review. I never saw a face fall like that. We got him back to the table and he said, 'I don't understand it . . .' Then Hope began crying and Monty said, 'That's all right. They don't understand. That Crowther! Who cares about him?' trying to comfort her—and she was sad for him! Later, when we were alone, he just crumpled. 'Oh, my God, my God . . .' "

Crowther had said, "Mr. Clift is strangely hollow and lackluster as the sensitive Jew. He acts throughout the picture as if he were in a glassy-eyed daze." The other critics were kinder, however. Typical was Beckly of the *Herald Tribune*, who said: "Clift is superb in his inarticulate anguish as he walks with his girl's father who had never met a Jew. He is no less so in the trying and brutal scenes in the training camp . . . By far the most engrossing of the romantic episodes is the courtship of Montgomery Clift and Hope Lange, which, despite the presence of Marlon Brando, made Clift's performance for me the most outstanding in the movie."

Before the accident Monty drank continually, but he was not always drunk. Now he was—day and night. Shortly after the completion of *The Young Lions*, Marlon Brando paid a call. He had been talking with Maureen Stapleton, and they both thought Alcoholics Anonymous could help Monty, as it had Maureen and many others they knew. Brando sat down with Monty and said, "Look, Monty, you're killing yourself." Monty protested that he wasn't an alcoholic. Brando said, "I'll go with you to AA. I'll go with you to every meeting . . . We'll sweat the whole thing out together. I'll do *anything*, Monty." He went on for quite some time. All the while Monty drank vodka, pouring himself whole tumblerfuls, as if to show Brando how senseless the visit was. Brando left.

Jack Larson tried, too, suggesting that Monty dry out in a sanitarium. Monty looked at Jack tearfully, and then began to shake his head slowly. "No, Dr. Silverberg thinks I shouldn't. He says that I don't have a drinking problem."

It worried everyone. How could Monty be seeing this psychiatrist every day in his perpetual condition, without Dr. Silverberg's acknowledging either to his patient or to anyone else that Monty had a drinking problem as well as an equally severe addiction to drugs?

They called him, and his reaction was always the same. He had no idea what they were talking about. Marge Stengel says: "The shoemaker on the corner knew that Monty was full of drugs when he went to see Dr. Silverberg, but when I called Silverberg, he would say, 'How did I know that Monty was full of drugs? Would I make him a list of what Monty took?' "

Monty bragged on several occasions that Dr. Silverberg even let him drink during the sessions with him.

At the age of sixty-one, Dr. William Silverberg's international credentials were prestigious, and his reputation certainly important within his own Skinnerian-behaviorist school. It was hard to believe that a man of such impor-

Sensitive Vittorio de Sica looks at the silver award that Italian film magazine editors gave Monty for his performance in *A Place In The Sun*. To receive the award Monty had to sit through a preview of *Ghengis Khan*. (Credit: UPI)

Monty, Burt Lancaster, and Frank Sinatra during a break in the filming of *From Here to Eternity* in early 1953.

Both Donna Reed and Sinatra got Academy Awards for their supporting roles, which Monty, through his relationship with both actors, helped to enhance. But Monty himself did not win the Academy Award for his Prewitt, which he deserved. For two and a half years following *From Here To Eternity* he stayed away from films. (Columbia)

Facing page:
Top: With Fred Zinnemann and Frank Sinatra at Schofield Barracks in Honolulu. Fred and others on the film were shocked by the voluminous drinking which Monty and Frank did together. Bottom: Monty, Libby Holman (right), and locals at a party Libby threw at her hotel in Florence. This was several years after *Eternity* and Monty was living off money he was borrowing from MCA. He should have been working.

Above and at right:
The Seagull production of 1954 at The Phoenix Theater was Monty's last appearance on the stage. Its illustrious cast and confused production values are still remembered by theater-philes. From left: Mira Rostova (Nina), Monty (Konstantin), Sam Jaffe (Sorin), Kevin McCarthy (Trigorin), Judith Evelyn (Madame Arkadin, Konstantin's mother), George Voskovec (Dr. Dorn), John Fiedler (Medvedenko), Maureen Stapleton (Masha), Will Geer (Shamraev), and June Walker (Polina). (Credits for all 3 photos: Vandamm Collection)

Broke and heavily into MCA's debt, Monty finally agreed to do a movie, *Raintree County* with Elizabeth Taylor. He hated the script but thought that he and Elizabeth could make it work. They couldn't. (MGM)

On the night of May 13, 1956—during the Hollywood shooting of *Raintree County*—Monty smashed up his Chevrolet just after leaving a dinner party given by Elizabeth and Michael Wilding. Monty's face was severely damaged. Kevin McCarthy, who had been driving in front of Monty, remained at the accident site to answer police questions. (Credit: Wide World)

Production on *Raintree County* was held up for several months while Monty's face healed. Libby Holman came to Hollywood to take care of Monty. She begged him to abandon the film and come back East with her to protect his health, but he felt he owed too much to too many people to just walk away. (Credit: UPI)

During the rest of the filming Monty was in physical and psychological agony. All the drugs he took still couldn't quell the pain.

Brando and Clift in the same film! During the making of *The Young Lions* in 1957 Dean Martin was in awe of those two heavy weights, and spent almost every evening in tete-a-tete dinners with Monty—who had a kind of Platonic crush on him. Despite the rumors, Marlon and Monty were truly fond of one another. Marlon even offered to help Monty sweat out the rigors of Alcoholics Anonymous. Monty, of course, refused.

During the 1959 production of *Suddenly Last Summer* there were stories circulating about dissention between director Joe Mankiewicz and principals. This gag shot for the press was supposed to show how silly the reports were. But Katharine Hepburn was in fact furious with Mankiewicz for not sympathizing more with Monty's "illness" and for favoring Elizabeth Taylor over her. (Credit: UPI)

Monty, delicious Marilyn, Eli Wallach, Arthur Miller, Gable, and John Huston are an imposing galaxy during the making of one of the great films, *The Misfits*. Monty and Marilyn understood one another's torment. (Credit: UPI)

Monty as the Nazi-castrated retarded Jew was superb in *Judgment at Nuremberg*. He had the d.t.s at the time Stanley Kramer was filming and couldn't remember his lines, but Monty's defects only added to the poignancy of the performance. (United Artists)

Monty and Judy found camaraderie on the enormous *Nuremberg* soundstage.

To some, Monty and director John Huston seemed to enjoy their sadomasochistic relationship during the 1961 filming of *Freud*. The lawsuit that followed wrecked Monty's career. He couldn't work for the next four years.

Monty, while portraying *Freud*, was suffering from a cataract problem, which threatened him with blindness, and his memory was poor. Yet none of Monty's troubles are visible in the film, which shows both his eyes and his mind as lucid. No one could fault his performance. Incidentally, the audience never knew that David McCallum was playing a homosexual. Most of the Freudian sexuality was removed either by Huston or the cutters, along with the film's guts. (Universal International)

Monty and Mrs. Walter Huston, John Huston's stepmother, were close friends. John knew this, and it probably irritated him. Monty felt comforted by the friendship of older women. (Credit: UPI)

Elizabeth, Richard Burton's father Phil Burton, and Monty at the premiere of *Night of the Iguana* in July of 1964. Monty, who had learned that Elizabeth had gotten him hired for *Reflections in a Golden Eye* by putting up her own salary to insure him, was terriby grateful to her. He hadn't worked since *Freud*. (Credit: UPI)

Monty agreed to star in a low-grade spy film called *The Defector*, to prove to Seven Arts that he could handle *Reflections In A Golden Eye*. Throughout the filming in Munich he was quite ill. (Seven Arts Associated Corp.)

Everyone begged the failing Monty not to do his own stunt work, but Monty insisted, and his condition grew worse. One night (April 25, 1966) he was swept downstream by the current of the icy Danube during a dangerous "escape" sequence. He was finally rescued by German soldiers aboard a patrol boat. (Credit: UPI)

Upon completion of *The Defector*, Monty was depressed and ghostly in appearance. This is the way he looked right afterwards, during a stopover in London. (Credit: Anthony Crickmay)

Several weeks before his death, Monty spent a weekend at his Fire Island house with singing coach Ray Buckingham (center), and Monty's male nurse Lorenzo James (left). Ray's wife, Ann, took this photo, Monty's last. Monty was deeply upset over what he considered to be the failure of his performance in *The Defector* and went into prolonged despair. (Credit: Ann Buckingham)

Edward Montgomery Clift died on July 23, 1966, at the age of 45. Services were held three days later at St. James Episcopal Church. (Credit: UPI)

Ethel Anderson Fogg Clift, Monty's mother, coming from St. James. (Credit: UPI)

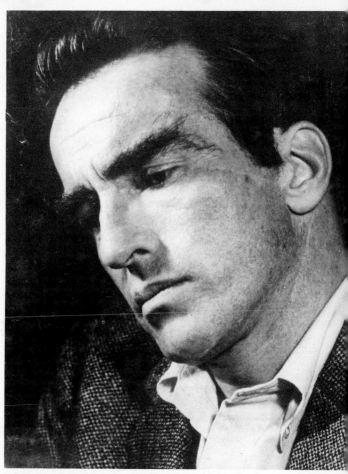
(Photo credit: Anthony Crickmay)

tance could handle a time-bomb like Monty callously. As Marge Stengel points out: "People around Monty had different theories. Some people thought what was happening to Monty was Silverberg's fault, but others felt that Monty might not have stayed afloat without him. I was with those who thought he was a bad doctor. Monty was with him for eight years and he was getting worse. If a psychiatrist isn't helping a patient after that long, I think it's his responsibility to give the patient up, to let another psychiatrist have a try."

It is accepted practice for psychiatrists to charge their patients for sessions they miss, since the hour has been set aside for them. It is, however, entirely peculiar for a psychiatrist to charge a patient for months of time while the patient is out of town. Monty would shrug and say to his amazed friends, "But I have to pay him while I'm away making films. He says he leaves the hour open for me in case I should fly back to New York unexpectedly from a location."

Hearing this from Monty (and one wonders if Monty wasn't, in this way, leaving signals for others to "save" him), the anti-Silverberg friends made certain assumptions: that William Silverberg had found himself a gold mine; that he was going to continue working it by keeping his patient dependent both on the bottle and himself; and that, as perpetual bait, he would keep telling the patient only what he wanted to hear. To satisfy Monty's discriminating intellect—so the belief went—Silverberg gave Monty theories about goal-achievement, and to satisfy Monty's need to quash his conscious mind, he permitted the drinking.

They also suspected that Dr. Silverberg was attracted to Monty homosexually. Kevin says: "Silverberg is a strange case. Monty used to go up and visit him in his place in Ogunquit. I heard that Silverberg was a homosexual and Monty was his young prince. I doubt if there was actually a physical relationship." Marge: "I think that Silverberg was in love with Monty." Mira: "There was talk about Silverberg being homosexual and that he liked Monty for that reason." Dr. Silverberg was divorced from his wife in 1936 and never remarried. Someone who lived near him in Ogunquit remembers the doctor living with another man of his own age. Dr. Ruth Fox, Silverberg's friend and protégé, today verifies Silverberg's homosexuality—though, at the time, it was merely a good guess among Monty's friends.

Monty simply would not listen to any criticism. He talked of Silverberg as if he were some sort of intellectual god, and sprinkled his descriptions with such expressions as "charming," "brilliant," "a man of great wisdom," "rare," and "witty." Fearing that he would wind up dead from a hepatic and/or sleeping pill coma, friends would call Monty's other doctors, asking them to lure him away from this rare man. "People would try to convince me to use my relationship with Monty to get him into other hands," says Dr. Kennamer. "They thought Silverberg was a bad doctor. But not knowing him, I felt I wasn't in a position to make any recommendations." In any case, Monty kept seeing him. To this day, no one really knows for sure what effect he had.

At one point a little conspiracy was arranged against Dr. Silverberg, with Marge, Roddy, and Dr. Arthur Ludwig as chief accomplices. Monty was told he looked so awful that he was probably suffering from some virus. Dr. Ludwig went through the theatrics of blood tests and what-not, and told Monty that he had hepatitis. Since Monty was promiscuous, it could well have been true; he was so high on pills and in such perpetual discomfort that he could not easily distinguish one malady from another. Dr. Ludwig put Monty in Mt. Sinai Hospital, giving strict orders—because of Monty's "hepatitis"—that the patient was to be forbidden even a drop of liquor. It was all a ruse to get Monty to dry out for several weeks. But he got his booze anyway. One of his friends felt "sorry" for him and sneaked bottles of liquor into the hospital.

Monty's health and physical constitution had always been borderline. A typical ectomorph, he was thin, frail, nervous, and more prone to physical ailments than most. It is not surprising how quickly Monty's health now began to deteriorate. The things that went wrong in his body could fill a medical compendium. He had peculiar blood pressure: it could soar to dangerously high levels one moment and sink to only slightly above normal the next. He developed sebaceous cysts, which were so deep they caused pit-holes after they were removed. His intestines had already been partly wrecked by the amoebic dysentery and colitis; what the liquor was doing to them now was anybody's guess. Monty also had a thyroid condition. Hyperthyroidism intensifies nervousness and causes bulging of the eyes. It is caused, most doctors feel, by excess stress. The same is felt to be true of high blood pressure, also known as hypertension. Everything Monty suffered from seemed to be "hyper."

In addition, the pains in his head from the accident had never disappeared, and the substances he took to deaden them caused hangovers which made them worse. He told the Zinnemanns that the head pains were excruciating, worse than migraines, and that they never went away.

Still, Monty had not fallen apart totally. He could still be bright, captivating, charming. Bill Gunn, today a fine screenwriter and playwright, met Monty when Bill was a mere twenty, newly arrived from Philadelphia and anxious to find a niche for himself as a black actor in a theater world that had little use for blacks. Monty liked him, recommended him to Mira, and would help Bill with his scripts, going over every line, painstakingly discussing motivations and choices almost word by word.

Monty would slam down whole glasses full of vodka, talking non-stop, going from one idea to another like an express train. What he said always made sense, but there were so many ideas Bill really came away with not so much a concept of a scene as a concept of a stunning, brilliant individual.

"I think he knew that I was studying him. He was the teacher and I was the boy who was learning. After a while almost every idea I had about style and attitude came from Monty. Here was a guy who was completely drunk, and yet every word, every movement caught you. He was so full of wit . . . the drinking only seemed to sharpen it. He had a vast knowledge of literature, and a great command of the language, and yet it was part of his approach to go out of his way to simplify his words . . . and if he did use the big words he knew, he would say them in a funny way, almost mispronouncing them, so that he wasn't calling attention to the fact that he was using them. I studied the way he dressed. My god, I can see it now! Always the same. He wore a lot of tapered Western shirts and denim shirts that had snaps rather than buttons. I once asked him why he didn't wear buttoned shirts, and he laughed and said, 'So when I get drunk and I get paranoid and tear my clothes off, I don't pull off all the buttons.' Everything was

183

simple, but in the best of taste. The house was the same way. My idea of drunks was that they left beer cans and messes all over the place and looked like hell themselves. But the apartment, no matter how much he was drinking, was immaculate, like him. There was nothing that was out of place, nothing that was excessive or cheap-looking."

After *The Sea Gull*, Bill saw Monty regularly. Monty had a rather singular attitude toward this young black. It was quite rigid. He had made up his mind that Bill had had a deprived life and thus had to be nurtured and protected from harsh realities—to Monty, all blacks were spat upon, all Jews superior, all writers flawless miracles. The fact that Bill came from a middle-class, very *un*deprived family did not make any difference.

One of the harsh realities of this world from which Monty felt he had to shield Bill was Monty himself. "Monty's bisexuality was practically legendary. I think that's what made him so exciting to people in theater—just about everybody felt they had a chance with him. I didn't really understand what his interest in me was, and I expected that he would eventually make a pass. I probably would have had sex with him, too, because I never knew anybody like him before, and I was open to anything. Monty was affectionate with me. He was the kind of guy that when he saw you, would throw his arms around you and kiss you right on the lips. But there was nothing sexual about it. It was just a gesture. We got *so* close, and it could have happened. But Monty never let it."

His evenings with Monty were, putting it mildly, different. As soon as he arrived, Bill would have to rush right to the bar and make himself a gin and tonic, because he knew Monty was already drunk and there was no way they could talk unless Bill had a few himself. Then Monty would begin talking and Bill would listen and watch. As more and more liquor went down, Monty might become sad about something he had read in the paper that day—a world problem, the trouble that someone was in. Monty was, after all, talking with an "underprivileged" black, and it was right and reasonable for him to break down at the thought of a sorrowful world. Then the tears would start streaming down Monty's face as he talked. No matter how much vodka was in him or how much he cried, however, Monty was always lucid. If the slightest hint of disgust appeared in Bill's eyes, Monty sensed it immediately and grew tense. It was all, in the best sense, an exquisite performance. The tears seemed timed, yet natural. Monty moved his hands as he cried with a director's dream of physically perfect movements.

What Monty said was only a part of the effect. You had to see his body move to appreciate the complete communication. When he walked across a room, he never staggered. Instead, his body took the shape of a question mark: pelvis pushed out, shoulders crouched and slouching. He was saying something with the looseness and vulnerability of his posture.

If the crying went on too long, Bill would tell Monty that he wanted to leave. Monty's immediate response would be, "Oh, no. Don't go. We'll do something else." The crying would suddenly stop. Sometimes, he would go upstairs and bring down parts of a children's book that he was writing and read sections aloud. The worst thing in the world was for anyone to leave him alone before he was ready to pass out.

Sometimes, they would go out to a nearby Italian restaurant for dinner or more drinks. Monty would inevitably act badly, they would go home, and Monty would collapse. Bill would carry him up to his bedroom, undress him and put him under the covers. Often he would stay, because Monty would break out into a sweat and start talking so wildly that Bill felt he had to be there to make sure that Monty made it through until the next morning. He would himself undress and slip under the covers, but there was little chance for sleep. Monty's antique bedroom clock rang "ding . . . ding . . . ding" every half hour, and the air conditioner was inevitably blasting away, making a terrible racket. Monty made noises at night—frightened gasps, thunderclaps of sound, words without apparent connection like pieces of a scrambled jigsaw puzzle. Suddenly his body would spring to a sitting position, eyes open saucer-wide, and he would cry out as if he saw something terrible. "Monty, are you all right?" Bill would cry. It was like a fever delirium. Sweat would pour down; he would be griddle-hot in the ice-cold room. Finally, things would settle down. But an hour later, Bill would open his eyes and find Monty gone. Bill would find him, naked, opening up doors and cabinets in the kitchen, still half-asleep. Bill would put him back to bed.

Eight o'clock the next morning Monty would suddenly

jump out of bed, run into his bulging clothes closet to grab some things, and lock himself in the bathroom. He would be in there quite a long time. Meanwhile, Bill would look around. The night before, Monty's clothes had been thrown on the floor, and now they were gone. Someone had come in and hung them up before Monty and Bill opened their eyes. Monty always threw his clothes on the floor, but by morning they were always mysteriously back in the closet.

By the time Monty came out of the bathroom, he would be jumping with energy. Marge would be already at work in the study, answering phones, typing. Monty's frantic day had begun. If Bill brought up the previous agonizing night, Monty would say, "I don't remember."

Bill would sometimes remain after the previous night, and would notice the constant tension in the apartment on Monty's behalf. Monty would leave the room, saying he was going to get something to drink, and the next thing one heard would be a crash in the kitchen—but Monty would come walking lithely out of the accident site as though nothing had happened, perhaps with an additional mark on his face. Or he would come tumbling down the stairs, bouncing from step to step on his buttocks, because he had slipped on the first step. Someone would come running over to him and ask him if he was all right, and he would think nothing of it. Or he would fall in the shower, on the bathroom floor, and in countless other places. It was rare for Monty not to have a Band-Aid around his finger, or on his face, or an extra bruise the next time one saw him.

There was an edginess in the group when Monty was around for fear that something terrible, *this* time, would happen to him. And yet he maintained himself. His intense physical and emotional effect on others amounted to nothing less than captivation. No weakling, no mere walking accident, could have drawn others to him the way Monty did.

During the day he would be a madcap of energy, totally preoccupied with work. Then, in the evenings, his emotions would catch up with him again, and he couldn't bear to be alone. He made endless phone calls in the wee hours of the morning. Bob Thom used to get them. Shortly after *The Young Lions*, Bob, a writer in his mid-twenties, and his wife, Janice Rule, became regular guests at Monty's dinner parties. At three or four in the morning, the phone would ring. Bob's hand would grope for the receiver. For a second, no sound would emerge, and then there would come this long, *endlich* sigh, a whoosh from the utter depths of the diaphragm. Seconds would pass. Bob would say, "Monty . . ." And then another sigh. It was a signal that Monty had called just to talk; he was preceding his "visit" with his own personal calling card of anguish. Bob would gird himself. When Monty called, you *couldn't* remind him that it was three in the morning and that you were fast asleep. The conversations would sometimes last for hours, and were seldom about anything in particular. They were just "stroking" calls. Bill Gunn got them. "I would be asleep and Monty would call. After half an hour or so he would say, 'I woke you up, didn't I? Why don't you just hang up on me?' And then I'd say, 'No, you hang up. I don't want you saying that I hung up on you.' And Monty would say, 'No, you hang up.' Finally I'd say, 'Listen, Monty, this is silly. I'm wide awake now and I won't get back to sleep for hours. Why don't I just come over?' Monty sometimes liked the idea—'Great, come on over!'—or he would recoil and tell me I mustn't do that. I never knew why he would sometimes have me on the phone for hours like that rather than have me over. It could be he was protecting me from something he didn't want me to see. So we would talk and talk for a few hours and then suddenly there would be this silence on the other end . . . and then the sound of snoring. I'd quietly hang up."

Aloneness seemed Monty's *liebehass*. He went out of his way to arrange his life so that he would only have people around when he needed them.

His drinking tore down the walls around this exquisite structure of isolation, however. What he wanted in the clear Apollonian sunshine, he despised in the murky bacchanalian shadows of the night. He often walked the streets along Third Avenue near his apartment. The creatures he picked up ran the gamut from nice young boys to violent hustlers. Monty didn't want to be discriminating; that would have meant involving his whole psyche in these adventures. He wasn't good sex when he was drunk, and one hears accounts of unsavory types messing up his bedroom and walking out in anger. Monty would not know who they were, and it would startle him, waking up in the middle of the night, to find some stranger sleeping next to him or walking around the apartment. Bill Gunn called him from Maine, once, and Monty said that someone was in the apartment and he was frightened. He had been at Libby's that evening, gotten very drunk, and on the way back, met someone.

"He's still in the house," said Monty, "and I don't know who he is!"

"Well," said Bill, "call a friend . . . call the police . . . call Kevin . . ."

"No, no. I don't want to call Kevin. I'm afraid. You've got to come."

"But Monty, I'm in Maine."

"Where are you in Maine? Let me write it down."

Monty took down the name of the small town, and hung up. Bill was in a play, and after the performance that night, a driver waited for him at the stage door. "Mr. Gunn," he said, "I'm to take you to Mr. Clift's." Bill packed a bag and the driver drove him to a small airport where a private plane waited. The plane flew him to New Jersey, where another car and driver waited. By 3 a.m. Bill was in front of Monty's house. He banged on the door; nobody answered. Totally confused and frustrated, Bill went into Daly's, across the street, and called the house. The phone rang and rang. At last, someone picked up and a fuzzy voice said, "Yeah?" Bill said, "Monty! It's me, Bill."

"Who?"

"Bill Gunn."

"Where are you?"

"I'm downstairs at Daly's."

"What are you doing in Daly's? I thought you were in Maine."

Bill was going nuts. "Who is in the house? Is anybody in the house?"

"No, I don't know what you're talking about."

Suddenly Bill realized that he was stranded. "Look, I sublet my apartment. You've got to let me stay at your place."

Monty went down to open the door, but by the time Bill got to the bedroom, Monty was out cold. The next morning, Monty said he hadn't the slightest idea what had happened. He remembered making arrangements to have Bill flown down from Maine, but didn't know why. He arranged to send Bill back by car, helicopter, and plane.

The street was not the only way Monty met partners. A mere look or word of kindness from some young, attractive bellhop or cashier might move him to offer dinner or an evening at the ballet. During these more lucid encounters, Monty went to great pains to find common ground for communication. Monty once picked up a handsome young Puerto Rican who worked at an airlines counter in San Juan. "He was very kind and affectionate," says the man. "He wasn't good in bed, but I didn't care. He was a sad man. He talked a lot about other people taking advantage of him because he was so famous. He said that it was hard for him to find love."

Monty needed love, but so much love that no human being could have gratified the need. He was, in essence, a superchild whose requirements were so oceanic that he couldn't help but walk around with an aching emptiness. The simple matter of taking on a steady partner was no less a task than rebuilding his emotional life from scratch. How many people had Monty told, "I don't feel loved"? How many had attempted to make him feel loved and failed? In view of Monty's titanic need to relive the mother-loving of his formative years, or compensate for the lack of it, the mere act of sleeping with this one or that could have been no more satisfying, or less fleeting, than the temporary kick he got from a glass of vodka or a Demerol.

If the love of no one person, no matter how genuine or extensive, could have given Monty peace, he was, at least, still game for a good try. After *The Young Lions,* he met a young Frenchman by the name of Jean. Jean put up an incredible campaign to win Monty, calling maybe a hundred times and writing long love letters.

He became Monty's first lover since the two-year disaster with Dino, which had ended some five years before. This time, however, Monty did not make the mistake of having Jean move in with him. He was extremely discreet about being seen with him or talking about him to friends. But somehow Jean managed to be around quite a bit, staying with Monty at night, doing things for him around the house in the day, and generally making a great fuss about his well-being. Those who knew Jean and Monty together were convinced that Jean was mad about Monty, although how Monty felt never seemed that clear.

One writer, who knew them both, put it this way: "I didn't feel that Monty loved Jean. He was an attractive, pleasant young man but shallow. I think, with Monty, it was like a man having a pretty girl whom he would be sorry to lose only because she was such a dish."

The word "girl" is used loosely, for Jean wasn't effeminate, although he had a superficial elegance and a streak of hysteria which was easily activated. He once called Marge during a quarrel with Monty and told her that he had taken a whole bottle of aspirins to end his life because he couldn't live without Monty. He could break down in tears quite as easily as Monty, but for utterly different reasons and in a much more womanly way.

Jean was in his mid-twenties, had dark hair, spoke with a heavy accent, and claimed to be the offspring of a well-to-do and well-known French family, the cousin of a celebrated countess. No one really knew if Jean was full of baloney, but the story he told was fairly consistent and convincing. He was, he said, an American citizen now; his respectable French family, unable to bear the shock of his giving up his French birthright, had cut him off without a dime. That was why he was struggling as a dress designer in the garment district.

Jean was used to better sex than Monty offered and would stray, yet he never flaunted it in Monty's face. He was timid and exceedingly careful in such matters. Jean did love him; there was no doubt about that.

It is, however, uncertain whether Monty really needed Jean and whether the relationship was, on the whole, good for Monty. If anything, Jean's personality seemed to aggravate Monty's drinking and pill-taking. The addictions that Monty imposed upon Jean and that Jean seemed to intensify in Monty, may have wrought more destruction in the long run than if Monty had decided to continue alone.

CHAPTER EIGHT

Bottoming Out

MONTY'S next film was *Lonelyhearts*. It was an execrable script but Monty decided, against all advice, to accept it, partly because he liked the writer and producer, Dore Schary. Nancy Walker read the screenplay and begged Monty not to do it. Maureen Stapleton, who was to be in the film, told Monty over the phone that she was disappointed with it. Monty's answer was irrational: "Oh, I don't know . . . I'm used to being disappointed."

Dore Schary had misread Nathanael West's short novel about an advice-to-the-lovelorn columnist who truly tries to help the poor creatures who write to him, and is destroyed in the process. He turned what was supposed to be a bitter commentary on the ineffectiveness of young idealism in a brutal world into a sweet, sentimental story. In the screenplay, *Miss Lonelyhearts* became a series of clichés which made West seem like an author with little more to offer than one or two basic ideas on how the world could be changed for the better. Schary had been, a decade before, the author of such important films as *Boys Town* (for which he won an Oscar), *Young Tom Edison*, and *The Farmer's Daughter*. The failure of the writing in *Lonelyhearts*, however, was probably less a matter of declining talents as of a change in the cinematic taste of post-forties America. Audiences, then, wanted sentimentality, and the studios always gave them what they wanted.

This was Schary's first independent film, and United Artists had financed it on condition that he keep it under a budget of one million. The cast was filled with important names: Monty, Robert Ryan, Myrna Loy, Jackie Coogan,

Maureen Stapleton, and Dolores Hart, all friends of Schary's or friends of others in the cast, and they had all agreed to do the film for much less than their normal fees. Monty was getting $200,000 per film now, but settled for well under $100,000—a figure so low that Schary today prefers not to reveal it.

If it wasn't the most praiseworthy project, it was at least a friendly affair. Vincent Donehue, a stage director now doing his first movie, called two weeks of rehearsals before shooting began at the Goldwyn studios. In the mornings, the actors sat around a large table reading from their scripts, and in the afternoons Donehue blocked all the scenes, just as if he were handling a play. Monty loved this little coterie and during rehearsals he was charming, usually relaxed, enthusiastic and full of constructive ideas.

Billy Wilder's *Some Like It Hot* was about to go into production in another part of the Goldwyn studios. Monty had been aching to meet Marilyn Monroe ever since he had seen her brilliant performance in *Bus Stop* in 1956. As with so many other opportunities, he had turned down the male lead in that film. At the time, he had thought Marilyn nothing more than a sex commodity—but when he finally saw her in the movie, he felt wretched that he had missed a chance to appear opposite her.

Rex Kennamer had known Marilyn long before her name became an American byword and contacted her about a dinner meeting with Monty. Coincidentally, Montgomery Clift had been *her* idol for years. With her artistic consciousness raised and the Actors Studio a new fever in her blood, Monty was like a god to her.

It was a strange evening. Wildly insecure, Marilyn couldn't talk to Monty, nor he to her. While Marge and Kennamer carried the conversation, Monty downed one straight Scotch after another while she drank pretty pink rum cocktails with flowers floating on top. "They were both getting bombed," says Marge. "Poor Rex! Oh, here were these two strange people trying to communicate! At one point Rex had to take Monty for a walk outside while I sat with Marilyn. What an evening!"

But soon after, they crossed the barrier. In no time, Marilyn would come into Monty's dressing room and the two of them would hug and kiss so much, people would think they had known each other for years. Monty was a kindred spirit. Marilyn could bitch and laugh and feel as

192

uninhibited as she wanted around him. One day, she complained bitterly about the rushes of *Some Like It Hot:* "I'm not going back into that fucking film," she said, "until Wilder reshoots my opening. When Marilyn Monroe comes into a room, nobody's going to be looking at Tony Curtis playing Joan Crawford. They're going to be looking at Marilyn Monroe." (Her instincts were right. After Wilder reshot the opening, it was much better than before.)

Shortly before they met, there was a good deal of talk about the two of them co-starring in the film version of *Cat on a Hot Tin Roof.* Although Monty had turned down the Broadway play, he would have jumped at the excuse to work with Marilyn, but producer Pandro Berman axed the idea. He didn't think Monty could make it through.

If there were any producers in Hollywood who didn't know about Monty's increasingly troublesome condition, they all knew by the time *Lonelyhearts* was finished. Monty's debilitating fatigue began in the early afternoons. Dore Schary and Vincent Donehue were quick to spot Monty's low work tolerance, and arranged a shooting schedule that allowed them to work without him. Around 2 P.M., "We could see that he was finished for the day," says Clarence Eurist, the assistant director. "He would lose all energy and spontaneity. Monty would realize it himself, but he'd want to keep on going. Either Vincent or Dore would stop the scene, and we'd work it out diplomatically, so that Monty didn't realize he was being dismissed. We'd just tell him we had something else planned. But he wouldn't go home right away. He would curl up under the camera tripod and watch the other actors in their scenes. About three-thirty he'd go home."

Monty couldn't get himself to function as well as he had in *The Young Lions*. He had trouble remembering his lines. He would go to the script girl and ask her to write them on little pieces of paper so that he could hold them in his hand. But pieces of paper couldn't get him through his speeches without the use of constant cuts. Donehue shot a lot of "pick-ups"—lines and fragments of lines to be spliced in later, covering stumbles. He was also forced excessively to cut to other actors while Monty spoke, creating a choppy performance overall.

Monty was in bad physical shape. His eyes bulged, his face was drawn, his look sickly, all of it absurdly inconsistent with the wonderful, handsome, idealistic young man the script suggested. What was worse, Monty played the part in his old romantic fashion, his speech replete with long hesitations, and it didn't work for the character. He became grim. He couldn't seem to find the flexibility and spontaneity he needed for the role; it made him constantly anxious. Nothing quite like this had ever happened to him before. He found himself having to run lines all day with the script girl, and even suffering mild delirium tremens—a source of great embarrassment.

Monty needed help and he received it from old and new friends. Ben Chapman was there, hired by Schary as the production trouble-shooter. Libby Holman came out for a short time, and Nancy Walker appeared for a full three weeks. She was having personal problems of her own, so they cheered each other. Every evening Monty would send a car over to get her, and they would sit and talk until all hours. She came on the set every day. When Monty got into a funk over not knowing his lines, Nancy would lock herself up with him in his dressing room and get him over it. As Joel Freeman, Schary's nephew and the film's production supervisor, recalls: "The crew would laugh hysterically at the language coming out of Monty's dressing room. It was loud and very dirty. They had a great time, laughing and cussing and swearing."

The attitude of the cast and crew is best summed up by Clarence Eurist: "Monty was our baby." Everyone mothered him; everyone did the best they could to help him without embarrassing him. Myrna Loy, whom Monty respected, got hooked on Monty—it was so easy for a woman with strong maternal instincts. She talked with him quietly and stuck with him when he got the shakes in the afternoon. With Monty one could not simply help a little, one had to take him completely under one's wing. Loy had reserve, compassion, and that little something extra—maybe a kind of weakness itself—which drew her to Monty. She often joined him for lunch, and Bob Thom, who was now briefly working in Hollywood, remembers once, "Monty spilled tea all over the tablecloth and he went right on talking. I'm sure Myrna was aware of it, but she didn't even look at the spilled tea. The conversation continued as if nothing had happened."

Bob Thom was one of the regulars, but after six months he still had to learn the peculiar ropes of being Monty's friend. One night, he drove Monty back to the Bel-Air.

"It's difficult enough for most people to drive in L.A.," says Bob, "and with me, worse, because I have no sense of direction. So here I was trying to find my way back to the hotel with Monty and I was lost and frustrated. Another car passed us. Monty was always so afraid that there was going to be a crash. He dropped his head in my lap and said, 'Don't! Stop the car! Please stop!' I said, 'Monty! For Christ sake, you'll get us killed . . .' I'm sure he was afraid, but at the same time there was that Peck's Bad Boy humor in him that made him do it."

Learning the "ropes" with Monty also meant getting used to listening to endless recordings of Frank Sinatra and Ella Fitzgerald. There were no other records in his collection. At the New York apartment, the voices of Frank and Ella dominated every gathering. Bob dared suggest that there were other singers. Monty looked utterly surprised. "Who?" Bob was on dangerous ground. When it came to questions of taste, Monty didn't hold opinions, he held truths. "Billie Holiday."—"Oh, *oh*," said Monty, tormented at the very idea. "How *can* you listen to her and still go on living? That *pain*." Bob found himself feeling cheap as Monty registered agony all over his body and face.

One night, while the voices of Ella and Frank filled the cottage, Bob came to pick Monty up for dinner. Monty was nearly gone by the time he arrived, and Bob suggested they call it off. No, Monty said, he would be fine after a shower. Bob heard the shower running. When he next looked up, a dripping wet, fully naked Monty was doing a forty-yard dash through the living room, out the door, and into the night. Bob rushed after him and brought him back in. Six months of Monty was like a crash course in how to be a male nurse, bodyguard, fellow sanitarium inmate, and friend.

Monty often saw the Zinnemanns. After a while, Renée began to serve dinner at home, because Monty would behave so badly in restaurants. Aside from his silliness with food, he had a habit of greeting waiters with such gracious remarks as, "Hello, fuckface."

Lonelyhearts took forty-five days to shoot, and shortly afterwards, United Artists released it. It did nothing in the box office. The critics made more of a fuss over it than it deserved, trying hard to say something nice about a film that displayed such important actors, but today it lies in the archives, a curiosity, to be taken off the shelves for the Late Show at 2 A.M.

Emotionally and physically, Monty was bottoming out. For those who cared, the fact that his work was suffering and his career all but wrecked was less important than the ever-present danger of sudden death. The pill-taking and drinking had reached unbelievable proportions. One braced oneself for the news over the radio, or by phone, that two or three sleeping pills and gallons of vodka had finally done it. Back in New York, just after *Lonelyhearts,* Maureen Stapleton came to one of the "pass out" dinners. Monty went on and on about his milk-glass tabletop, delightfully exuberant; ten minutes later, his face hit the thick brown rug and he just lay there. Maureen began to cry. It was particularly hard to bear when just minutes before Monty had been so charming and lively. She looked at Roddy. He said, "There's nothing any of us can do. You can only hold his hand to the grave."

Libby, who possessed more tolerance for Monty's suicidal habits than most, stopped seeing much of him after her engagement to painter Louis Schanker in late 1958. Monty's relationship with her became more nostalgic than current. A year later, he would talk of her as if she were merely an old, dear friend who had existed in the distant past. Other people, too, drifted away from him—Myrna Loy, Elizabeth, Kevin and Augusta.

Worry over Monty still pervaded every corner of Marge Stengel's life, however. It was a great strain. She had her eyes on him every second, to make sure he did nothing dangerous. When he'd stumble drunkenly in front of her, her quietly efficient, unperturbed manner made others think she wasn't paying attention. But as soon as he'd start to do something harmful to himself, she'd rush to him.

She knew every name in Monty's phone book, even those he tried to hide from her. It was an important part of watching over him. She became intimately involved with and knowledgeable about his addictions. When Marge first went to work for him, in 1954, she was naive about anything more stupefying than a Bloody Mary. She found herself thrust into a world crammed with multicolored little capsules and tablets and hypodermic needles filled with depressants. She found out the difference between Nembutal—the most common sleeping pill, which Monty hated —and Demerol, the depressant he was most fond of. She found out about amphetamines, whether Monty was on an "up" or a "down".

"When it came to drugs," says Marge, "I did everything I could to shut every door that Monty would open. He would find a new drugstore that would supply his pills. They would call me to come down and pick up the stuff, and I would tell them that before I did, I would have to call Monty's lawyer to find out if it was legal. Oh, that would stop them cold. They would just tell Monty, after that, that they couldn't supply him anymore. I don't know if Monty ever knew that I was doing that, but if he did, he never mentioned it to me. But Monty always found new doctors to prescribe his pills and new drugstores to give him his stuff without prescriptions. It was the same with Marilyn Monroe, when I worked for her just before she died. Her apartment was littered with half-empty pill bottles—made out to my name, her name, friends' names. Some doctors will just do that for you, if you're rich and famous enough.

"It was just so easy for people like Monty to get pills. I never knew who those doctors were—certainly not Rex or Dr. Ludwig—but I did know the drugstores. Some of them would charge unbelievable prices for the most inexpensive drugs. I guess they just figured that, well, here's this rich movie star who doesn't give a damn. I'd see a bill: seventy-nine dollars for a seventy-nine-cent bottle of aspirins. If I didn't see the bill, Monty would just pay it. It was a safe way of overcharging. They could always claim it was a typographical error. These places still hold me in awe. Today—many years later—I might call a drugstore and say, 'This is Marge,' and there will be a pause, and then, 'Marge Stengel!' Oh, they remember me, all right."

If Marge read about a new drug in *Time* or *Newsweek*, invariably she knew Monty had already tried it. He loved visiting doctors, but he also loved to diagnose and treat himself. He had a shelf full of medical books and would sit reading them for hours, the way others read novels. There were hundreds of different drugs in the apartment. He had an enormous jug full of "reds"—sleeping pills— which he would give out to friends or acquaintances, telling them the exact dosage like a doctor giving out samples to complaining patients. He always carried his bag when he went visiting, and if someone complained of a headache, he would snatch a codeine tablet from the bag and offer it with sincere medical advice.

During this period, Monty's house was the scene of a perpetual, ongoing play, an intense social happening. Around Monty's drunken *angst*, psyches were torn, feelings exposed and wounded, weaknesses revealed. There was much telescoping, as in a well-constructed drama; one could spend but a few hours and come away feeling that one's whole world had been exploded and reconstructed. Arthur Miller, Truman Capote, Arthur Laurents, Norman Mailer, and Bob Thom came to Sixty-first Street. Before their eyes, a magnificent creature writhed in pain, and forced others to feel it in themselves. Monty may have been failing in front of the cameras, but in front of intelligent eyes, his ability to captivate, move, and change was even greater than before—for, of course, the audience was smaller, the contact more intimate.

Each writer saw something different in Monty which reflected his own nature. Arthur Miller, inclined toward social questions of morality and guilt, saw a man struggling with a certain "problem" (the same problem that is often hinted at in his plays). "I think he was struggling with his homosexuality," says Miller. "He lived in a period, unfortunately, when these things were unacceptable in any disguise. I thought later on that if he had been born ten years later, he would still be alive. He was extremely sensitive on that score, and had that social sensitivity been different, or the social situation less unacceptable, it may well have made a big difference. This struggle that he secretly fought caused him great guilt. He never discussed it with me but I could sense it, because he wasn't that inscrutable. That was what was so moving about him sometimes."

Arthur Laurents agrees with Arthur Miller, but adds to the analysis his understanding of Hollywood's effect: "Monty was miserable. He was tremendously guilt-ridden about his homosexuality. The time Monty spent out in Hollywood only made it worse. It said to him, 'You are a pariah if you pursue what you want.' That was a tremendous problem for him. Hollywood brings out all kinds of fears and guilts and very false values."

Bob Thom saw something quite different. He noticed no guilt. Instead, he saw someone who was "pre-sexual," tortured by the extreme sensitivities of the precocious adolescent. "Monty drank," says Thom, "because he couldn't grow up. He had to keep himself that dazzling adolescent, whom you did want to help protect and who you did feel was vulnerable and open to be rendered in these terrible ways. He had to drink because he couldn't let knowledge accumulate."

James Jones (reflecting upon his earlier friendship with Monty): "I got the feeling that Monty was *consciously* self-destructive and I don't think that homosexuality was the basis of it. Like a lot of us, especially when we're younger, Monty was almost incapable of accepting the universe and the human race the way it was: the bald indecency with which people treat each other, and the way the universe treats its creatures. I don't think it was an adolescent sensitivity, but it could have been an outgrowth of it. I think all adolescents go through a period when they begin to realize that the world is a sort of shitty place. Some people grow thick skins and get over it and some never do, and some learn just to live with it. I don't think he learned to live with it."

Each of these people fed Monty through their finely honed systems—and each came away with special personal dilemmas. One senses a guilt about Arthur Miller when he says, "I would try indirectly to help him, to be supportive of him. There would have been no bottom to it. I didn't want to get in a position where I would have to support him totally. After all, I wasn't his father or his brother. I couldn't promise what I couldn't deliver. I wasn't prepared to become his nursemaid. And he sort of liked the idea that when he was with me he'd have to control himself. Because I would let him know that he couldn't use me as he did other people."

Bob Thom found deep responses in himself for Monty's brand of cruelty. At one point, he would tell his analyst by day how much he hated Monty, and at night wind up dutifully at the duplex for more torture.

Bob and his wife Janice Rule were just leaving Monty's one evening, when Monty took Rule's face in his hands with devastating compassion, as if he were going to kiss her. He said, softly, "I don't understand how you can be so beautiful and not have any feelings." Rule was then at a low point in her career, and the way Monty said this, as if it flowed from him only out of love for her, made the wound cut even deeper. Bob admits that there was a terrible truth to what Monty said. Rule was then playing Miss

Sweetness roles, which didn't suit her nature and gave her an emotionally stilted appearance. At the time, however, all he could think of was Monty's cruelty. "I'm never going to see you again!" he yelled into the phone later, sandwiched between a lot of four-letter descriptions of Monty's character. Monty claimed he was drunk and couldn't remember what he had said.

Monty called Bob again and again, apologizing profusely each time, and—what else?—Bob and Janice were back at the dinners. But they had already established a pattern which involved cruel truth-games. With Monty, the original basis of a relationship seldom changed.

Everyone was abused by Monty, with the exception, perhaps, of Marge, with whom he usually treaded carefully. During dinner, he would aim hurtful remarks at the sorest spots of those around him. He probably loved no one better than Nancy Walker and yet, in front of nine or ten dinner guests, he would hurl monstrous comments about her looks. She would be visibly hurt, but neither she nor anyone else would retaliate. If people were sensitive and intelligent, they usually understood. If he dug into a sore spot, it was so he could sympathize with it. He had to bring hurts out into the open because *he* was hurting so much. If one wanted to be around Monty, one had to suffer along with him. He forced that.

His generosity could be just as extreme as his cruelty. It was all the same thing except for different packaging. It was part of his effort to reach others deeply.

One afternoon, Monty asked Nancy to help him pick out a gift for Renée Zinnemann. Jean came along and the three of them went to Buccellati, a chic jewelry store on Fifth Avenue. Monty said, "How about a necklace?" Nancy said, "I don't know the lady. It's so difficult . . ." Monty described Renée as a small woman, about the same size as Nancy, so she began trying on various necklaces as if she were Renée. Finally, they decided on a little emerald necklace with pearls at the end. He said, "Oh, it looks marvelous," and disappeared to the back of the store. Nancy was still unsure about Mrs. Zinnemann's taste: "It's perfect for a small woman. But it really should be shortened." Jean turned to the salesman and said, "Would you shorten this for Miss Walker?" She said, "What?" He said, "This is for you." Nancy let out a fishwife scream. She became hysterical in the middle of chic, proper Buccellati. "Take

this necklace off!" she cried. "Get it away from me!"
Monty came flying down the hall when he heard the commotion: "What's the matter?" Nancy was crying: "How
dare you do this to me?"

Says Nancy, "It ended up that he had wanted to get me
something to celebrate my first year in analysis. He was so
happy that I had done so well in it. But he didn't know
how to give me the present. He couldn't have just come
out and given it to me because he knew I would have
rejected it, which indeed I did, like a big Screaming Mimi.
The poor counterman was saying, 'But this man wants to
buy it for you.' And I shouted, 'You shut up!' This was
very late in our relationship, and we had never given one
another anything in the material sense. It shattered me in
some way. My screaming was also not knowing how to
cope. I finally took the necklace because Monty started to
cry.

"Now I had to go home and explain to my husband how
I got it! David became very upset—as well he should have
been. He felt it was a little untoward. So Monty came over
to the house and apologized. He said he wanted me to keep
it. 'After all,' said Monty, 'it's only a string of beads.' In
one sentence, he had pulled the whole overblown thing
down to its essence. I'm sure if we had passed a place and
I had gotten excited about cheap little coral beads, that
would have been the gift. He just didn't know how else to
do it. I loved him for it, because he had suddenly made
the incident so unimportant except for his thoughtfulness."

Occasionally, when Monty was drunk, he would become
sloppily sentimental and write Marge Stengel a large check,
which she would always tear up. He would give her expensive gold bracelets, which she made him take back.
Once RCA tried to deliver a monstrously large color TV
set to her home. She had quite an argument with the
delivery men to convince them she wouldn't have it.

Monty spent an inordinate amount of time hunting for
things to get people. They were often expensive, luxurious
gifts—like the costly Buggati compact he sent Renée Zinnemann with the note, "I love you. Monty"—but they were
just as often simple items. Any gift Monty bought was as
well thought out as a line of movie dialogue. How to give
a gift was also important. Bill Gunn was once broke and
asked Monty for forty dollars to pay his rent. Monty's face
fell, but he immediately went into his pocket and pulled

201

out the cash. When Bill saw how Monty's face had fallen, he hated himself for having asked. He knew what was going through Monty's mind. He killed himself to get the money back to Monty a few days later. Monty protested, saying that he had no recollection of having given him anything, but Bill made him take it. A day later, Monty called Bill up to his bedroom. There was a beautiful corduroy jacket lying on the bed. "I just bought it this morning and it doesn't fit. Let me see how it fits you." Bill tried it on. It not only fit, it looked like a million. "I don't feel like bringing it back," sighed Monty. "Why don't you just keep it?" Bill knew Monty was lying. He had made a special trip to an exclusive men's store because he was so touched by Bill's paying him back the forty dollars.

Not everyone was aware of Monty's career problems. Friends would come to the house and see his study desk piled with movie scripts. It simply seemed that Monty was looking for something special. Nancy would ask, "Anything yet?" And Monty would answer, "No, not yet." But it was apparent to Monty that everything he was being sent was junk: spy films, horror films, and other low-budget nonentities. What was not apparent, not even to Monty himself, was that he was being sent small-vehicle junk because he was considered unusable and uninsurable in major films.

For stars like Monty who were in trouble with alcoholism or other addictions, the question of insurability—or "bankability"—was tricky. Starting in the mid-fifties, no major movie company would use a star who could not be insured against sudden inability to work. Marilyn Monroe was a special case. Although there was the constant risk that she would wind up dead from sleeping pills or in a sanitarium, there was also the inescapable fact that she was one of the biggest money-makers in Hollywood. With Monty, however, as with Judy Garland, there was no longer the same guarantee.

Monty knew something of the problem, but he had no idea how bad the trouble really was until the truth finally came out. For months, Bob Thom had been holding it back. While Monty had been filming *Lonelyhearts*, Bob had been in and out of producers' offices at MGM. Pandro Berman was casting *The Brothers Karamazov* and casually asked Bob: "Who would you cast in it?" He answered: "Paul Muni as the father and Montgomery Clift as Dmytri, one of the brothers." Berman replied: "You can't use Monty in a film. He's unusable. He should never work again. Only a fool would hire him." Selznick, to whom Monty was suggested for *Tender is the Night,* replied in a letter to his wife, in January 1959: "Monty Clift has, I think, become so impossible to work with that I'm afraid he would throw you higher than a kite, although there are many things to recommend him for the role . . ." According to Arthur Freed, even Lew Wasserman, Monty's own agent, referred to him as "unusable."

That *was* surprising to Thom. Monty had depended enormously on Lew Wasserman. He saw him as a father figure who would look out for his interests and protect him, no matter what. His voice and manner would suddenly become boyish when he talked about his agent-cum-father: "Oh, Lew will take care of that for me . . ."

One night, Monty was disagreeably drunk and provoked Bob into a dreadful mood. Behind the mood was also the frustrating realization that this man who had once been *the* most highly prized member of his profession was throwing it all away. He believed Monty still had a chance. He wanted to shock him into seeing the truth.

"You should commit yourself," said Bob.

Monty was stunned. He looked like a wounded animal. He groaned like a wounded animal.

"Oh, I'm all right," he said. "Lew is setting things up for me . . . He's lined up all these offers . . ."

"Monty," said Bob, "are you crazy? Lew Wasserman is telling people that you can't be hired. He's telling MGM that you're not fit to work and they shouldn't hire you."

It was a tremendous blow. This time, Monty was on the receiving end of the cruelty.

Toward the middle of 1959, Monty finally did receive an offer to do a decent movie, through the intercession of Elizabeth Taylor. Her commitment to MGM was virtually over. As a free artist who could choose her own movie scripts, and as the biggest box-office in Hollywood, she now had the same power Monty had had in the late forties and early fifties. Her first choice as an independent was *Suddenly Last Summer,* from Tennessee Williams' one-act play. She told Columbia and the producer, Sam Spiegel, that she had to have Montgomery Clift as her leading man.

Spiegel agreed, providing the insurance company would back him.

Monty accepted immediately. He loved the idea of playing with Elizabeth and Katharine Hepburn, and he considered the Gore Vidal script a poetic and tasteful mingling of abnormal sexual psychology, demonology, and darkly evocative characterizations. But bankability? That was going to be a problem.

Marge went with him to several insurance doctors in New York, but he was so nervous and incoherent, among other obvious problems, that they would not pass him. Sam Spiegel could only hope that by the time Monty got to London, he would be in better shape.

The film was to be shot almost entirely in London's magnificent Shepperton Studios. Marge had already been with Monty on three other films, and each time had seen him slip deeper into a dependency on others, including herself. She dreaded accompanying him to London; she had vivid foreboding of what it would be like, with Monty depressed and an important production depending on his stability. And yet she didn't dare let him go alone. On the plane to London, she sat with him, making sure he drank little and took no pills. At Heathrow Airport, however, his nervousness made him unsteady, and early news reports announced that Monty had left the plane so bombed he was collapsing. The same day, Spiegel called Marge into his office. "He's going!" he told her. Marge assured Spiegel that he had *not* been drunk, and guaranteed that she would get Monty through the film. Spiegel seemed placated, but the tension did not lessen.

Monty was still uninsured. He arrived two hours late for his first doctor's appointment and missed the examination completely. Another appointment was set up. This time, he arrived at the doctor's office so over-medicated for his nervousness that the doctor told Spiegel he couldn't possibly recommend him for insurance. Sam Spiegel finally had to begin production without insurance on one of his top principals.

At the beginning of every film, Monty liked to go through elaborate procedures to make friends with certain fellow players. He was like a pointillist painter, building up amorphous, compelling structures with thousands of tortuously placed oil-paint dots. He made dozens of small gestures to cement relationships. This time, he chose to pay particular court to Katharine Hepburn. Hepburn had taken a house in Brompton Square, at some distance from the Savoy where Monty and Marge were staying. Before production began on May 25, 1959, Monty went through the city on a flower-shopping spree. He was intent on buying a bouquet, but not *just* a bouquet—it had to be the most special, the most hand-picked bouquet in the whole world. He spent the whole afternoon stopping at florists, foraging for one flower at a time. The production went on for hours! When he had finally amassed a marvel of color and scent, it was time to write the note. Monty slaved over every word. Marge watched over his shoulder. Was he using the right phrase? Was a dash better than dots (Monty did not like periods)? Finally, after all this effort, he went over to Brompton Square and up Hepburn's steps. He rang. A maid appeared and Monty put the flowers in her hand. He ran back to the car and the chauffeur drove off. The ritual courting gesture was complete.

Hearing that Joseph Mankiewicz, the director, was ill, Monty also went to his house to pay a first formal call. He was quite charming and, despite all the talk of uninsurability and instability, Mankiewicz respected Monty as an artist. Grateful for Monty's kind gesture, the director invited him to dinner. That was a terrible mistake, but how could he have known? A disciplined, work-oriented man does not easily sympathize with idiosyncratic behavior in others. Mankiewicz was appalled at the sight of a grown man reaching for food on the plates of others, throwing it around, blurting things out to strangers, eating with his hands, and engaging in other acts of embarrassingly infantile behavior. As Marge succinctly put it: "That dinner finished it all." Never again did Mankiewicz suggest social intimacy between them. His attitude became one of formal politeness—a kind of coldness that Monty would find disconcerting, at times even paralyzing.

Suddenly Last Summer was not, as Mercedes McCambridge observes, a happy film. Its dark thematic material seemed weirdly counterpointed by the disturbances in the lives of those who were creating the movie. "Everyone connected with it was so unhappy. The ambience and the vibrations were upsetting. I'm glad I wasn't in it more than I was. *I* was bitterly unhappy. Elizabeth was still mourning Mike Todd. Miss Hepburn was suffering through Spencer Tracy's illness. Albert Dekker died soon afterwards. Joe had something wrong with his hands . . . a skin disease . . . and he had to wear gloves all the way through the picture. I don't think you would think of Gore Vidal or Tennessee Williams as particularly happy people. Of course, Monty was in torment. Everybody connected with the film was going through some kind of personal anguish and it showed."

Gore Vidal's screenplay kept intact Williams' thickly metaphoric language, which transfigured a brutal plot about unspeakable sexual acts into a series of tantalizing metaphysical suggestions. Wealthy Mrs. Violet Venable is willing to build a new wing for a hospital, providing the hospital's talented brain surgeon, Dr. Cukrowicz, performs a lobotomy on her seemingly psychotic niece, Catherine. It appears that Sebastian, Violet's beloved poet son, died suddenly last summer in hot, sultry Cabeza de Lobo, while using Catherine as bait to lure native boys to satisfy his own lusty homosexual desires. Sebastian is finally cannibalized by the boys who, in terms of the play, take revenge on Sebastian's cruel cynicism by literally devouring the evil. The knowledge of his death is what drives Catherine crazy and makes Aunt Violet plot to "cut the truth out of her brain."

Vidal wisely decided to preserve the compactness of the play by dividing the movie into a small number of extraordinarily large scenes. In this way, all the emphasis is put on the language and the actors. For Monty, however, the long scenes were exhausting, and often nearly impossible. In one scene, he was supposed to perform a delicate brain operation in front of a gallery of students. He had a half-page of dialogue to be delivered—in one take. Monty tried. He would manage one sentence, and blow the next. In the end, Mankiewicz was forced to break up the scene into fourteen different takes, each one representing about one line of dialogue. Only a few were finally used in the movie.

Mankiewicz started demanding that Spiegel replace Monty, and Spiegel was often ready to comply. "We were frequently tempted," says Spiegel, "because it became increasingly more difficult to work with him on certain days. And then there were days when he was considerably more relaxed. I was very fond of him . . . I spent hours and hours during the picture practically nursing him—postponing the shooting until I knew that he was calm and we had given him enough coffee and enough counter-medicines to counteract whatever drugs he was taking. He would become extremely agitated. And of course I knew that he was not capable of memorizing lines when he was that agitated." Part of the problem also was that Mankiewicz could not, or would not, pay Monty the personal attention he required to get through his scenes. Again, according to Sam Spiegel, "Mankiewicz is an excellent director but devoid of a great many human considerations when it comes to weaker beings than himself."

With the exception of Mankiewicz, Monty evoked the company's sympathy. During the day, he developed the sweats and shakes. He drank his "orange juice." This particular summer, London was an inferno. The heat in the studio was even worse. Monty, sitting or standing around with the sweats and the d.t.'s, looked as if he were a man with a fever suffering from a violent chill. Mercedes McCambridge, who played Elizabeth Taylor's mother, had battled alcoholism herself and knew exactly what Monty was going through. "I can see him now," she says, "with his shoulder blades hunched and pinched in in that way of his. It wasn't that he was round-shouldered; it was as if, no matter how loose he seemed in the rest of his body, there was always that terrible tension. He was dripping wet all of the time. I can remember mopping his brow several times trying hard not to spoil his makeup. Once in a while, I would go over to him and stand behind his chair and put my hands on his shoulders and keep them there for a while. My heart ached for him."

One day, when Monty seemed extremely disturbed and ill, she went over to Elizabeth and asked: "Is there anything that you can do?" Elizabeth answered: "I don't know. I've tried to get through to him and I just can't." She was obviously deeply concerned, but at this point in her life, Elizabeth didn't have the time or the emotional means to help Monty. Her personal life was a shambles. She had just made the supreme mistake of marrying Eddie Fisher, whom she didn't love. Neither Fisher nor Elizabeth felt secure. She forced herself to parade her new husband around the studio, making a spectacle of her affection for him. In the evenings, she holed up with Fisher in a big house in Surrey, to which Monty did not come and from which she did not stray.

Besides Elizabeth, the strongest influence on Sam Spiegel

to retain Monty was Katharine Hepburn. She practically became his nurse. "Katie has a brisk appearance," says Spiegel, "but under it is an extremely soft heart . . . She really spread her motherly wings over him." She sat with Monty, ran lines with him, and attempted to rebuild his confidence as she had often done in the past with Spencer Tracy.

The two longest and most difficult sequences came at the very beginning of shooting and at the very end. The first was the primeval garden scene with Monty and Hepburn, and the second was Elizabeth's brilliant monologue in front of the whole cast. For the garden scene, hundreds of exotic plants were brought to Shepperton, and arranged in an extravagant set that represented Mrs. Venable's symbolic transfiguration of her son's voracious sexual appetite into a garden filled with insectivorous growths. Monty, as Dr. Cukrowicz, had to react to Hepburn's chilling speech about the slaughter of baby turtles by carnivorous birds. For Sebastian, this had represented nothing less than the savage nature of God. The speech had to be slightly overdone, because Mrs. Venable was nearly as hyperbolic as her words, but not so much so that it wasn't convincing.

Extreme concentration was necessary. The temperature was in the upper nineties. Assistant director Jake Wright says, "It was agony trying to get Katharine and Monty into their costumes and onto the set at the last possible moment to shoot, because if Hepburn was in her costume twenty minutes too early and walking about, the thing was just drenched. She had to go off and have a cold shower and start again." Once they got into the scene, Hepburn would deliver a difficult passage and Monty would stumble at a place where the camera simply couldn't cut. They would have to start all over. Anyone but Hepburn would have been climbing the walls, but she was positively saintly about the extra effort he caused her.

Monty's exhaustion was so total that Roy Pryce, his chauffeur, put pillows in the back seat so that Monty could sleep en route. Sometimes he was unconscionably late in the mornings, and yet he was just as likely to be the first to arrive. In the evenings, he was usually in bed before ten.

Only occasionally did Monty roam around London during evenings and days off. During the day, Monty donned dark glasses and a funny hat—the whole movie-star bit, but the nights were different. A few items in the London papers about the leading man's nocturnal outings came to Spiegel's and Mankiewicz's attention. One had to do with Monty's passing out in London's posh Stork Room. He was reportedly carried to the manager's office on a stretcher when he could not be brought around, but by the time the doctor arrived he was fully conscious and ready to resume his drinking. The manager wouldn't hear of it and had two waiters escort Monty to a taxi, where he howled old sailor songs as he was driven away.

Monty wasn't especially friendly or witty. He was much too sick. But there was often a gleam in his eyes, and he sometimes displayed a kind of low-grade gallows humor. One dreary, rainy morning, around 6 A.M., Monty and Mercedes McCambridge drove to Shepperton. On the way, they spotted a house of detention—ugly, gray, wet, and desolate—standing next to a cemetery called Wormwood Scrubs. The landscape matched the way they both felt. "I don't think those stones had ever been dry—just the most awful place," says McCambridge; "and to think that people were in there for the worst crimes that any one of us was capable of committing. We would talk about the horror. One day, Laurence Harvey came on the set. He looked so pompous in a terry-cloth robe. Monty yelled out to me, 'Wormwood Scrubs!' If something funny went wrong, and we saw the incongruity of whatever it was, one of us called out to the other: 'Wormwood Scrubs!' This little code of ours was a great equalizer. It would bring us back to the reality of the foolishness that was going on."

Elizabeth Taylor got her Oscar for the wrong film. Her work in *Suddenly Last Summer* was the best of her entire career—with the exception of the fine performance she gave in *Who's Afraid of Virginia Woolf?* The stunning monologue which closes *Suddenly Last Summer* is by far the single best speech she ever gave, and the first time that the many hours of work between Monty and Elizabeth finally bore fruit. The hesitations for emphasis, the tension, the deliberate running together of certain words—these are all pure Montgomery Clift. She also used a bit of the Method, too, however. After the exhausting monologue, nearly everyone rushed to congratulate her. She burst into tears. She was inconsolable because she had used her grief for Mike Todd to do the scene.

There is a story that Katharine Hepburn spit directly into the face of Joseph Mankiewicz. It is true, and so embarrasses him today that he prefers to say that she spat at the floor. It happened on the last day of shooting, after the very last take at Shepperton was done. "Are you quite sure we're finished?" she asked Mankiewicz several times, and each time he told her, perplexedly, that they were quite finished. Then she spat into his face. She did not, as Garson Kanin reported in *Tracy and Hepburn*, spit at Sam Spiegel as well. She felt that Mankiewicz had mistreated both her and Monty. It's hard to say whether Mankiewicz, an accomplished artist who had proven himself countless times prior to this film, deserved such contempt. "At the time," says Spiegel, "Mankiewicz was anxious to court friendship with Elizabeth, who later rewarded him for it by insisting that he direct *Cleopatra* (which became his punishment instead of his reward). He was downright disrespectful to Katie. To please one girl he was disrespectful to the other."

After the film, Mankiewicz was blamed for his treatment of Monty, but those closest to him on the set were aware of his particular situation. He could not, in all honesty, find it in himself to act fatherly and warm toward Monty—because he didn't understand Monty's problem.

Suddenly Last Summer, released late in 1959, was a knockout at the box office. The film's suggestions of incest, homosexuality, rape, and cannibalism put off a number of prestigious critics, but tantalized the public. This *was* the end of the fifties, a period when the public was eager for more candid sexual situations, while the Establishment still refused to admit to the change in public taste. The movie's undertone of titillating perversions camouflaged its higher artistic qualities. Williams' poetry was provocative, the direction superb, and the performances by the three principals nothing short of glorious. Katharine Hepburn, as Mrs. Venable, managed to transmute her usual balanced qualities into those of a supernatural creature, capable of both psychotic cruelty and metaphysical consciousness. Monty gave Dr. Cukrowicz a sensitive objectivity, and, above all, a stature that counterpoised the neuroses of the two warring ladies. When he listens to either one of them, it is as if his whole body is concentrating—precisely what is needed in a story where painful verbal revelations create the interest. His physical presence in the film is magnificent. His face, with all of its irregularities, takes on a special romantic interest. How astonishing: That Monty could have photographed this well while existing in a state of utter physical misery and decay.

In early September, Monty returned to 209 East 61st Street.

On a Thursday evening, the twenty-fourth of the month, Libby and her fiancé, Louis Schanker, were just returning to her town house when they saw fire engines on the next block. Libby, who had a way of second-guessing Monty's troubles, was sure that it was Monty's house. It was. By the time they got there, the fire was already out. Libby told the firemen, "I'm Miss Holman and I'm a friend of Mr. Clift's. Please let me through," and, when she entered, found the vestibule and much of the first floor completely gutted, with choking smoke still pouring from the walls. When they reached the second floor, the first level of Monty's apartment, Libby called out. She heard Monty's voice from the bedroom and there were Monty and Jean, sitting up in bed. Except for a touch of smoke poisoning, they insisted they were fine.

Apparently, painters working in the vestibule had set off a flash fire with their acetylene torches. Monty and Jean had been trapped and escaped only when firemen hoisted a ladder to the roof of an adjoining building, crossed over to Monty's building and rescued them through the skylight. After the blaze was quashed, Monty and Jean climbed through the wreckage of the stairwell and went back to bed.

The next day, the morning papers ran front-page reports on the close call, describing Jean as an "unidentified male companion." It was embarrassing for Monty, who had been conscientious about keeping Jean's presence in his life a secret.

For days, Monty and Marge cleaned soot from the books and furniture that had not been destroyed by the fire. Half the building still stank from smoke, but Monty insisted on remaining in that gutted atmosphere. He seemed content with mountain-climbing up the crumbling, scorched stairs that were partly disengaged from the melted walls. Monty loved that place, burnt or whole.

More than once Monty had told people that, of all the directors he had ever worked with, Elia Kazan was the one he most admired and respected. Kazan had already offered him a number of exciting scripts—among them:

On the Waterfront and *East of Eden*—which Monty, for one reason or another, had turned down. It was a pity that the movie they finally did turned out to be one of Kazan's lesser achievements and a commercial loser: *Wild River*.

Production on *Wild River* started two months after *Suddenly Last Summer* ended. Kazan had been working on the script of *Wild River* sporadically for nearly five years. But the idea of doing a movie or a play concerning intractable do-gooder government agencies versus the needs of flesh-and-blood people had come to him in 1941, while he was working with the Department of Agriculture.

Wild River's theme was a good, simple one, even if potentially undramatic: The rights of one individual are as important as society's right to progress. The film does not condemn, but does note the tragedy of eminent-domain laws. In the script, big-city TVA man Chuck Glover comes to a small town in the South to convince elderly Ella Garth to sell her house and land so that it can be submerged as part of a dam system the TVA has created to protect local residents from flooding. While he battles Ella Garth's stubborn pioneer sense of the homestead, he becomes romantically involved with her granddaughter Carol.

It was a mood story, and most of the interest had to be supplied by the performers. For the old woman, Kazan picked Jo Van Fleet, who had brought fire to his *East of Eden;* for Carol Garth, he chose Lee Remick, who had impressed him in his *A Face in the Crowd* and had just become known to the public in *Anatomy of a Murder*—and for Chuck Glover, the pecking order had been reversed. Kazan preferred Marlon Brando over Monty because, he said, "I can't work with a drunk." Brando's unavailability made him choose Monty, but not before he got a promise from Monty that he would stay dry. Monty's respect for Kazan gave substance to Kazan's order. He did not exactly dry out for *Wild River*, but as the weeks of production went on, he drank less and less and became stronger. Kazan, who knew how much Monty needed to drink, was impressed by Monty's reliability. Charles Maguire, the assistant director, cannot remember seeing Monty inebriated once.

The picture, which began in November 1959, was shot exclusively on location in Cleveland, Tennessee—a little town of about 20,000. Monty was accompanied by Donna Carnegie, whose function was more or less that of a companion. As Marge explains, "I had already been with Monty on four films, and this time I wanted to stay behind. Actually, the only important thing was that *someone* be there with him. In the past, if I hadn't been there, Libby went, and before my time, Mira used to go with him. It was always less a matter of being a secretary than just being around when he needed you." Donna Carnegie was a beautiful young actress who had come to a number of Monty's dinners with an actor friend, Ben Piazza. Like so many other beautiful young women with much to offer, she had been taken with Monty and put up with much on his behalf, both during the filming and afterwards. There is no evidence that Monty himself was drawn to any of the luscious, bright, enthusiastic females who, at this point in his life, would still have become Mrs. Clift at the merest sign of interest on his part.

Everyone in the cast, and a good many in the crew, stayed at the Cherokee Hotel in Cleveland. The first time Gadge (Kazan's pet name) introduced Lee Remick to Monty, Monty's only response was: "God, she's so young!" She loved him from the start—what woman didn't love Monty from the start?

Says Lee Remick, "His body was bird-like. He was very thin and all bones. He was practically not there. If you put your arms around him, you were practically hugging yourself . . . He was a slight man with a beautiful face and gorgeous eyes. And he was so sensitive. I would stop myself from saying things like, 'You need a haircut,' because he would take it as a sign that maybe you didn't like him. He did inspire in me, as he did in most women I suppose, the feeling of wanting to look after him. He was like a wounded bird—so vulnerable. He was clearly a troubled soul. He made me feel needed."

The script was minimal when shooting began. Kazan had decided to flesh out his scenes after seeing how his actors responded to one another and what their attitudes were toward their characters. He would sit with Monty and Lee Remick and chat with them about personal matters, then slowly turn the conversation toward the particular scene they were going to play, and start an "idea" rehearsal. Monty became mercurial at these sessions. He would sit in a corner, dropping out of the conversation as Remick and Kazan talked about a scene, and then suddenly jump out of his seat spouting a barrage of suggestions. They were often exceptional and helped Gadge forge the film.

The scenes between Jo Van Fleet and Monty conveyed Kazan's theme and were remarkably well done, but it was the peculiarity of the love scenes between Lee Remick and Monty that, in the released print, created the excitement. Originally, Carol was supposed to be an awkward, rural girl who falls in love with the man who is dispossessing her grandmother. There was no indication in the dialogue as to which of the two was to be more dominant; one simply assumed it would be the man.

Remick says, "Insofar as Monty was incapable of being the dominant partner in a male-female relationship, my character always ended up literally above him. In every love scene, his head would end up on my shoulder. It was the way he was. Instead of forcing Monty to play a dominant male, Gadge went along . . . I think in the end, the film showed a very different kind of relationship than what one usually sees."

One exceptional scene—a scene personalized, as it were, for Monty—was completely improvised in rehearsal. At the end of the movie, Albert Salmi beats Monty in a fight and Remick pounces on Salmi's back so hard that she, in effect, saves Monty. Then, while she is tending his wounds, Monty says: "Damn it! Can't I just win one fight?" Remick replies, "I don't care if you ever do. I just want you to marry me. I'll defend you for the rest of my life." The dialogue and action were based on the relationship that Monty and Lee had developed in previous scenes.

Elia Kazan had no problem with Monty forgetting his lines. That was part of the mystery: Why on one film, or during one period of time, Monty seemed on the brink of expiration, and on the next, appeared as normal as anyone else. His physical stamina, however, was not good, and to function normally he had to seclude himself in the hotel in the evenings. Before going to bed, he ran lines with Donna, and when he got up the next morning at six A.M. he knew his dialogue cold. He made it through until five P.M. every shooting day. On weekends, he would drive to Chattanooga, his father's home town.

The film should have been finished by mid-December, but weather problems caused delays in shooting; the weather was bitter cold, and the company was anxious about having to work through Christmas. Lee Remick's personal tragedy ironically solved the problem. A few days before Christmas, she was notified that her husband, producer-director William Colleran, had suffered severe injuries in a car accident in California. She left the location for a week, and all filming stopped. Before she left, Monty rushed into her room. "It was all so fast," she says. "The day I got the telegram was the day I left. But Monty was there in the room—like *zap!* He was wonderful, because he had been through all that himself. He was the soul of empathy—just inside your head and heart, whatever your problems might be. He put me onto doctors. He was seeing me off saying, 'Make sure you call Rex Kennamer. Do you want me to call him for you? If you're not happy with him, call . . . And I'll make sure . . .' and so on. I was absolutely crushed and destroyed, but he was just like a rock."

After Lee returned and the film resumed, Monty began to drink again. Donna had gone home for Christmas and hadn't returned. The film was dragging. On many days, because of snow, there was nothing much to do but sit around. Monty was restless and worked on his thermos. It was late in the film, so it presented no major problems, but Kazan did become upset when, three days before the film ended, Monty walked up to him to say hello and fell flat on his face.

Kazan spent six months cutting his movie, which Twentieth Century-Fox released in July 1960. A number of critics admired it, but it was not financially successful.

Monty had already signed for his next film anyway. *The Misfits* was Arthur Miller's first original screenplay, and Monty was fanatically enthusiastic about the script. At first, he had been less than sure about it. As always, he sent it to Nancy Walker for her opinion, and she had told him, "Oh God, it's gorgeous!" Monty read it that same night and would make no general comment, only picky objections to some of the writing. Nancy thought that Monty was out of his skull, and called him a "stupid son of a bitch" for being so blind, and the two of them proceeded to have a screaming fest over the Arthur Miller script. Then, shortly afterwards, Monty decided that he loved *The Misfits* and gave his agents the go-ahead.

Getting Monty insured, as Miller points out, was not easy. Strings were pulled at United Artists, just as they had been pulled on his last two films, and somehow he got past his physicals.

In January 1960, Monty was informed by the owners of 209 East 61st Street that he would have to move. The fire damage had been too great. He was heartsick. It was his home! He didn't want to live in a big apartment building with doormen. But, by a stroke of luck, he discovered a townhouse for sale not three doors down from his gutted building. It was ideal, though Marge noted that the stairs leading up to the bedrooms were quite a bit steeper and higher than the stairs at the old apartment. One couldn't help but notice such things, for Monty's sake. Monty's permanent address became 217 East 61st Street.

With the change of address came a change in his domestic situation. Jean had lost his job as a dress designer, and, since Monty was by now supporting him anyway, he asked Jean to move in. The change in living status meant, naturally, that Monty could no longer hide Jean from his friends. As far as Jean was concerned, having people know that he was Monty's lover was not an embarrassment, but a symbol of prestige. He rather enjoyed having others know.

The tenor of Monty's relationship with Marge began to change—subtly but steadily—the day that Jean became a permanent resident. He began to take over some of her functions around the house: answering phones, bringing things to Monty as she would have, even typing. There was a pushiness about Jean that one could only notice after knowing him for a while. Marge was aware of it and found herself resenting having her duties usurped. But her concern went deeper. She knew of Monty's weaknesses and, without interfering, could serve as a buffer. Jean, on the other hand, was even weaker than Monty. Instead of buffering Monty, he tended to exacerbate his problems. If Monty took too many pills, Jean reacted by taking pills himself. If Monty was drinking, Jean would begin drinking. Marge knew that was exactly what Monty didn't need.

Although Jean may have wanted to become Monty's helpmate, his tendency toward hysteria made that impossible. One day, Marge saw Monty at the top of that high, steep staircase. She thought he was simply going to walk down. When she looked up moments later, he was hanging by his toes from the top of the stairwell! Marge wondered later how Monty could have gotten himself into that insane

216

position in so short a time. He would have had to climb over the banister, clamp his toes around the bottom of the banister slats, and then slump over the side. It was so high up that, had he fallen, he could have been killed. Jean saw Monty at the same time Marge did. He began to cry and scream. He was paralyzed with fear. Marge instantly ran up the stairs, grabbed Monty's legs and pulled him up, somehow managing to get his limp body over the banister. Jean was still sobbing hysterically.

Jean's continual presence was only one of the things that made Marge begin thinking of leaving. Monty's was such an all-engulfing, consuming personality, that Marge confessed to some of her friends: "It's either his life or mine. I've got to leave before it's too late." She began to prepare Monty by slipping little side comments into their conversations. "You know," she would say to him, "I won't be here forever."

In June 1960, a month before Monty was to fly to Reno to start *The Misfits,* Marge told Monty that she would be going. She said that she was glad that Jean was there because Monty would have someone to look after him and take care of things as she had in the past. She did not explain, but when Roddy and Libby begged her to stay, she told the truth: There would soon be nothing left of her life if she didn't leave. She could not bear to go on living in Monty's nightmare world. "What will become of him without you?" Roddy asked.

Monty pleaded with Marge to come to Reno with him. She insisted she had made plans to visit relatives in California. She gave him her number. After Monty checked into the Mapes Hotel in Reno—where most of the cast was staying—he called Marge in Los Angeles. Wouldn't she stop by Reno on her way back to New York? "I told him I couldn't," says Marge. "I wanted to, but I knew that if I stopped off, I would have been done for. I would have been right back in the same situation. When you finish a thing, you just finish." A whole year passed before Marge Stengel thought it safe to talk to Monty again.

He arrived at the Mapes Hotel in Reno well before the picture was to begin on July 18, filled with his old youthful excitement. He was going to play a rodeo cowboy—Perce Howland—and he was determined to learn everything he could about rodeos and bronco-busting. In Pocatello, Idaho, he watched a real rodeo and mingled with the riders. There,

217

while helping a cowboy climb onto the back of a Brahma bull, he was bruised badly on the bridge of his nose. The injury couldn't have been more appropriate. Perce Howland was supposed to receive exactly the same one in the rodeo sequence of *The Misfits*.

The story of a divorcée and a group of has-been cowboys—all losers looking for some kind of dignity through love or work—*The Misfits* had been tailor-made for Marilyn Monroe. For several years, she had been the center of Arthur Miller's life and work. It also appeared to those who knew of Miller's long-time friendship with Monty that he had written Perce Howland with Monty in mind. Perce is a mama's boy, awkward with girls and masochistically self-destructive. In the opening scene, he tells his mother that his face has been smashed up; and in another scene, after getting banged up in the rodeo, he has his head in bandages, is drinking, and doped on morphine. In a piece which appeared in *Esquire* after Monty's death, Bob Thom wrote: "How ghoulish of the cold-blooded Arthur Miller to have Monty, in the telephone scene in *The Misfits*, say to his mother that she would not recognize his face, it had been so badly beaten up." Arthur Miller, however, vehemently denies that the thought of Monty even entered his head when he delineated Perce Howland in the script. "I had known cowboys like Perce. Casting Monty in the part was strictly an afterthought."

Monty wasn't much interested in the question. He told James Goode, "I have no misgivings about this character. Someone said, 'My God, it's exactly like you.' Now it's just a question of can I do it? It's a wonderful part and if I don't do it justice, I'll shoot myself."

About a third of the way through *The Misfits*, Monty did the scene in the telephone booth, his first take in the movie. He was extremely tense. Photographed in the same frame with Monty were Marilyn Monroe, Clark Gable, Eli Wallach, and Thelma Ritter—all sitting in a car listening to Perce talk with his mother. It was "frightening," Monty later described it, doing what amounted to an "audition" in front of the gods and goddesses of the performing arts. The director was John Huston, not quite George Stevens, but a minor god himself and well known for his impatience with actors.

Monty got the long, awkward, hesitating speech on the first take. He was unbelievably brilliant. It was a feat comparable to a high-wire artist accomplishing a perfect triple somersault without warm-up. Arthur Miller was stunned. Gable was completely won over. He came over to Edward Parrone, Frank Taylor's assistant, and said: "This guy's great!" For the duration of the filming, Gable treated Monty affectionately and with obvious respect.

John Huston said nothing, but everything about his behavior indicated that Monty had overwhelmed him. He had been caught by surprise. After he and Miller had agreed on Monty for the part, John had been warned by friends in the profession about what to expect. He had figured on headaches—not only from Monty, but from Marilyn, which indeed he got. Working with such actors presented a directorial challenge which John almost seemed to enjoy, as a way of dispelling his increasing reputation as one of Hollywood's most difficult directors. Some actors cringed at the very name of John Huston. Says Doc Erickson, Huston's close associate on a number of films, "I think with *The Misfits,* John was trying to live down some of his own past criticisms of being trying on actors. His most recent films were not cleaning up at the box office. The one he did before *The Misfits—The Unforgiven,* with Audrey Hepburn and Burt Lancaster—had lost money. I think he was trying to prove himself."

For one who was himself trying to live down a bad reputation, Monty's instant disproval of the lurid stories concerning his own behavior must have been utterly moving. At the end of the filming, Huston made a point of telling the press that Monty had been as good as Gable, and that no other living actor could have played the part of Perce Howland as well.

Waiting for Godot was nothing compared to waiting for Marilyn. The general mood of the company became deliberate, premeditated patience, as hours, whole mornings and afternoons, and sometimes days went by while she attempted to pull herself together. John Huston decided that he was going to be a saint, and he was just that. His attitude helped establish the psychology of the entire company toward her enormous insecurity and the day-long semi-comas that were the result of her addiction to sleeping pills. The presence of Arthur Miller and her coach Paula Strasberg—her umbilical cord to the Actors Studio, which so dominated her psyche on this film—seemed only to increase her insecurities. At one point in late August, after

Marilyn's intake of Nembutal had increased to four capsules, and sometimes more, per night, the whole production closed down for two weeks while she was hospitalized in Los Angeles' Westside Hospital.

The parallels between Monty and Marilyn were strong and visible, but only on a certain superficial level. That they both had their addictions was an obvious fact. Monty's, of course, were more wide-ranging, in that he used many more chemicals and for different effects, and had used them for a longer period of time than Marilyn. They also used drugs for different reasons: Monty's had more to do with personal demons, while Marilyn's sprang into being out of a violent insecurity caused by her sensational fame and professional self-doubts.

"They were similar and yet different in many ways," observes Arthur Miller. "Neither one of them was capable of dealing with the situations they were in. They were terribly sensitive people. They never knew when and how to make the compromises that had to be made in the movies they appeared in. So they would make drastic compromises at the wrong time and refuse to make the ones that would have been helpful at the right time. But Monty was less paranoid than Marilyn. He was a little better capable of running his life and could continue to work, no matter what the conditions. He was far more advanced as a technician, and could be more objective about his performance because of his theater background.

"Marilyn had never been on a stage, had never learned the discipline he learned. She was a native talent who was trying to find some way of rationalizing it and controlling it . . . The Actors Studio disfigured a lot of her working time. It didn't support her. It didn't make her feel secure with her talents. It always left her with a feeling that she wished someone were there to tell her what to do . . . After all, before the Studio she was a very good comedienne. In *The Misfits,* her performance as a dramatic actress was extraordinary, but I'm not sure if all that torture was worth the result—all that agony. It's not worth anything . . .

"I was never sympathetic to the Actors Studio. I just didn't like the way the training cut the actor loose from his obligations to what he was doing and made the whole performance a question of his feelings. It made work extremely difficult for actors who had trouble with discipline —so that doing those lines and those actions at that moment became next to impossible for them. Monty disliked a lot about the Studio also. He had a powerful awareness of the need to get the scene done, and never thought of himself as using the Method. He thought that Studio people were self-indulgent, and he fought that part of himself which was self-indulgent."

Whatever the difference in their strengths, working habits, and psyches, the two actors were drawn to one another. "Marilyn always pitied Monty—she recognized a kindred soul, as he did," says Miller: "all sad people." Marilyn herself said to a reporter: "I look at him and see the brother I never had and feel braver and get protective." John Springer, who knew both of them, said to writer Lyn Tornabene: "Even to Marilyn, the most vulnerable person in the world, Monty was someone who needed protection. You should have seen them together. They were like two babes in the woods."

Marilyn gave Huston trouble all through the film with constant line-blowing and retakes, but in her most difficult scene—a five-minute take with Monty—she behaved like Hollywood's most experienced professional. In Huston's book of credits and debits, this was obviously another big credit for Monty.

The scene was shot on September 8 and was to be done in one take without a cut—the very longest single take John Huston had ever shot. The general feeling in the company was that it would take him days to get that scene. In the story, Perce and Roslyn—Marilyn's character—have been dancing and, because of the injury to his head in the rodeo, Perce becomes dizzy. Roslyn takes him outside the saloon. The five-minute take started here, with Monty putting his head on Marilyn's lap, while she, in a revealing white dress, sits on a broken car seat. Empty beer cans were scattered all around. Everyone watched: Clark Gable, Arthur Miller, Paula Strasberg, Frank Taylor. Marilyn was extremely nervous. As Edward Parrone observes, "Monty and Marilyn were both nervous people, but Marilyn's nervousness was very different from his." Hers was an urgent, primitive nervousness, based largely on fear; Monty's was associated with tension. At Marilyn's request all strangers had to leave, and she also asked that no one stand in her line of sight during the scene. Even the still photographer was instructed to stay at an abnormal distance so she would not be distracted by the clicking.

Marilyn and Monty had long speeches—his the longest. He had to do a moody monologue about how his father had died and how the man that his mother had remarried had not only taken legal possession of the ranch, but had undermined his mother's affection for him. Marilyn had to show more than just sympathy; she had to hurt along with him as he spoke.

It wasn't until the third try that Huston got a whole take. Marilyn turned to Monty and said something reassuring, that he was good. It was marvelous, seeing her attempting to build his confidence when all around stood her own confidence-building entourage. Then Huston wanted another take for good measure. Marilyn blew it, and then Monty blew the next one by going up on a line. Marilyn laughed and hugged Monty like an understanding sister. Take number six was perfection and the one that Huston printed—done in less than a day.

It was obvious that Monty and Marilyn not only comforted one another, but intensified each other's concentration and work. Shortly after her death, Monty was to say that of all the people he had worked with in twenty-eight years, Marilyn gave the most and with all her soul. "Working with her was fantastic . . . like an escalator. You would meet her on one level and then she would rise higher and you would rise to that point, and then you would both go higher."

The Millers had all but split up by the time of *The Misfits,* and were simply waiting until the end of the filming before announcing the divorce. Halfway through, Miller even took a separate room at the hotel. When Monty socialized at all, it was usually with Marilyn alone, and one reporter, who happened to walk in on Monty and Marilyn in a litttle club near Reno, overheard her confiding her marital problems to him. The whole thing was later overblown by the fan magazines, which fabricated tales of a romantic liaison between them. Like the romantic stories that had linked him to Elizabeth, he rather enjoyed reading these concoctions and kept the magazines.

Most evenings, he locked himself in his hotel room and prepared for the next day's shooting. He drank night and day—grape juice and vodka—but only moderately, which, as any alcoholic will confess, takes great strength of will. When he was sufficiently motivated, he had tremendous will power. No one thought of him as a drunk. Arthur

Miller remembers Monty as the most reliable performer he had ever worked with.

Yet Monty's seeming new hold on himself was deceptive. The physical demands on him were at times strenuous, but they were not continual. During the two months that he actually worked on *The Misfits*, he exerted himself only briefly. In fact, that was one of the things that attracted him to the script. He had told Henderson Cleaves of the *World-Telegram & Sun:* "I decided to do *The Misfits* because I don't appear on the screen until page fifty-seven. In my last two pictures I was on the screen constantly." Undoubtedly, Monty was able to perform brilliantly in *The Misfits* because he could concentrate his energies on a few key scenes. Had he been in nearly every scene, like Monroe or Gable, his endurance could not have held out. And once exhaustion hit, pills, boozing, and failing memory were the inevitable results.

Monty gave the appearance of new health and stamina. It seemed, with his partial abstinence, that he had reached the deepest regions of his personal hell and was on his way back. Perhaps he was returning from that inferno, but if so, the journey was treacherous indeed. Clearly, the best course Monty could have taken at this juncture would have been to stick to parts he could handle.

There was a mild flurry of activity in the company the day producer Wolfgang Reinhardt and agent Paul Kohner came on the set to huddle with Huston about *Freud,* Huston's next film. It was known that Huston hadn't yet chosen the actor to play Sigmund Freud, and that the meeting had been arranged expressly to discuss casting. As a gag, Eli Wallach donned a beard, mid-nineteenth century suit, and top hat, and paraded around in front of Huston and others in a gleeful parody of an actor trying anything to get a director to cast him in a part. It was only a joke—but Wallach did want the part. As it would later turn out, however, Huston had someone entirely different in mind . . .

Filming over, Monty returned to his town house in Manhattan, which he and Jean were still furnishing. Shortly after his return, Stanley Kramer approached him to appear in *Judgment at Nuremberg*. Based on the Nuremberg trials of former Nazi judges accused of sanctioning atrocities, *Judgment at Nuremberg* already boasted Spencer Tracy as the American judge, Maximilian Schell as attorney for the defense, Burt Lancaster as a prominent citizen who had been one of the Nazi judges, Marlene Dietrich as a German general's widow, and Richard Widmark as prosecutor. One of the picture's two cameo witness roles was to be played by Judy Garland. For the second—that of a retarded Jew, Rudolph Peterson, who has been castrated by the Nazis—a casting man at Universal, Jack Bauer, suggested, "You ought to take a look at Monty Clift for that part, because you won't believe it." He meant that by now Monty already looked the part.

Kramer sent a copy of the script to MCA, which declined even to send it to Monty because the deal called for only $50,000 for a seven-minute appearance. Monty had been paid $200,000 for *The Misfits*, and his agents advised him not to take less for even a minute on film, lest it establish a precedent. Kramer circumvented the agents, called Monty directly, and they decided to meet.

Kramer had been prepared for Monty's appearance, but he was still shocked at what he saw. Monty had been boozing heavily, and was nervous, shaking, and ill at ease. It struck Kramer that, indeed, Monty was perfect for the role.

He described the part and Monty immediately became enthusiastic: "I'll do it!"

Kramer reminded Monty that MCA was asking $200,000 for seven minutes on screen, far more than he could afford.

"Don't worry about MCA," said Monty. "I'll do it for nothing."

Kramer was taken by surprise. "But you can't do it for nothing even if you wanted to. There are minimums."

"Then let's do it for the minimum."

Monty felt he was satisfying everyone. It wasn't as if he were negotiating for less than his current fee—it was almost like making a free appearance at a benefit.

Well, not quite. He did ask Kramer for certain other things: such as picking up the tab for Monty and whatever friends he chose to bring to the Bel-Air Hotel in Hollywood; transportation for two; a chauffeur; and whatever amount of liquor he would order.

Monty knew that he was talking about a script that he hadn't even read, so he asked Kramer if he could change some of his dialogue if he felt it necessary. "I told him that we would certainly be flexible. I had already checked around, and I think he suspected that he wasn't going to be too good on big, long speeches." It was only to be a five-day role (it actually took ten because of Spencer Tracy's illness), and Monty had no intention of going through the agony of drying out just for that.

When Monty told his people at MCA that he intended to sign for the film at no salary, there was shock. Monty was reminded that he had not read a word of the script; he impishly lied and said that, oh yes, he had, and loved every word of it!

Monty was exceptionally nervous his first day on the set. He didn't even bother with the thermos charade. He made the world's most primitive screwdrivers by dumping out most of a supermarket carton of orange juice, and then filling it up to its original level with vodka. Except when he was in front of the camera, he drank from the moment he came on the set until the moment he left, and freely admitted what he was doing. Since the soundstage at Universal was so huge, portable dressing rooms for the stars were set up near the courtroom. *Nuremberg,* with its phenomenal script—penned by Abby Mann—and its luscious cast of Hollywood legends, attracted all sorts of celebrities to the set simply to watch the shooting. Dozens of important people who had once known Monty in Hollywood came into his dressing room; he managed to greet them happily through a thick, shaky haze.

By the second day, Monty was ready to do his first take. As he approached the witness chair, you could see him shaking quite badly, extremely agitated. All the principals in the film—Dietrich, Garland, Widmark, Lancaster—sat in the courtroom and watched, along with the countless extras who comprised the jury and spectators. A full crew, many visitors, and numerous members of the press also watched. Spencer Tracy sat in the judge's chair as he did throughout the movie.

Monty had about ten pages of dialogue, seven of which were rapid-fire questions and answers between himself and Maximilian Schell. Three of Monty's ten pages were solid monologue. The whole seven-minute sequence was written with dramatic precision. At a certain point, Monty had to break down during Schell's relentless questioning, and admit that he had been castrated because he had been a threat to society.

Monty was having great difficulty—not only with the

actual words but with the delicate timing. He missed cues. Several times during the struggle, Monty went to Kramer and said: "I don't know if I can do this thing." And Kramer, whose bedside manner was excellent, would reply: "Well, what you're doing is all right until you find out how to do it better."

Monty's pathetic shaking and uncertainty got to Spencer Tracy who, more than anyone else in the company—because of his own past alcoholism—understood what Monty was going through. He said to Monty: "Just look into my eyes and do it. You're a great actor and you understand this guy. Stanley doesn't care if you throw aside the precise lines. Just do it. Do it into my eyes and you'll be magnificent." And Monty did just that: he looked into Spencer's eyes.

Kramer did four different takes of the seven-minute sequence. On each take, Monty's breakdown came at a different place, and what he said was different.

On the fourth day, Monty performed with such stinging pathos that after Kramer yelled an emotional "cut," the entire courtroom broke into waves and waves of applause. Real life and acting had mingled to perfection. He performed the monologue as a series of excruciating hesitations, "Yes . . . yes . . . and they made me . . . me . . ." Monty had trouble with the pronunciation of certain diphthonged words which, combined with the d.t.'s, and his tortured appearance—made all the worse by the crew-cut he wore for the film—helped him create a needle-sharp characterization. Says Kramer, "Monty was playing a man who was a little retarded and stumbling. Monty's condition gave the performance an aura as though it were being shot through muslin: the way the words tumbled out and the disjointed, sudden bursts of lucidity out of a mumble. It was classic! It was one of the best moments in the film!"

The cameo gained Monty his fourth and last Academy Award nomination—this time for Best Supporting Actor. Nancy Walker and David Craig went to see the film. When Monty's part was over, Nancy got up and said: "Let's go, David. Nobody's going to beat that."

Throughout the filming, Kramer used a 360-degree camera rotation for the testimony of the witnesses. He used the device during Monty's testimony a great deal, and a few press members button-holed Kramer and asked: "Is the 360-degree stuff designed to cover for Monty?"—implying that, in desperation over Monty's trouble with lines and cues, he intended to dub in lines later. That was absolutely false. In fact, Kramer used that entire five-minute take on the fourth day without a single bit of editing.

Judy Garland and Monty became close during their few weeks of contact during the film. "Everyone," says Kramer, "felt compassion for Monty and got along well with him, but I think Monty and Judy understood each other best. Both of their careers had reached a low point, and they were each struggling to find their ways back. They both had incredible problems, and in this there was obvious camaraderie."

Monty could have left Hollywood immediately after his cameo, but he seemed to want to stay with the cast. During Judy's sequence, he sat huddled in corners, unobtrusively drinking and watching her work all day. She played a German hausfrau. At the time, she was overweight and her unattractiveness fit her part. Her performance was deeply touching. As Judy broke down on the stand, Monty wept openly, tears drenching his cheeks. After she finished Monty came over to Kramer, his eyes and cheeks still wet, crouching in that defenseless way of his. With that special irony which only Monty could conjure, he said: "You know, she did that scene all wrong."

Monty hung around the set for a full extra week, much to Kramer's irritation. Monty's stay-over at the Bel-Air was costing him large sums of money. In the end, Monty and Jean ran up a bill of $15,000—which included cases of champagne and expensive presents. Kramer could not very well have asked Monty to leave, but after he saw the bills, he felt it might have been easier to have paid Monty the original $50,000 after all.

In Hollywood, Monty didn't seem all that anxious to be with Jean, whom Kramer didn't know. "Whoever it was that Monty had brought with him from New York," says Kramer, "Monty was basically lonely. He hung around us all the time."

Monty finally returned to New York—and immediately upon arriving, made one of the worst decisions he had ever made.

CHAPTER NINE

Freud

JOHN Huston—irrationally, perhaps even perversely— had decided that he wanted Monty to play the lead in *Freud*. By now Monty was having his greatest successes with shorter appearances. There was every indication that he could not undertake a long, demanding role. If Huston couldn't see the evidence himself, there were many others who did.

It is easier to understand why Monty was so anxious to accept. Here was the chance to prove himself; he would revive his career with his first deeply intellectual role. It must have seemed tailor-made. He had been seeing Dr. Silverberg since 1950, had long been involved with Freudian theories, and fancied himself a doctor of sorts. He believed his failing mind, body, and spirit would somehow find the strength to get him through; this was *the* film. But it was sheer folly. The filming of *Freud* destroyed whatever was left of Monty's life. When the five months of celluloid grotesqueries were done, Monty was a walking cadaver.

Sigmund Freud had groped his way through the darknesses of the human mind to help mankind. He would have been aghast at the dismal exercise in sado-masochism that was conjured up by misguided Hollywood filmmakers in his honor.

For all the effort that went into the making of this, the only filmed biography of Sigmund Freud—years of planning by John Huston, hundreds of hours of script-writing by Jean-Paul Sartre, rewriting and painstaking research by

Wolfgang Reinhardt, an endlessly protracted period of neurotically tense photography in Freud's homeland—the final print, at least the one released in the United States, was stiff and unimpressive. Its distribution was poor, and the public hardly cared. Monty's portrayal of one of the most important men of the century, although virtually the only interesting thing about this wooden movie, was far from his best.

In the end, *Freud* drew a blank as a provocative account of the man who had probed the depths of the human psyche, but ironically the people who made *Freud*, in their personal encounters and their interactions with the material of the film itself, created a behind-the-scenes story so dramatic, so psychologically anguished as to make their film seem pathetic by comparison.

That story began during the years of the Second World War. John Huston had been hired by the War Department to film a secret documentary on the rehabilitation of shell-shocked soldiers called *Let There Be Light*. Remembered Huston: "We went through the whole process, from the time a fresh batch of psycho-neurotics arrived at the hospital to the time they were discharged. We watched the slow rising of their spirit. Most people could stomach a film about amputees, but a wounded psyche is much harder to watch. It was almost too personal. Making that film was like having a religious experience." He and screenwriter Charles Kaufman were so deeply affected they began to consider making a major movie dealing with the realm of psycho-neuroses. Eventually, they decided to go the whole route and do Freud's life. The problem was, as Wolfgang Reinhardt points out, that what Huston had gleaned from his experience in filming *Let There Be Light* was not sympathy for Freud's theories or real understanding of mental illness, but merely a view of one method for treating psychoses: hypnosis. When Reinhardt and Jean-Paul Sartre, who had agreed to write the screenplay for *Freud* in 1957, met in Paris to go over the script, one thing puzzled them —why on earth would John Huston want to do a film about Freud, whose theories were mainly sex-related? In his first meetings with Huston, Sartre was amazed that Huston had almost no idea that sex was a dominant part of Freudian psychology.

As Sartre understood it, no attempt would be made to

commercialize *Freud* by putting it in the hands of a Hollywood company seeking normal distribution. This was to be a vast saga, a monumental art film that would have enduring value. Sartre's script ran to 1,600 pages, or about ten hours of film, but when Huston received the translation, he was stunned by all the scenes involving homosexuality, incest, masturbation, prostitution, molestation of children, and sexual aberrations of every kind. Huston simply had no idea. It was shocking territory for a man who had lived his whole life out of a Hemingway novel. He shot wild game in Africa, drank hard, followed boxing religiously, dealt sympathetically with women and strictly "man to man" with other men. He directed films which were action-oriented, such as *The Maltese Falcon, Treasure of the Sierra Madre, The Asphalt Jungle, The Red Badge of Courage, The African Queen, Moulin Rouge,* and *Moby Dick.* The material in *Freud* simply was not in Huston's range.

After Reinhardt succeeded in boiling down Sartre's tome to a mere two hundred pages, Huston read the material and began to argue for drastic changes. He couldn't believe that Freud had been so involved with sexuality and perversions. "John kept telling me that it all seemed fallacious," said Reinhardt, "and would argue against what Sartre and I were saying about Freud's life and theories. I had read all the books on Freud, and John hadn't, and so these became such useless sessions. He kept asking me, 'What does repression mean?' over and over. Even when we were filming, he'd ask that in front of the actors, as if we never talked about it. These arguments took place in Hollywood, at John's castle in St. Clerens, after the filming began and during the whole course of production. It was embarrassing for me. He'd call in expert after expert, psychiatrists, to read this script and prove that I was wrong, but instead they all confirmed that the script was accurate. What could John do, finally, but go along with it?"

Sartre's view was that Huston was using the movie as a way of exposing his own repressions and inhibitions to himself, but that he was fighting the process as well, as would a patient in analysis. Reinhardt says, "There was a point in St. Clerens, just before we began the movie, when I thought that John had finally come to grips with the idea of sexual repression and what we were really filming. Later, on the set in Munich, I'd get reports from some of the young ladies who had visited him in St. Clerens that John had become a kind of teacher, lecturing them about the unconscious and how sexual suppression can cause deep-seated neuroses which are revealed in analysis. But he was always quick to point out that he was totally healthy that way, had no such problems, and certainly had no need to see a psychiatrist."

The pre-production quarrels did not stop there. It had been understood that Huston would get independent backing for the film, and go nowhere near a Hollywood studio, which, in those days of the Johnson office and the lust for the "seal" of approval, would surely have watered down the sexual material in order to get widespread distribution. There were independents willing to back the film without the seal, but they wanted Huston to share in the risk himself by not accepting a salary—and Huston simply couldn't afford it. Strapped for cash, he was forced to sign the picture over to Universal International. "This is a rank betrayal!" Sartre announced, and immediately withdrew his name from the movie. Huston was already settled in Munich when Reinhardt conveyed Sartre's reaction.

"Well, go to Paris and persuade him to change his mind," he told Reinhardt.

"What am I supposed to say to him? He's made up his mind. And really he's right. You did go back on your word."

Huston insisted, and with Universal backing him, he had all the power. Reinhardt meekly went to Paris to see Sartre, who was irritated at Huston's insolence. "He doesn't seem to understand your reasons for turning him down," said Reinhardt apologetically. "Then I will explain my reasons," said Sartre, immediately sitting down to compose a sixteen-page exegesis of his motivations, attacking Huston for selling out the high intellectual ideals of their project. When Reinhardt brought the letter to Huston, he threw it on the floor and scowled, "Why the hell do you bring me something like this? Are you trying to ruin my film?"

This was not an unusual scene. Relations between the two of them had been deteriorating for a long time. It seemed to Reinhardt that Huston was arguing constantly about the script, refusing to take advice about casting; and there was always that eternal question, accompanied by a perplexed look: "Wolfgang, explain to me again this business about repression."

And so the stage was set for Monty's arrival in Munich.

Monty was in fine spirits as he flew from New York to London with Jean in the beginning of August, some six weeks before principal photography began. Since this was a period film, the costume fittings would take weeks, and on one of Monty's first days in London the production supervisor, Doc Erickson, took him to the house of Doris Langley Moore. A handsome, sympathetic, middle-aged woman, Miss Moore had the double distinction of being one of England's most esteemed costume designers and a noted Byronic scholar. When Monty first walked into her living room, he saw several other people there and was, at first, slightly intimidated; even now, in his early forties and a movie star of more than ten years standing, he was still the shy boy with strangers. However, as he stood there, he became aware of something special. It had happened before in Monty's life: he knew in an instant that a complete, new relationship had suddenly been offered him.

Miss Moore recalls, "He came here first about his clothes, and of course here I was, a designer whom he had never seen before, and I could see that he was a very nervous, sensitive person. He sat on the sofa, and I went up to him, after we had had a lot of discussion about the clothes, and I said to him quietly, 'Just have absolute confidence in me.' Something about my saying that to him utterly won him over."

Monty relaxed. There was something about a warm, sincere older woman that seemed to offer more palliation than any number of tranquilizers. Although a striking individual in her own right, she offered yet another version of the perennial mother figure. Add to this qualification her enormous literary intelligence and her status as a writer—and Monty was bound to admire her with abandon for the rest of his life.

Monty fully expected weeks of tedious fittings, and would probably have drunk himself into one long anesthetized stupor, but with Doris personally taking him around to the tailors, Monty couldn't have been more soberly delighted. They were quite close during those weeks of fittings, and later, during the filming, when the sweat of desperation and fear began to fall from his temples, she would become his closest friend and confidante.

They often talked about the film. Huston had finally sent Monty a shooting script, and Monty thought the dialogue dreadful, replete with cheap lines and non-idiomatic phrases. Huston, aware of Monty's objections, had assured him that the shooting script was temporary and would be totally revamped, and, with that, Monty was filled with the celebration of Sigmund Freud. He, like Doris, had read all the major biographies and was tremendously excited over what he thought would be the most important film of his career.

Toward the end of August, Monty flew to Huston's majestic Irish home in St. Clerens for his first direct conference with him about the film. Huston was about to leave for Munich to begin production. Who can say what would have happened in the ensuing months if Monty had not decided to take Jean with him? It was probably the worst single tactical mistake of his life. Monty had been out of the closet for several years, and probably felt he could relax, especially in England where such relationships hardly raised an eyebrow among people in the arts. Monty hadn't counted on Huston's prejudices. Huston had behaved like a father to him on *The Misfits;* perhaps Monty wanted to "admit" everything to such a father figure. Or perhaps Monty simply wasn't thinking.

Up until then, Huston had had only positive feelings about Monty. He had seen him behave beautifully on *The Misfits,* and after that, "It was as if he felt that he had had some sort of wonderful influence over him," says Reinhardt. "He thought he could do anything with Monty now, because Monty had such great respect for him. I told John that Monty was simply not right for the role, and that he might not get through it. John was naive and egotistical and insisted that Monty could do it because of him."

Huston had already heard that Monty was homosexual, but refused to believe it. He considered it simply malicious gossip. Hearing gossip is one thing, however; seeing with one's own eyes is quite another. The evening of Monty's and Jean's arrival at the castle, they talked about the film for hours, and then the two guests retired to one bedroom and the host to another. Early the next morning, Huston opened the door of the guest bedroom without knocking.

Reinhardt, to whom Huston told this account, describes

233

the rest. "John surprised Monty and Jean and was aghast at what he saw. John said to me, after we met in Munich, 'Did you know this about Monty?' 'Yes, of course I knew,' I said. 'I think it's disgusting! Why didn't you tell me?' he asked. But why should I have told John? It wasn't his business. After all, Monty behaved like a normal man. If he had been swishy or something, obviously he wouldn't have been able to portray Freud, and I would have had to tell John. And, well, Freud himself said that he detected homosexuality in himself and in most men. So it was all very out of place of John to have over-reacted—especially on *this* film. I really think that John would have fired Monty on the spot if Universal's backing hadn't depended so much on John's casting a major star like Monty in the role, and who else could John have found at that late date?"

Reinhardt feels that this incident, aggravated by Huston's growing subconscious horror of the material he was filming, made Huston despise Monty from that moment on.

Monty flew to Munich in early September with Angela Allen—the script girl Huston had used for years—and a Miss Kennedy, a pretty secretary Monty had just hired. It was wisely decided that Jean was not to come to the set. During the flight Monty drank, but was not obnoxiously drunk, as the German papers reported it that evening. Apparently one of the more imaginative Lufthansa stewardesses telephoned the papers with the "scoop" that Monty had been collapsing in the aisles.

The next day, Reinhardt and Monty went over to Huston's suite in the Four Seasons. Huston had just read the papers and wanted to straighten Monty out before another day passed. Reinhardt carried a briefcase into which he had stuffed a letter written to a neutral friend about all the troubles he was having with Huston. When they arrived, he put the bag down *somewhere*—he'd forget, later, exactly where. The atmosphere was strained, and after a time, Huston said, "You'd better leave us alone, Wolfgang. I have something to say to Monty." Reinhardt picked up his briefcase and left, but ". . . after I got outside John's door, a strange suspicion came over me. I opened up my briefcase and the letter was missing! How I got that suspicion, and how on earth John ever knew that the letter was even there, and how he got a chance to take it in those few minutes, are questions that to this day I can't answer."

He about-faced, knocked on the door, and asked if there was a letter on the floor that had fallen out of his briefcase.

"Hell, no!" said Huston, who made a small effort to look around.

Suddenly, Monty got down on all fours and began looking under the cushions and under the rug and behind tables. He picked up easy chairs and put his whole head underneath them. He looked absolutely insane, like some nervous dog looking for a lost bone.

"Could it be here?" said Monty, wide-eyed, his facial expressions turning rapidly from perplexity, to sympathy, to anxiety, and then back to perplexity. "Where could it be? Could it be under this?"

Monty's hands and body moved wildly about while John just looked on, flabbergasted. Reinhardt knew what was happening. "Monty was one of the most sensitive souls I have ever met, and he caught the tension between me and John after I came back into the room. In his own way, he was trying to help by taking it all on himself. John could not have understood."

Wolfgang, letterless, left them, and then Huston, Old Testament style, began to lay down the Law. Monty was not to behave in a homosexual manner, or to have any kind of homosexual relationships while he worked on the film. He was to behave in a normal manner. He was not to drink or take pills. He was not to have dependent friendships with older women.

Monty was stunned both by what Huston said and by his brusque manner. Nevertheless, he agreed to the demands. He still respected Huston, and believed in him, but this was the first time he had gotten any hint of Huston's drastic change in attitude toward him.

Meanwhile, the letter still preyed on Reinhardt's mind. The next morning, he called Huston to tell him that unless the letter were returned, he would quit. Huston hesitated a moment, then said, "All right. Come on over and get it."

The battle lines were clearly emerging.

Setting-up in Munich was a task. The problem was in getting three nationalities to work together in a cooperative effort. The actors were mostly American; the cameramen, English; and the trained studio crew, German. They all tried to get along at first, but with the language difficulties and the natural animosity between the Germans and the English, the amenities did not last long.

During the first few days of filming, everyone got a look at the eerie material they were to live with for the next five months. The first set was the Salpêtrière Hospital in Paris, and Dr. Charcot, played by French actor Fernand Ledoux, was to hypnotize patients suffering from such extreme hysterical symptoms as shaking of the whole body and paralysis of the legs. Huston had hired Dr. Steven Black, an expert on hypnosis, to act as consultant on the film and the patients in the scenes were his own, brought over from London. The actual scene was simple. Freud was to look on, wordlessly, as Charcot hypnotized and affected his cures. The execution of the scene, however, was not so simple. While Monty and M. Ledoux waited, Dr. Black went through the hypnotic process again and again. The patients were instructed that the next voice they heard— that of M. Ledoux—would be the voice that would control their actions. Mesmerized themselves, the crew looked on as tremors and paralyses appeared, then stopped, then started again, and even transferred between patients. The whole process was agonizingly long, and took days. Occasionally, during a take, one of the patients, presumably in a deep hypnotic trance, would turn to an assistant director and complain, "But we did it differently yesterday." After the initial curiosity, the actors and crew began to growl among themselves that Huston was being taken in, and at great expense. As Doris Langley Moore remembers, "Most of us felt that any good professional could, after a brief demonstration, have done what the amateurs were doing."

But, in fact, Huston wasn't taken in at all. The final print of this scene, the best in the whole movie, is a testimonial to what most assuredly was his original vision: a deeply enthralling drama of the inner sanctum of the unconscious. The hypnotic subjects were upsettingly real. As Charcot tells a woman that she is going to be *"shak*ing . . . *shak*ing," and the symptoms indeed develop, one truly feels the icy presence of the hidden parts of the mind at work. In this scene, Huston showed his true genius for detail and realism, which, had it pervaded the rest of the film, might have made *Freud* a classic.

Whatever else one may think of Huston's work on the film, it is terribly important to understand that he had come into the project with the intention of doing an important film, an extraordinary film. He went to great lengths to hire psychiatrists, hypnotists, patients; he insisted on shooting chronologically, so that the actors could feel the intensity of Freud's mind building; he planned his scenes meticulously in terms of long takes, so that the audience would be drawn into the minds of the characters without being distracted by cuts. Compromise, at this stage, was out of the question. But in working with Monty, compromise was the only possible way.

The first real sign that Huston was going to take a hard line came a week after the Charcot scenes. It was during an exterior scene in a café garden, supposedly the Stadtpark coffee house, where Freud and his wife, played by Susan Kohner, were to talk. It took forever to get the scene started. A noisy crowd had gathered; the crew kept shouting in German for silence. Neither Monty nor Susan Kohner felt comfortable about the scene anyway because Huston, not wanting to distract from the real import of the film (and normally disliking love scenes anyway), had insisted that it be played without affection. He wanted it in one long, uncut take. Monty blew a line. Huston asked them to start again. Monty missed again. It became clear that the only way Huston was going to get a take was to give in and cut midway; but he refused, and the day was wasted.

A few days later, Monty was to give a rather long lecture to more than a hundred extras dressed as physicians. Monty hadn't bothered to learn his material by heart since the script indicated that he would be lecturing from notes. Just as they were setting up to shoot, Reinhardt made some comment to Huston about Freud's habit of speaking impromptu. Suddenly everyone heard Huston tell Monty that he had to do the scene without notes. Over and over, Monty tried to give the lecture without looking down, and every time he'd falter, and Huston would yell, "Cut. Try it again, Monty." Monty was perspiring, and embarrassed at the foolish figure he was cutting. The take wasn't made that day. By the next day, Monty had memorized the speech, but Huston kept yelling, "Cut!" at the slightest deviation from the text. That morning, too, went by without a print.

During lunch break, Monty confessed to Doris that Huston had yelled at him the night before about his not being able to deliver his lines; it had seemed to him that Huston only did this to wreck his confidence.

That afternoon, Huston finally got the take he wanted, but Monty was thoroughly shaken and plagued by the idea that Huston was out to get him. Monty wasn't the only one who felt that. By now, the company of *Freud* had become polarized into separate factions: those who saw Monty as Huston's victim, and those who believed Monty to be a disintegrating, brain-damaged alcoholic who was devastating Huston and his important film.

The factions seemed to divide by nationalities. Almost to a man, the English were on Monty's side. The Germans were generally for Huston. The Americans, who included representatives of Universal, tended to be for Monty privately, but against him publicly.

The English have always had a weak spot for Monty and his introverted brand of vulnerable, suffering masculinity. British women love to mother, and British men recognize Monty's type among their species and extol it: Hence the almost fanatical and protective devotion of the British press (which can be ruthless toward American stars). Desmond Davis, the English camera operator, will never forget his first meeting with Monty. "It was the first day of shooting and we were all very nervous about meeting one another. Monty appeared in a dark suit and beard, and he sort of wandered up and introduced himself to me. 'It feels like the first day at school,' he said. He was very nervous himself, and I thought that sort of surprising: He was a very big star." In no time, Desie (Monty's nickname for him) had gotten close to Monty, along with Doris, and soon Monty had a circle of English friends around him. They would eat together in the evenings, and there would be much head-shaking about the day's events. As Desie puts it, Monty and his group became "incestuous."

The Germans had no such predisposition toward Monty and sniped at him constantly, usually angling their stories at Monty's alcoholism and supposed hatred of women. Monty was considered a Jew by many of the working-class Germans in the studio crew because of the roles he had played in *The Young Lions* and *Judgment at Nuremberg*, and now, of course, he was playing the Jewish Freud. Later, when Universal would file its lawsuits against Monty and the insurance company claiming that he had single-handedly forced the film to double its budget, it would be the German assistant director, Laci Von Ronay, who would fill his deposition with venom. He would carefully select details of Monty's inability to work, and omit every mitigating factor; Monty would be made to appear hardly more balanced than the patients in the film.

The American attitude toward Monty can best be summed up by an incident during the lecture scene. Doris watched Monty struggle for four and a half hours, with Huston calling for retake after retake. Finally, beside herself, she went outside to complain to Doc Erickson. "I have the most vivid recollection of the conversation. Mr. Erickson was, I think, not without sympathy for Monty, and he replied, referring to John Huston, 'You know and I know that this man has been absolutely laying waste his life and his talents.' He said something unequivocal about Huston's extravagance and destructiveness, and then added, 'But he can still get any star he wants to work with, and when the chips are down, you've got to go where the money is.' "

According to Desmond Davis, Monty had been "moderately good" with his speeches during the first weeks, but toward the end of September, his memory began to falter. It became nearly impossible for Huston to get those long, uncut takes he wanted. But Monty was on the wagon and he wasn't drugging. Reinhardt felt that it was Monty's own sensitivity to Huston's indifference and intolerance that was causing him to break down. Huston, however, did not know what to think of Monty's problem. In *The Misfits*, he had seen Monty breeze through lengthy takes, some lasting as long as four minutes, and trying to save his film, he summoned psychiatrist Dr. David Stafford-Clark to examine Monty.

Dr. Stafford-Clark had been to the set before as a consultant, and unlike Dr. Black, whose hypnotic probing had made many people uncomfortable, he was well-liked. Shortly after Stafford-Clark's second arrival, Monty's camp barraged him with complaints about Huston's manhandling of Monty. He did some investigating and concluded to Monty's friends that it was Huston, not Monty, who was in need of psychiatric treatment. He said that John envisaged himself in the role of benevolent father figure to Monty but, frustrated by the difficulties of transforming the cowboy from *The Misfits* into the bearded Freud, had developed a love-hate feeling for him.

Of course, by now, in this atmosphere heavy with psychiatric jargon and probing, it was Freudian amateur night. Members of the cast and crew stood around theorizing. Was John a suppressed homosexual? Was Monty a true masochist who secretly loved John, or vice versa, with John the sadist? John, no fool, knew what was being said. Laughing, he muttered to Desmond Davis: "Yeah, I know, they're all saying I'm a repressed homosexual."

Dr. Stafford-Clark recommended that any attempt to have Monty treated would only make matters worse. He thought there was no reason why Monty couldn't finish the film, provided he were handled delicately. It was a not-too-subtle hint that Huston revise his approach. Huston, however, was convinced that Monty had a problem which needed treatment.

At the very beginning of October, Susannah York came on the set and, for a time, the atmosphere relaxed. All of Huston's attentions shifted from Monty to getting York started in the role of Cecily, the patient whose dramatic cure, first through hypnosis and then through psycho-analysis, inspires Freud to formulate his theory of infantile sexuality and to explore the role sexual repression plays in neuroses. The role of Cecily was complex, requiring an actress who could reveal, scene by scene, through specific and well-chosen mannerisms, the different levels of her neuroses as she comes to grip with the sexual material her conscious mind does not wish to confront. Miss York was then only nineteen and quite inexperienced. She had done only one previous movie, and there was nothing in her background to indicate that she could handle Cecily. However, she did have an ingenuous, British wholesomeness about her which, it was hoped, would take some of the repugnance away from such ideas as Cecily's repressed desire to have intercourse with her father. Susannah herself was quite insecure about the part and, in the beginning, put herself totally in Huston's hands.

His first task was to carry York through the opening sequences. He took great, loving pains with her on the set, and in the evenings immersed her in talk about the unconscious. An amateur hypnotist since the days of his War Department documentary, Huston tried to hypnotize her, and while he didn't succeed in putting her into a trance, he did raise her receptiveness and energy levels to such a peak that she became utterly responsive to all the ideas, words, and deviant behavior patterns which were being

240

tossed at her. As she says herself: "I was afraid of making a fool of myself, and so I had to learn quickly. I had lived a sheltered life. Hypnosis was a new word to me. I didn't know anything about Freud or the dark, labyrinthine corners of the soul. I must have known them instinctively, of course, but plunging into them was another matter."

Plunge, she did, and extraordinarily well, according to Wolfgang Reinhardt and other witnesses. In her first rushes, she gave a brilliant rendition of a hypnotic subject, which must certainly have impressed Huston, as it did the others. But Dr. Black wasn't pleased; he felt her trance a mere impersonation, not at all the real thing. Huston, somewhat hypnotized by Dr. Black himself, took his word and ordered a total retake.

Reinhardt was surprised at Huston's insensitivity, especially when the new rushes revealed no more than a humdrum, romanticized trance, such as one sees young actresses do in grade-B Dracula films. Evidently, Dr. Black was pleased and, therefore, Huston; and the German assistant directors all concurred in chorus. The contrast between the realistic trances of Dr. Black's patients and York's fake trance is so striking as to make one wonder why Huston couldn't see the mistake. Such errors marked all her scenes, from first to last.

The closer the script came to the film's real substance— the material dealing with sexual repression as the cause of neurosis—the more Huston insisted that the script be revised. Hours before a key scene between Monty and York, he would meet with the two actors and his producer for a conference. "What does this mean . . . well, that just doesn't work," he would say, and either Huston or Reinhardt would start rewriting on the spot.

Reinhardt says, "The problem was, John couldn't rewrite these scenes because he was essentially trying to hide the truth, while pretending that he was trying to improve the quality of the film. All day long, I had to write and rewrite and debate with John, instead of doing my job as producer and supervise the production. It was *terribly* hard for Monty to learn these rewrites given to him just hours before photography. Monty had already told John that he was a slow study. He was the sort of actor who needed to ponder and study; and, remember, these were complicated psychiatric terms. Some actors of Monty's stature would simply walk off the film if scripts were handed to them in that haphazard way."

Monty and Susannah York settled into a kind of grim routine. In the evening, they would receive the third or fourth revision of the script, have a late supper, work on the scene until three or four in the morning, go to bed, then get up three or four hours later for their call. York was enthralled by Monty's dedication and almost masochistic insistence that they do what Huston required of them. "I think I existed on about two hours sleep a night for about five months. It took me nearly a year to reachieve any sleep pattern and, my God, I *did* begin to understand what neurosis was. I loved Monty's generosity of himself, I loved his demands on me and other people, but I was under no illusions about him. I think he was determined to give back to John whatever John was giving to him, but in his own way. I think Monty was made of the same steel."

In the mornings, Monty seemed almost an amnesiac in front of the cameras. Forty, sometimes fifty, takes were required to get a decent print. Everyone got edgy. Often Monty didn't seem to understand Huston's directions and was incoherent when he tried to explain himself. The production was slowed to a crawl. Huston was out of his mind with impatience.

One day, Reinhardt was sitting in his office when someone rushed in and said to him, "You must come at once." As he lurched through the door, he could hear loud, high-pitched noises coming from Monty's dressing room. By the time Reinhardt got there, the commotion was over. Monty came walking out, saw Reinhardt, and said, "I pity this man." What Reinhardt saw as he peered into the dressing room chilled him—mirrors were broken, every chair smashed, the couch torn apart, broken glass all over the place. In the middle of it all stood John Huston.

"I sure taught that little bastard a lesson," Huston said. "I had him trembling in a corner. Maybe he'll start to remember his lines a little better now." He finished with a stream of four-letter words.

Reinhardt left Huston in the middle of the wreckage and went in search of Monty. When he found Monty, upset yet surprisingly lucid, Monty's verbal account differed widely from Huston's. "He came into my dressing room and told me to take my choice. Either I'd remember my lines or he'd break every bone in my body. I just stood there quietly—didn't raise an arm—and told him, 'Why don't you hit me? Why don't you strike?' " According to Monty's account, Huston looked totally disarmed at the dare. Monty kept asking, "Why don't you hit your leading man?" and then Huston, in frustration, began demolishing the room, destroying one piece of furniture after another as if he were destroying pieces of Monty. There was no trembling; he calmly observed John Huston revealing the beast in himself.

It was here that whatever authority Huston had had with Monty vanished. From then on, the two barely spoke, a bizarre situation since Monty was in nearly every scene. Now one could never be sure whether Monty truly couldn't remember his lines, or if, in a campaign of passive resistance, he simply hadn't bothered to learn them. To Reinhardt, Monty seemed to be behaving like a naughty boy—although not without justification. At times, Monty would come in for morning call and calmly announce that he wasn't ready. He would lie on his stomach in the middle of the set, mouthing and pretending to learn lines he thoroughly despised, while Huston sat off in a corner reading for hours, or playing pool—almost forcing himself into a state of pathological calm while his dream, his movie, went down the drain. Later, Monty might get through the scene or he might not. Or Monty might start the day by telling Huston that he simply could not say the rewritten lines, and York, who had made the difficult decision to take Monty's "side," would agree. Invariably, the lines were those that Huston had rewritten, and Huston, lashing out, accused Reinhardt of prejudicing Monty by telling him who had done the rewrites. "But I never discussed them with Monty," says Reinhardt. "Monty could tell . . . They were just so poor." John complained bitterly to Reinhardt in private, "He's sabotaging my film!"

Monty was well aware that he was gaining sympathy. It is revealing to see how he played on those around him in this peculiar sado-masochistic war with Huston. Despite all the desperation of getting through scenes, Monty still retained a sense of precisely what to do and say to gain the desired audience effect.

There were elaborate preparations for the mountain-climbing dream sequence, filmed shortly after Huston's blowup in the dressing room. Dream analysis was a major factor in Freud's work, and the film presented numerous examples, all exhibited in the same way: Freud has a dream; he encounters disturbing symbols; he interprets them as horrifying sexual truths about himself. In this particular dream, Freud climbs a mountain (on thick, rough ropes—penis and umbilical cord symbols) and meets a young male homosexual patient, played by David McCallum, at the top. Freud identifies with the young man and, in his own disgust at the realization, they both fall.

The setting for a major confrontation between the two *real* participants in this drama was almost too perfect. The huge mountain set, the rough ropes (also eternal S & M symbols), the complicated physical labyrinth which put Monty up high and forced Huston to shout to him from below, the eerie wordlessness of the scene—all combined to create a psychological scene, the content of which both of them must have understood. The movie scene was unimportant (the explanation in the script that the young male patient was homosexual would later be cut, destroying the whole impact of the scene); the real confrontation was played to the rafters before a packed house of actors, cameramen, technical crew, and managerial assistants. There were nine separate takes. In each, Monty would climb up the rope, slip a bit, and then struggle to the top. The palms of his hands were sensitized by the skin grafts done after the automobile accident. It was obvious that Monty was in pain and exhausted, but Huston asked for a cut and a retake. Blood spotted Monty's hands. Someone told Huston; someone else asked Monty if he didn't want to take a rest. Huston insisted on going ahead; Monty refused to stop; he was Prewitt again in *From Here to Eternity,* or Ackerman in *The Young Lions,* the determined, lovable masochist out to prove a point or die, and he was terribly convincing. By the seventh or eighth take, his hands were a bloody mess, and the blood streamed onto the rope. And again Huston asked for a retake, and again Monty refused rest.

As they bandaged Monty's hands at the end of the day, Monty may have looked like the ravaged one, but it was Huston who had lost. Monty had succeeded, probably quite consciously, in turning the company, almost as a body, against Huston. The crew buzzed for days afterward about what Huston was doing to Monty, but they seemed to miss how well Monty was fighting Huston back with such tactics.

By the time the company moved to Vienna for two weeks of shooting in Freud's home city, Susannah York's relationship to the film had changed drastically. Instead of taking direction from Huston, it was Monty's guidance she sought. Seeing that he had lost York to Monty, Huston was now as indifferent to her as to his leading man. She recalls, "During my scenes, John would be doodling and drawing. He didn't seem to be focused. He'd removed himself, and I found that terribly destroying for me." She also had great difficulty with the lines, and it was Monty, not Huston, who often got her through.

"I was being given rewrites with new lines that were banal and purplish, or lines that didn't actually relate to scenes I had done earlier. This upset me and I physically couldn't do it. I remember on our first day in Vienna . . . I could *not* get the words out, I was so embarrassed. It got to take nine, take ten. It got desperate and John was very angry. And Monty was saying, 'Come on, come on, Susannah, you must do it.' We got to the tenth take, and suddenly he changed. Up until that point, he'd been quiet and calm as Freud, but suddenly he shouted out his lines in a completely hysterical fashion. This shook me out of my self-consciousness and I gave it right back to him. He had made an absolute twit of himself before the camera, shouting his lines in a way that was completely out of character in front of crowds and crowds of people. But by his doing that, he roused me to a peak of response that got the scene for John Huston. I admired him terribly for that and I was tremendously grateful."

With Monty and Susannah York slaving until four in the morning six days a week on newly-doctored scripts, and then coming to Huston the next day with their *own* rewrite of the day's scenes, it was inevitable that Huston would accuse them of collusion against him. He made his suspicions clear to them and to others. The victim game could be played both ways.

One by one, the men and women involved in the filming of *Freud* underwent psychological suffocation. For months, they were, literally and figuratively, shut into a small, airless room, and forced to ponder truths about themselves and their relationships to others. The film had only one main location, in a city where most of the principals, unfamiliar with the language, were forced to keep to themselves. Day and night, actors, cameramen, director, producer and technical people ate, slept and breathed Freud. Filming went on until seven or eight at night; at the Mark and the Four Seasons, endless talk about repression, the unconscious, Monty and Huston, and rehearsals filled the air. The specter of Sigmund Freud haunted and pervaded. Sigmund himself could not have survived long in such a psychological hothouse.

Monty acted as a dangerous catalyst in this environment. His manner of appearing helpless, without walls, anxious to send to and receive from others on sensitive wavelengths, coaxed others into letting down their guard—a sometimes rewarding, but also potentially lethal, exercise. On the set of *Freud*, his manner released a Pandora's box of pity, sadism, love, hatred, self-doubt, sympathy, compassion, sexual reawakening, and sexual bigotry.

He even had a peculiar effect on the very people who should have been immune to his power for disruption. A week before the company arrived at Vienna, Dr. Black suddenly became quite interested in Monty. He presented himself as a friend, but this new friend, who insisted on having lunch with Monty every day, kept asking all sorts of personal questions about his background and his problems. Monty was exhausted by what should have been a relaxing break in the day's shooting. Dr. Black asked Monty if he wouldn't help him with a little experiment. Would Monty agree to let the good doctor put him in a trance and then try to learn some lines? When Doris asked Monty how he could possibly have agreed, Monty said, "It wouldn't look good if I didn't go along with them." Not wanting to hurt Dr. Black's feelings, Monty feigned being in a trance and was so convincing the doctor thought he had succeeded. Meanwhile, Dr. Stafford-Clark, upset by Dr. Black's courtship, found out what had been going on, and a sort of rivalry started. Both doctors began discussing their interpretations of Monty's "problems" around the set (though Stafford-Clark only confided to a select few within Monty's camp, like Wolfgang Reinhardt). Doris finally got so upset she asked Doc Erickson why he permitted it. Erickson replied that he was only waiting for Monty to complain.

None of this is meant to malign the two doctors, who came to the film with excellent reputations. The story simply shows how Monty's power to disrupt could undermine ordinary standards of behavior in this unique atmosphere.

October 17 was Monty's forty-first birthday, and his friends decided to throw a small dinner party. Huston, probably feeling that things had gone too far between them, decided that *he* would do a bit of acting himself. He insisted on giving the party in his suite at the Imperial. Among the guests were Angie Allen, Huston's script girl (but also a member of Monty's camp, which annoyed Huston); Doris Langley Moore; Miss Kennedy, Monty's secretary (who was now in Huston's camp, which annoyed Monty); Wolfgang Reinhardt; and Monty. That whole evening, Huston was tremendously charming and entertained everyone with jokes and anecdotes of a kind that only he could pull off. At one point, he looked at Monty's hands, still showing their injuries from the ropes, and said in a loud voice, "Well, son of a bitch! Did I do *that* to you?" Monty was deadpan.

During those two weeks in Vienna, Doris Langley Moore walked off the film. She couldn't stand the wasteful extravagance. Huston, probably because he was trying to compensate for the small-vignette, "drawing room" look of his film, would call for one and two hundred extras in many scenes that required only one or two dozen. Doris would conscientiously individualize and fit each one in the brief week or so before the scene was to be shot, only to have completely different extras arrive for the actual shooting. It required hours of frantic last-minute juggling to make sure they looked halfway believable—and then it made little difference, anyway, since the rushes showed only a handful of them. Doris knew there was a kickback situation between the company that supplied the extras and the German members of her own costume department. Reinhardt pleaded with her to come back, and in the end she relented.

It was only a symptom of a general financial malaise, however. Universal had agreed to a budget of $2,000,000 for roughly three months' shooting. It was now the middle of October, the picture was far behind schedule, and the budget had already been blown on retakes, extras, costumes, and general extravagance. The executives in Hollywood writhed. They had backed *Freud* purely on John Huston's word that they would get a high-class, low-budget, commercial psychological thriller—and so they sent George Golitzin, an experienced production trouble-shooter, to investigate. On his arrival, Huston's camp immediately informed him that Monty was to blame, but Golitzin could see for himself that a good deal of the trouble lay with the last-minute rewrites. Huston showed him the script and, incredibly, Golitzin himself was soon enmeshed in the destructive wickerwork of rewriting. Given all this, it would be most peculiar when later, as part of Universal's suit against Monty, Golitzin would claim that it was indeed Monty who was responsible for the inflated budget. Clearly, Huston's extravagance and inability to deal with the film's ideological content were at least half responsible. The move to Vienna had been incredibly expensive—and, typically, nearly every foot of film shot there would later wind up on the cutting-room floor.

On October 26, the day before the company came back to Munich, Monty was slapped in the face in a scene and accidentally hit in both eyes. Soon after, he began to complain about blurred vision and saw a physician in Munich who told him the accident had caused cataracts, but that they were not very serious. Universal's executives in Munich insisted, however, on their own doctors, and they changed the diagnosis to long-standing bilateral cataracts having nothing to do with an injury. He was told that he might go totally blind. At Monty's insistence, Reinhardt took him to London to see another specialist.

When Reinhardt's telegram from London confirmed the diagnosis of a serious cataract condition, there was ghoulish happiness outside of Monty's camp. The set was abuzz about a big insurance claim. Monty's own makeup man, Bob Schiffer, who had now joined the opposition, told Doris what "good news" it was that Monty's troubles were too serious to have been caused by a slight accident. Doris never spoke to him again. Susannah York spotted John Huston and some yes-men assistants laughing. Wanting to be included in on the joke, she asked, "What are you laughing about?" Huston replied: "Oh, we're getting ready to save up to get Monty a guide dog for Christmas." York began to cry hysterically and couldn't go on with her scene.

The point of all this glee had to do with the bizarre tactics Universal was already mapping in an attempt to recoup the millions of dollars they expected to lose by the end of production. Huston and his followers were convinced that something had been wrong with Monty long before the film started, and now that "something" had been found—a debilitating condition caused by Monty's anxiety over the prospect of going blind, which was preventing him from learning lines. It had nothing to do with Huston or *Freud* or Universal. It was obviously all Monty's fault.

After Huston's merciless joke, any good fellowship between Huston and Susannah York collapsed. To have disaffection with a forty-one-year old male movie star who already had a reputation as a difficult boozer was one thing, but to be leered at as a sadistic enemy by a sweet young girl was quite heartbreaking for Huston. York had already told him that she was outraged and wouldn't forgive him. His reaction was to send her a huge bunch of expensive roses with a request that she have dinner with him. At dinner, Huston tried his best to salve the hurt and to give an honest explanation for what he had done. He told her how difficult it was for him to have affectionate feelings toward people; that the only two people he had ever loved were his father, Walter, and his son, and that he couldn't feel anything for Monty or anyone else. Huston said he knew it was wrong, but in all honesty this was the way he was and Susannah mustn't expect more. Her reply was perfunctory; she was unmoved by the evening and the gesture.

During November and December, the production crawled snail-like. Monty, upset, depressed, and worried, spent whole days trying to deliver simple speeches. In the evenings, at dinner, Monty, Desmond Davis, Doris and Susannah York made a point of not discussing his eyes, but he would say, in a despairing manner quite uncharacteristic of him, over and over: "This film is going to shorten my life by ten years." His premonition was uncanny. Monty's friends thought him extremely courageous in his determination to finish what was so obviously an impossible film. Courage aside, Monty knew that walking off *Freud* would finish his career forever.

Monty had been drinking almost nothing throughout the film, but now that the pressure was building, he began to consume a bit more. Perhaps Jean's appearance on the set at this time had something to do with Monty's going off the wagon. Even now, however, he watched what he drank— which did not stop some of the Germans from trying to

249

make him look like an unsavory alcoholic. Doris would have dinner with him at the Mark, and she says, "Whatever he did there, it was reported that 'Monty was drunk at the Mark.' We used to go to a very good restaurant in Munich, Humpelmeyer's. I never saw Monty drink more than a glass of wine there, but it was reported to John Huston by one of the German chauffeurs, that he had heard it direct from the manager of Humpelmeyer's that Monty was so drunk and raving that he had to be turned out of this restaurant. This was a lie, because after this supposed incident Monty, Susannah and I went into the restaurant and were treated with perfect respect. That chauffeur was an absolutely odious character, a kind of universal spy. You have no idea what lice crawl about in film studios." There seem to have been a number of sycophantic chauffeurs running around the set with nothing better to do than communicate gossip about "drunken" movie stars.

Sensational reports about Monty's "behavior" spread all over Europe, and appeared in publications like *Paris Match, Rome Espresso,* and especially in German papers. *Bild Am Sonntag* ran a piece in early December which stated that Monty was in a continuous state of drunkenness on the set and drank two bottles of whiskey a day in Vienna.

A translated excerpt reads: "Hidden under the bed stood a white plastic cup, invisible to the film camera where, in Geiselgasteig's newly built giant studio, they were about to shoot a difficult love scene between Montgomery Clift and the blonde English girl, Susannah York. Monty often fluffed, and every time he did he reached with an unsettled, nervous, almost addictive movement for the plastic cup and drank. 'Tea,' he insisted smilingly when asked about the cup. 'Whiskey,' said the others. When, finally, the bed scene in the Sigmund Freud picture worked out satisfactorily, the full-bearded Clift suddenly behaved like a savage. He threw himself onto Susannah, who was lying there in her nightdress, and kissed her for minutes. Both rolled and turned in the studio as in a sensual love scene. 'My darling! My darling!' he panted . . . When on October 14, accompanied by his director, John Huston, he arrived for outdoor shooting at the airport in Vienna, all the waiting journalists asked him about a small leather case which he was gripping anxiously: 'What is in there?' In the case was a bottle with high-percentage contents, but Clift said: 'Little chickens!'

He was drunk, and said immediately after that, 'The script! At the moment that is the most important thing for me.' "

Monty was miserable when his chauffeur, Eckhardt, indelicately showed him this pack of lies. The *Freud* press crew wouldn't budge an inch to help Monty squelch these stories. Doris urged the chief press representatives, Ernie Anderson and Phil Gersdorf, to go with her to Humpelmeyer's manager, who said the story about Monty getting kicked out was false; Monty had always been a perfect gentleman. Astonishingly, Huston, days later, told Doris that he never heard what the manager said. Doris, soon after, overheard several people in the press crew talking about Monty in the same absurd way the *Bild* story had been written. Monty's camp strongly suspected that the damaging stories came from the *Freud* press representatives themselves.

Monty had a few days of all-too-brief respite from the "airless room" of the Geiselgasteig psychiatric concentration camp when, on December 13, he was permitted to attend the premiere of *Judgment at Nuremberg* in Berlin. For the first time in months, he was his old self again: lovable, warm, laughing, secure in the good fellowship of the people around him. On the night of the premiere, held at Kongress Halle and televised, a distinguished international audience gave Stanley Kramer, Spencer Tracy, Judy Garland, Richard Widmark, Maximilian Schell, and Monty a full, twelve-minute standing ovation. Mayor Willy Brandt made a dazzling, emotional speech, praising the film and saying to his fellow Germans: "This film is a reminder that it is the responsibility of peoples everywhere to act whenever right is trampled upon." All the stars hugged and showed their teeth in grandiose Hollywood-premiere style. Stanley Kramer permitted a barrage of photographers and reporters to attack his big stars with cameras and streams of questions. It was a gigantic amphetamine shot for Monty's ego. In Munich the press crew treated him like a cretinous relative who had to be shut in an attic. Press interviews were strictly Huston's prerogative. In Berlin, after it became apparent that he had given one of the best supporting performances of the year, Monty was joyously besieged by reporters. Monty desperately needed approval, and now that he had it, he was charming, articulate, and happy.

On his return to Munich, the mood broke like shattered

glass. Monty's frustration with the lines, his fear of going blind, the constant rumors that Universal would launch a gigantic suit against the insurance company and thereby make him virtually uninsurable on any other film—all this was a Sword of Damocles dangling over his exhausted mind and body. At night he clung to Jean. Monty needed him now, and Jean was always near him on the set, but discreetly off in the wardrobe department where Huston seldom went.

By now, the war between Monty and Huston had petered out. Huston even allowed mid-scene cuts and rearrangement of scenes so that they could get prints on a few lines at a time. Even then, there was trouble. Monty would say a few words, become addled, hesitate and then turn in Huston's general direction and say, "Oh, I'm sorry . . . It's gone again." But Huston wouldn't even bother to look up or watch what Monty was doing. He would read a newspaper. From where he sat at the opposite end of the huge hall, he would only say, "Go again," without even moving his head.

They had to use "idiot cards," with Monty's lines on them, pasted on the backs of every conceivable piece of furniture or prop. The boards had to be close enough so Monty could see without straining, yet out of the camera's view. Monty was dreadfully embarrassed but, more than that, he still feared that he would go blank on the next word or line, even with the boards there. Three or four times, he broke down completely and rushed off the set sobbing. Huston just went on reading.

It was always surprising, therefore, to see how good Monty came across in the rushes, even in those scenes where he had read every word of dialogue off the boards. There was a tremendously lucid quality about Monty's eyes—cataract-ridden as they were—and he projected a cerebral calm which amazed those who had seen his desperation.

In late January, as the film approached some sort of conclusion, Universal's executives on location demanded that Monty be examined by a battery of their own doctors. Since an insurance claim was shortly to be filed with the Fireman's Fund Insurance Company, Fireman's Fund also demanded that Monty be examined by *their* doctors. Dr. Stafford-Clark again warned that this sort of commotion would be unwise for Monty, but the executives couldn't have cared less at this point. Monty was vulnerable. Universal was thinking about its pocketbook. John Huston, a far stronger figure than Monty in the motion-picture business, was perfectly willing to place full responsibility for the blown budget on Monty and his mysterious "malady." The only task remaining was to prove what that malady was.

Monty called his lawyers, Polikoff and Clareman, in New York, and told them that George Golitzin and Benjamin Lorder, Universal's insurance manager, were pressuring him to "go along" with what the examining doctors had come up with: That Monty was suffering from an "anxiety" reaction caused by the diagnosis of cataracts, and therefore could not learn his lines. "Polly"—as Monty liked to call Benet Polikoff—told Monty not to go along with anything; he would personally fly to Munich to see Monty through the ordeal.*

Monty did agree to what he thought would be a simple eye examination. Dr. Marcelli Shaw, Fireman Fund's doctor—in the presence of Dr. Bruno Sarcletti, Universal's doctor—saw that Monty was in an agitated state and began to talk to him as if he were speaking to a child. Monty responded by mimicking him. Dr. Shaw then asked Monty how the accident with his eyes happened, and Monty did a dramatic monologue, playing, now with intensity, now with pained perturbation, every detail of the episode. The doctors were tremendously moved by the sensitive monologue; in fact, they were so moved they decided he was on the verge of a nervous breakdown! This was Dr. Sarcletti's view in his peculiar deposition on behalf of Universal.

A week and a half later, Universal's executives tried to get Monty to agree to a full medical exam, and when Monty flatly refused, they insisted he sign an absurd rider to his original contract with Universal, stating, in essence,

---

* It isn't clear how far the executives were willing to go to establish their addlepated case against the star. Members of Monty's camp claimed, in later depositions, that they found hidden microphones around the studio, running to tape recorders, presumably to tape Monty's incoherent talk and inability to say lines. If true, it was probably not Universal's idea. German film studios had been infamous for their habit of bugging stars' dressing rooms. Months earlier, the first thing Bob Schiffer, Monty's makeup man, did when he came onto the set was shush Monty with a wordless hand signal and make a thorough search of his dressing room for hidden bugs. None were found, and then he permitted Monty to talk.

that he could not later claim that the very fact that he was permitted to finish the picture nullified the suit.

Two days later, on February 10, shooting finally ended on *Freud*.

A week later, Monty agreed to a medical exam by Dr. Kenneth MacLean, with Polikoff present. Nothing abnormal was observed, except some shaking of the hands and tongue; later, during memory and learning tests, Monty scored slightly under par. Astoundingly, although Monty said he had been only momentarily upset by the diagnosis of cataracts, the doctor concluded in his report on behalf of Universal that, because of Monty's nervousness during the exam and borderline performance in a memory test, Monty must have been suffering from an "anxiety state" responsible for all the filming delays Universal claimed.

That last day of shooting should have ended the Geiselgasteig nightmare, but nobody could forget what had happened in Munich and Vienna. The cast and crew were to be haunted for months—some for years—by the trauma they had gone through. For Monty, the effect was even more devastating. The fatigue turned into something deep and terrifying that attacked his psyche. He refused to leave Munich. He kept Jean there for weeks and drank himself into a near-coma. Doris Langley Moore, who had finally left *Freud* for good at Christmastime, called Monty from London and, alarmed at the news of his binge, sure he would wind up dead in the streets, called him again and again to ask him to come to London. Three weeks later, he finally did.

The evening of his arrival, Doris held an exquisite dinner at her Regents Park house, prepared by her German *au pair* girl, Sabina, with lots of champagne for Jean, who liked to guzzle it. To her astonishment, Monty not only brought Jean along, but his chauffeur, Roy Pryce, and Pryce's wife. Doris thought this a wrong-foot-first way of beginning a stay at her home, to invite the chauffeur in as if he were an equal! But she was soon to discover, and learn to appreciate, Monty's total disregard for class when he liked a person. Monty came into the house "very, very tight," as Doris recalls, and during the evening ate little and drank a great deal. At one point, he got up from the table, walked mysteriously behind Doris, and put his hands on her neck. Everyone at the table gaped. Doris put her hands to her chest and found a beautiful diamond necklace sparkling there. She was filled with emotion, embarrassed and speechless at the extravagant gift which had cost thousands.

Monty did not stop drinking. After everyone had left or gone to bed, he still sat in the living room drinking whiskey and playing the record player very loudly. Doris knew that Sabina, the *au pair* girl whose bedroom was directly beneath, could not possibly be able to sleep.

"Won't you please come to sleep?" Doris begged.

"I will not," said Monty, like a silly three-year-old.

"But the records are keeping Sabina awake."

Monty's response was to jump up and down on the floor.

Monty could be charming when he was sober, but that wasn't often during those weeks at Doris' house. His presence began to upset her, and it hurt her because she truly loved Monty. In the daytime, he sat around the house drinking whiskey, while Jean drank champagne and fine wines. In the evenings, he pressured her into throwing parties for him and inviting all her celebrity friends. "After *Freud,* he wanted excitement, and we had to be continually on the go, receiving people and taking Monty around. So I got Michael Redgrave here, and Vanessa, and everyone I could think of who was interested in him and likely to interest him. He was pushing me to do this, for things to be going on every evening. It was very hard on a hostess with only one *au pair* girl. And Monty was always late for meals; he'd never turn up when she'd prepare something special for him. It was a hostess' nightmare. It grieved me because I had never seen Monty like this before. He had been cold-sober all during the film, while Huston had been making such demands."

It was impossible to get Monty to go to sleep at night. He was mixing drugs with his alcohol again—amphetamines—and Doris would hear him wandering around the house at night. She would get up and quietly ask him to go back to sleep. Sometimes he would be quite docile and say, "Oh, my dear, I'll go to bed," and other times he would simply keep walking around the house. "One time I was awakened in the middle of the night and I found him just wandering stark naked up and down the staircase."

Jean was also overdoing the drinking, but only because Monty drank too much. He loved Monty, so it was necessary for him not to show Monty up. Interestingly, he seemed to find Doris a rival for Monty's attentions and showed hostility toward her. Doris responded in kind. She seemed to feel, as so many others had, that he was a bad influence on Monty—perhaps because by his perpetual presence he fed Monty's guilt about his own homosexuality. There was a strange duality these days in Monty's simultaneous openness about Jean and his persistent attitude that his homosexuality did not exist. Says Doris: "There was a deep puritanism in Monty—the English aren't nearly so puritanical as Americans—because he would much rather talk to me about his affairs with women than his affairs with men. He knew that I knew that he slept with Jean, because they slept in the same double bed in my bedroom, but it wasn't as if he would ever talk about it. I believe all this made him self-destructive. It wouldn't' have mattered at all if he had been an Englishman. He would have had a very, very happy life." Perhaps.

The food-picking and food-throwing episodes in public continued as well. Though they had less to do with attention-getting than with Monty's need to relive his staid childhood, this time as an unmitigated brat, a part of him still did crave attention. He would get depressed if nobody asked him for his autograph when he was out on the town. One evening in Soho, a group of rough-mannered teenagers came over to the car—it *was* a Rolls in Soho—and peered into the back seat. One of them cried out, "You're Mon'-gomery Clif', *blimey*, ain't you?" Monty was delighted, rolled down the window and began speaking to them, and the boys promptly started rocking the Rolls. Monty was still trying to talk with them when Roy Pryce very wisely put his foot on the accelerator.

Around this time, Desmond Davis went with Monty to a performance by Ella Fitzgerald, Monty's idol. Suddenly, Monty vanished from his seat. Davis just assumed Monty had gone to the gents, but a minute later, Monty walked right onstage in the middle of one of Ella's songs. "Heaven knows why Monty did it," says Davis. There was no mistaking Monty's condition. Ella stopped singing, and was polite but visibly upset. Monty gave a little smile to the audience, and Ella said, "This is a great surprise to us. We have to introduce you to Mr. *Montgomery Clift*." The audience gave him a friendly round of applause and a member of the management quickly escorted him off the stage.

Monty could still behave when he wanted to. During a

side trip to Bath with Jean and Doris, he stopped drinking and proved a model of deportment, as charming and magnetic as at any time in his life—but once back in London, the whiskey demon took over again. He was once more the haunted, drugged creature prowling her house at night. There were terrible scenes. Finally, Doris told Monty that he simply must stop—it was wrecking her household. They argued back and forth, and then it was over. Doris' daughter, Pandora, finally told Monty, "Look, wouldn't it be better if you moved to a hotel?"

That was all Monty had to hear. He assumed that it was Doris' wish. The same day, he and Jean took all their baggage and moved into the Savoy. Doris couldn't bear the thought of Monty being turned out of her home, but at the same time she knew that Pandora was right. Perhaps it was even best for him; maybe he would drink less. But Doris underestimated Monty. He stayed as drunk at the Savoy as he had been at her house. He made no effort to call her or speak to her again before he left London, and she did not call him. In only a few months, Monty and Doris had undergone a process that usually took him years to live out with other friends. In all likelihood, Monty would never have spoken to Doris again, had the next few months' events not occurred.

Monty and Jean flew back to New York while those events were still brewing—in Hollywood.

Day after day, Wolfgang Reinhardt cringed in Universal International's cutting room as his four-hour film was surgically amputated into slightly more than two hours, and then later, just before release, into a mere hour and a half. Whatever intriguing sexual material was left, after Huston's puritanical script-doctoring, landed on the floor. In one key scene, a father has brought his paralyzed daughter to Freud for treatment; her paralysis has no known organic origin. During therapy the girl tells of being raped, and the father's tears are to be the giveaway. But Huston cut the take of the father crying because he didn't *like* the idea of a father raping his own daughter. Of course, the scene was rendered pointless. Many other scenes were cut because of similar pointlessness when the editors saw them. Several important dream sequences were eliminated, for instance, because they seemed to be dangling; the sexual analyses that had explained them had been rewritten out of the script in Munich.

Reinhardt says, "They were all so afraid of releasing a film that would emphasize perverse sexuality and violate the code. This was 1962, and the film industry was just on the verge of releasing films—for example, *Peyton Place*—that were to make fortunes simply because they did dare to violate the old puritanical norms and intrigue the public. I think if John had been more courageous and insisted on keeping what we originally had in the script, *Freud* would have been a tremendous success in every sense."

As released, the film was static and cold. Granted, the scripts, even going back as far as Sartre's 1600-page screenplay, never attempted, except in the most superficial way, to humanize Freud. The central theme concerned ideas, not a man. The big jolt in the film was to be the intrigue of a great mind discovering terrible human secrets, such as the Oedipus complex, the theory of infantile sexuality, and the weird tricks one part of the mind will play to hide its own sexual secrets from another part. Had that theme been adhered to, with its own built-in shock value and human appeal, *Freud* would have needed little more than the feeble characterizations it attempted. But with all the real shock removed from the film, the released print seemed little more than academic. As *Esquire*'s review pointed out, the film "might well be used in high schools as an audio-visual aid." (Indeed there is a heavy audio-visual demand for this film: it rents for approximately double that of other films of its vintage.)

Freud got generally dismal reviews from most of the important critics, who nevertheless condescended to give Huston credit for at least trying the impossible. Monty was given reviews a fraction more on the credit than debit side —but then what had he done in the film? There was no action to speak of, his dialogue was not dramatic, and he was left with little more than manner as his primary acting tool. He did use this tool superbly. During the film, one begins to forget the stilted words and to concentrate on Monty's magnificent expressions.

"There is an impressive stillness in the man when he acts," said a London *Times* writer, "as if he were held steady a thousand leagues below the surface by enormous subterranean gyroscopes. Whether he understands more of his lines than other actors do, only he could tell you. But he seems to." *Time* magazine added, "Montgomery Clift has the singular ability to make his eyes light up. This is an enormous convenience in *Freud*. Thinking, after all, does not lend itself to visual representation, and it would have been excessive for director John Huston to draw a cartoon light bulb over Clift's head to indicate inspiration. With Clift's odd physiological talent, however, Huston can show the instant of young Freud's conception of the theory of infantile sexuality, the theory of repression, and the theory of dreams. The technique is to give a generalized cue (Freud's mother, who calls her son Siggy, tells him: 'Memory plays queer tricks'), and then zoom into Clift's lit orbs." The *Times'* Bosley Crowther, who in the past seemed to have had some sort of vendetta against Monty, said: "Montgomery Clift gives an eerily illuminating performance in the title role," listing *Freud* as his choice as one of 1963's ten best movies.

The box office was decent in the big cities, but poor in the rest of the country, where it counts. However, Universal did not exactly lose its shirt. The film has been doing extraordinarily well in rentals for years, and the studio, known as a manufacturer of cheap Hollywood horror films, managed to gain some prestige. Among intellectuals, *Freud* is admired, probably for no other reason than that it is Hollywood's only attempt at taking a crack at Freud.

But the film caused much more damage than good. In shock at the butchering of the film, distraught at observing the virtual destruction of Monty's life during the filming of *Freud*, Wolfgang Reinhardt became so disillusioned that, by his own admission, he practically withdrew from the movie business. He has attempted only one film since. Angela Allen left Huston. For years, she had been Huston's confidante and script girl, but after *Freud* she announced bitterly that she would never work with him again.

Would it be stating the obvious to say that *Freud* was also John Huston's tragedy? It was his dream of a lifetime —the one film in which he could probe minds and emotions without the aid of an outdoor action setting, a vast emotional and professional risk—and it crumbled. After all that has been said, was Huston really to blame, not only for what happened to the film, but for what happened to Monty? If all the moral, social, and psychological questions were somehow brought into one all-encompassing court of law, the judge would simply have to throw the case out, shaking his head over the impossible prospect of sorting through the ambiguities.

No one person, thing, or state of mind, such as the concocted "anxiety reaction," was responsible. That was why the insurance lawsuit was absurd. No company can be expected to indemnify a motion picture studio for a psychological state of affairs in which nearly every member of a cast and crew seemingly breaks down and cannot function normally. Perhaps Lloyd's of London will one day issue a policy entitled "Insurance for Financial Loss Caused by Total or Partial Collapse of Interpersonal Relations."

After Universal sued Fireman's Fund Insurance Company for $628,213.52, Universal's lawyers had to support their claim with extensive sworn depositions of what had happened on the set of *Freud*. It took months to collect them. Those willing to swear that Monty was the cause of all the delays were John Huston, his assistant, Laci Von Ronay, and George Golitzin. They were supported by rather unconvincing reports from doctors who suggested that Monty was in a state of near collapse, while admitting that at least half of what they had learned had come from Universal executives themselves. The one doctor Universal really counted on, Dr. David Stafford-Clark, refused to "go along." Instead, his deposition for Fireman's Fund suggested that Monty had been harassed by executives. Doris Langley Moore, her daughter Pandora, actress Rosalie Crutchley, Desmond Davis, and Angela Allen also gave depositions for Fireman's Fund and, in essence, for Monty, who stood to lose both his career and what was left of his reputation if the insurance company lost.

As soon as Monty read Doris' deposition, he was moved to call her from New York, filled with gratitude for the detailed, beautifully written account of the film's atmosphere and events. He was also filled with misery over the way he had behaved in her home. "I feel awful," he said. "Awful. How could I do that to you in your own house?" The relationship was on again, but Doris could not help noting that Monty had only called her after he had read the deposition.

Monty himself was examined and cross-examined at the Waldorf-Astoria Hotel in New York on November 27, 28, and 29 about why he couldn't remember his lines. It was quite a scene in itself. True to his nature, Monty remained desperately determined to tell the truth.

In the following excerpts from the cross-examination,

the questioner is Joseph Dubin, attorney for Universal; the opposing lawyer is Raymond Stanbury, for Fireman's Fund.

DUBIN: "Can you give me any reason why you were unable to deliver your lines, if you were unable to deliver your lines, on that day?"

MONTY: "I hadn't memorized them. It's that simple."

DUBIN: "You also said that ordinarily when you rewrote dialogue you didn't learn it until you had a discussion with Mr. Huston?"

MONTY: "Yes."

DUBIN: "In other words, you didn't do any memorizing or learning of the dialogue until you submitted your proposed changes to Mr. Huston? Is the question clear?"

STANBURY: "This is objected to as an ambiguous question."

DUBIN: "Read the question back. If the witness doesn't understand I'll be glad to clarify it."

STANBURY: "It's ambiguous. Whether he understands it or not, it doesn't specify whether you are talking about the entire script or those scenes he found difficult to play."

DUBIN: "Read the question. If it's ambiguous I'll be glad to clarify it."

MONTY: "Are you talking about this scene?"

DUBIN: "Any scene."

MONTY: "That implies they were all changes of mine and I, consequently, never memorized."

DUBIN: "I'm asking you in connection with any scene which involved suggested changes by you."

MONTY: "Oh."

DUBIN: "Did you at any time know the original scene?"

MONTY: "No."

DUBIN: "You never bothered to learn the dialogue as contained in the original script?"

MONTY: "Not bothered, purposefully."

DUBIN: "Deliberately?"

MONTY: "Deliberately."

That was all the lawyers for Universal had to hear: Monty admitting that he had deliberately not learned lines. They immediately cut off Monty's salary of $500 a week. He was to have been paid $200,000 in installments for tax purposes, and had already received $25,000, but Universal determined that he would get no more. In retaliation, Monty's lawyers sued Universal for Monty's salary, and

261

Universal sued back for the same amount they had requested from the insurance company but now had lost.

In the middle of 1963, Universal was forced to give him his money, because despite Monty's admission of deliberately ignoring the script, the overwhelming evidence was in his favor. Ultimately, however, he was the loser. For nearly four years following the completion of *Freud* and the announcement of Universal's suit, he was not offered work in a motion picture. He was uninsurable. It was a great defeat for him at a time when he so much needed the sense of an ongoing career. There was nothing else in his life but his work. Without it, a deep and empty chasm opened before him. The demons were free to come at will, and stay as long as they liked.

CHAPTER TEN

Unbankable

MONTY stayed with Jean for a little more than a year after returning from Europe. The year 1962 was bleak. Monty underwent three operations for cataracts, as well as a serious operation to correct a hernia—the result of his sado-masochistic bout of rope-climbing with Huston. During 1962 and into the following year, he entered Mt. Sinai Hospital seven times, each hospitalization lasting from one to two weeks.

It was hopeless for him to try to seek work while the *Freud* lawsuit was in progress. He had had insurance problems before, but never like this. It was not so much John Huston's treatment that made him feel victimized as Lew Wasserman's. MCA, Monty's agents ever since *Red River*, had negotiated the deal for *Freud*, but during the making of the film, the government had filed an anti-trust suit against them. MCA had been operating both as a major casting agency and as a conglomerate producing company, and now they were forced to disband their agency. MCA owned Universal Pictures, and Lew Wasserman suddenly became its president. In essence, it was Wasserman, as head of the movie company, who was suing Monty. Monty, along with a good part of the industry, thought it ghoulish, especially since it was Wasserman who had arranged Monty's appearance in *Freud*.

Robert Lantz became Monty's new agent. Lantz tried, as best he could, to get Monty's career reinstated, but the prejudice of producers, the nearly insurmountable bankability problem, and Monty's continual drinking and sickliness made the task Herculean. Before Lantz could do anything about the bankability, he had to get Monty together with producers, to restore confidence in him—but he could hardly get Monty to come to his own office in a sober state. The only reason Lantz kept trying was that he liked Monty so much.

It was a vicious circle. The lack of work sent Monty into a depression which made him sit stone-silent for hours, and the depression, which often made him impossible to contact, robbed him of any chance to resume his career.

Jack Larson came to stay with Monty now, although because of his own busy writing career and personal life, he left Monty pretty much to himself—especially since Monty seemed determined to wallow. Oh, Monty did put on a great display of friendliness and forced enthusiasm for Jack's sake, as Jack came and went independently from his own room in the townhouse; yet as Jack began to leave for an evening out, Monty would abandon the forced smiles a bit too soon. Jack, turning around for one last look at him, like Orpheus, would receive the sting of the most agonizingly depressed expression.

He recalls: "Monty had to pretend everything: interest in people, interest in life, in the very words he spoke. Sometimes, I would pass Monty's bedroom. The television would be on, and Monty would be sitting scrooched on his sofa, crying, not paying a bit of attention to the television. That's how Monty spent his days. He didn't want to go out. He didn't want to see anything. Once, I brought him to a play, and right in the middle, Monty fell asleep. He woke up suddenly with a start, and yelled out, 'What do you mean?' Everyone, even the actors on the stage, heard him. It was really the last sentence of some dream conversation, but it sounded as if it were directed at the actors."

Sometimes Monty would feel a need to reach back into his past to feebly rekindle a friendship that had died. He made those long, late-night phone calls again to people like Bill Gunn. Bill was living with a girl now, however, and when Monty broke down on the phone and asked Bill to come over to see him through the night, Bill's girl became upset. The two of them would rush over to Monty's at three in the morning, just as Monty was ready to pass out, and Bill would tell her, over her protests, that he dared not leave Monty alone. Eventually, she became so distraught that she told Monty, when he called one night, not to call again. Bill heard and did not stop her. "It had gone too far," he says. "Monty's pathetic crying and carrying on—I just couldn't take it anymore. Monty wasn't the same as he had been. He needed the kind of help that I couldn't give him, and my trying to cope with him was breaking up a good relationship that I had. Monty didn't call me anymore and I didn't call him."

Jean was making Monty worse. He was drinking and drugging as much as Monty. He became prissy and pretentious, an outright bore. Monty only put him on display when they traveled. They seemed to have degenerated into a pathetic passivity, neither one strong enough to offer substance to what had become nothing more than a drinking partnership. They could not even achieve the free-spirited spontaneity that drunken sprees, for whatever they are worth, usually offer. Sexual passion was out of the question. Monty would glide from his gin and tonics into sexless oblivion.

He was too powerless, too drunk, to make Jean move out of the house. Both of them were getting too sick to take care of themselves or each other. Neither of them ate enough.

It was toward the beginning of 1963 that Monty began to see his mother again. Over the previous ten years, her calls to Monty had been unending. Marge Stengel remembers that the entire time she was Monty's secretary, Monty saw his mother no more than seven times, despite Mrs. Clift's pleadings. His attitude toward her ranged from total indifference to outright nastiness. The word he used most often about her was "calculating." He simply didn't trust her and her motivation for calling him. Once, Nancy Walker said that she would love to meet his mother, and he just shook his head with a large sigh and said, "Don't even bother." Nancy said, "That bad?" Monty said, "Yes."

On October 1, 1962, a tragic storm hit the Clift family. Suzanne Clift, the twenty-one-year-old daughter of Monty's brother Brooks, killed her boyfriend, twenty-seven-year-old Pierro Brentani. For four days, the New York *Daily News* headlined the story. Brooks could not afford to pay for the defense of his daughter, and his wife's family, still bitter over their daughter's marriage to Brooks in the first place, refused to help. Poor Bill Clift had to shell out and nearly went broke. The messy trial left the family emotionally, as well as financially, drained. Suzanne, pregnant by her slain boyfriend, was convicted, and later had her child in prison.

The tragic scandal brought Monty and his family together again. Mrs. Clift came over to the Sixty-first Street town house now, terribly grateful once again to see her son. She could see how he was living and wanted to help. She was not possessive or domineering, but quite relaxed, and Nancy Walker remembers that Monty remarked to her, during that time: "Not bad, Nanny. Not bad." He was surprised that he no longer felt hostile toward her.

Bill Clift also became reconciled with his son. When he found out what Monty had become—added to the immediate tragedy of his granddaughter Suzanne's conviction—Bill's spirit broke. He saw Monty and Jean together, and knew what it meant. Maria says, "For the longest time Bill refused to admit to himself that Monty was gay, but in the end he knew. He never came out and used the word, but he said he was disturbed at the kind of men his son hung around, and I knew immediately what he meant."

The thing that Bill and Ethel wanted most, now that they were seeing Monty again, was to help him survive. His drinking and his deteriorating health were the most obvious problems. Jean was another.

Jean's galloping alcoholism hospitalized him in mid-1963. Ethel called Billy LeMassena and told him that she was worried: Monty was all alone in the house now. Billy, who had remained close to the Clifts but who had not been in Monty's life for many years, told Ethel, "I'll take care of Jean when he gets out of the hospital. I'll take him to my place. But we've got to get someone to take care of Monty." The two of them went to see Dr. Arthur Ludwig, who said he would try to find a male nurse. Elizabeth Guenster, who had left Monty's employ in 1960, was now back with him as his cook, doubling as a sort of nurse, but that was only in the daytime. Monty needed full-time care.

Dr. Ludwig sent over a pleasant-looking black man by the name of Lorenzo ("Larry") James. Mrs. Clift and Billy hired him immediately, and he stayed with Monty twenty-four hours a day. Billy says, "He was a godsend. He would put Monty to bed, massage him and make him feel comfortable, and get him to sleep. He would make sure that Monty took his medicines. Monty had become helpless." Lorenzo had his own apartment, but he spent most of his time at Monty's house.

While Jean recuperated at Billy's apartment, Billy told him bluntly, "You and Monty just can't see each other anymore. You're dangerous for one another." Billy told him that he would have to get his own apartment and that Monty didn't want him back. Monty acquiesced to it all with childlike surrender.

For months, Jean fought the enforced separation violently. He went to Monty's and tried to get in, but Lorenzo James came to the door and coolly told him that he had orders not to let him in. That approach failing, Jean tried telephoning, but Lorenzo would not allow Jean to speak to him. Finally, Monty changed his telephone number. Meanwhile, Jean was drinking and mixing barbiturates more heavily than before, and becoming hysterical. One night, he called the fire department and told them Monty's house was on fire, then went to the house hoping that in the confusion Monty would come out and he could talk to him. Monty did, eventually, see Jean. Several times, late at night, while Lorenzo was either sleeping or unawares, Monty let him in. But by then, even Jean knew that it was over. He dropped out of sight completely. Perhaps he went back to live with those "wealthy" French parents of his. Every once in a while, Billy would get a call from Kennedy Airport, Jean's drunken voice would say, "Beel, I'm going to Paris. Beel, I love you . . ." Billy would laugh and say: "Stop drinking, Jean, and get on the plane."

Occasionally, Roddy McDowall and Nancy Walker saw Monty, but basically Monty did not have one steady friend left. He spent all of his time with Lorenzo, and went to movies. Billy would sometimes take long walks with Monty and try to behave as if things were the same as in the old days. At the behest of Mr. Clift, Ned Smith, too, came to see Monty frequently. It was as if the Clifts were attempting to wipe out all those years between Monty's early and late adulthood. Monty and Ned would talk about the old days. Ned always had been a little negative about show business, and since Monty was feeling depressed about his whole life and everything he had tried to do, much of their talk centered on Monty's gripes against the friends he had made in the business. He was down on Mira Rostova, down on Kevin, even down on a good, present friend like Roddy McDowall.

Billy had developed a drinking problem—nothing like Monty's, but serious enough for him to seek help at Alcoholics Anonymous. He told Monty how much it was helping him and begged Monty to go to meetings with him. For years, Monty had resisted any means of therapeutic support but Dr. Silverberg. He had sloughed off the idea of AA many times in the past, because essentially AA members want to stop drinking and Monty didn't. But after Jean left, and was replaced by conscientious Lorenzo, Monty was not so sure what he wanted. He did go a few times with Billy to Alcoholics Anonymous, but didn't like the idea of thinking of himself as "one of the alcoholics." He told Billy over and over, as he had told others in the past, that Silverberg had said he wasn't an alcoholic. It was as if a small, muddied-up boy were insisting, to a patient parent, that, no, he hadn't been messing around in the puddles outside and why would anyone want to think that?

Billy would come over for dinner, and they would get into one of their old conversations about ethics and logic. Monty hated to eat, but, with Lorenzo around, was doing better than he had been. Then Monty would start pouring glasses of Polish vodka, and Billy, who knew Monty was going to drink anyway, went along with him. The logic and lucidity of the old days would quickly get drowned. "Billy, Billy," Monty would say, tearily, "they're all corrupt —except you. You're the only really decent, honest person I know." Billy, stewed, would protest and confess to Monty all the hypocritical things he had done. Monty would shake his head. "No, it's true. You're the only honest person I know." Then Billy would take a good look at what the two of them were doing, and suddenly say:

"Why are you trying to kill yourself?"

"I'm *not* trying to kill myself."

"Yes, you *are* trying to kill yourself."

"No, I'm *not* trying to kill myself."

Billy says, "He always denied to me that he knew he was trying to kill himself. I don't see how he could have been that naive, not to realize what he was doing—but maybe he didn't. It's just that he wanted to remove life, to anesthetize himself against it. I used to get so mad at Dr. Silverberg because he would tell Monty that it was okay to drink. Psychiatrists who do that ought to be electrocuted."

Mrs. Clift got mad at Dr. Silverberg, too, but after thirteen years with the same analyst, Monty was not to be talked out of seeing him. Mrs. Clift, never one to concede defeat, decided to arrange a summit conference. The scene was a lofty one. Ethel, Jack Clareman—Monty's lawyer—

and Dr. Ludwig sat in a circle in Dr. Silverberg's office, staring militantly at the sixty-six-year-old psychiatrist. The big question was launched. What was he doing about Monty's drinking?

Dr. Silverberg asked the imposing trio: *"What* drinking?"

That ended the big summit conference.

Lorenzo James' function was simply to take care of Monty, not to become Monty's warden. He could not have stopped him from taking pills or drinking himself into a stupor all day without the silliness of hiding bottles and vials, which would never have worked with Monty. Several things, however, coinciding with Lorenzo's appearance in Monty's life did curtail his drinking. For one, Monty was becoming too sick for liquor to have any other effect than to make him sicker and more uncomfortable. For another, without Jean around, Monty's depression had begun to lift sufficiently for him to think about regaining a hold on his disrupted career, and his maneuvers involved periodic total withdrawals from liquor. More than anything else, Monty wanted his self-respect back.

Those sicknesses, though, were not helping. Monty had developed a new hormonal disease, rather rare, called *hypo-parathyroidism,* a condition known to exist in people like Monty, who have already been treated for thyroid trouble. The resulting calcium imbalance causes tetany—involuntary shaking of the muscles, especially of the hands and feet—and, often, cataracts. It cannot be cured, but it can be controlled by periodic injections of calcium compounds directly into the bloodstream, which Monty was receiving.

Then he developed phlebitis in both legs. It started as simple varicose veins—because Monty had been sitting around the house so much and not eating—which then became inflamed and had to be stripped in a serious operation in early 1964. The phlebitis made it incredibly painful for Monty to walk. The tetany effect of the calcium imbalance, plus the pain in his legs, made him unable to walk any distance without help; he had to hobble and lean on Lorenzo when they walked down the street. Strangers who passed them whispered, "Oh, that poor has-been!" The condition made Monty look perpetually drunk, although those days Monty would not have been walking in public if he were. Nancy Walker had lunch with him one afternoon, and later an acquaintance who had seen the two of them walking down the street said, "Isn't it terrible that Monty has become like that—always drunk?" Miss Walker quickly told the acquaintance she was a miserable s.o.b. for having jumped to such a conclusion.

Those who remembered Monty as he had been only ten years earlier were now overcome by an uncomfortable, tomb-like chill. It was like one of those horror movies that Roddy was always appearing in those days, only infinitely more disturbing. In a sensitive piece for *Backstage,* written in 1966, Ralph Zucker recalled:

"I saw him in 1964; his face had been altered by the terrible car crash he endured in 1956, his once lithe body was rigid, his movements constricted. And the face was a mask; the eyes were dull. He could hardly walk. A friend led him by the elbow. His hand trembled. He stumbled slightly as he moved along. He seemed as if he were in a trance, as if he were no longer with us, as if his overwhelming personal isolation were irremediable. And I remember thinking: he's a dead man."

This "deadness" was something Monty tried to fight; but the more he tried to force a sense of being alive, the more chillingly dead he seemed. He would encounter old friends in public places and make ludicrous scenes, in an effort to show that he wasn't yet embalmed. He had only been an occasional friend of Norris Houghton's in the past, and yet when he ran into Houghton at the City Center he shouted and screamed and threw his arms around him, as everyone looked up to see what was going on. Houghton was embarrassed. Lehman Engel, who also had not seen Monty for years, ran into him one afternoon in a chic barber shop in the basement of 30 Rockefeller Plaza. "When I got there Monty was in a chair in the middle of a haircut, sheet around him, all covered with hair. He made the most terrible, the most embarrassing, the most awful scene! Everybody knew who he was and was watching. He saw me in the mirror and he got out of his chair in the middle of a haircut, with this sheet around him and all this hair on him, and he came to the door and he took me by the arm and said, '*Mon vieux,* how are you?' I said: 'You're acting like a baby.' He said: 'No!' and then he said to the barber, Martin, 'Mr. Engel is much busier than I am. You take him and I'll wait, because I'm not busy at all today.' I said: 'Now come on, Monty. Martin will be through with you in ten minutes. Please sit down.' Monty's voice was slurry. Between Martin and me, we got him seated in the chair, and I stood there keeping him occupied with conversation until Martin could finish. Then he was staggering all over the place while he took out his money. When he got out the door I just wanted to collapse: I felt so incredibly sad, but relieved that he was gone."

For people who had only known Monty well during the glamorous years, this sudden horrific vision of him was all the more depressing; one just wanted to blot out the image.

Lorenzo suggested that Monty rent a summer place near the ocean to get some sun and revive himself, and to that end took a house in The Pines community on Fire Island. The house was a simple, three-bedroom affair, set quite a distance from the ferry landing and therefore from the hordes of homosexual young men who dominated the community. He did, naturally, have to take the ferry over, and land on the dock with everyone else. Monty's "walking" with Lorenzo—a half-carrying process—became a legendary gossip item during the three seasons Monty was there. He kept the house mainly for rest, but hated to be alone there with Lorenzo—especially during his bad depressions.

He fraternized with the local homosexuals, but not indiscriminately. Monty was incapable of sexual pleasure, even if he could have drummed up the strength for it; his main reason for going to some of the gay parties was sheer boredom. Almost universally, they looked upon him as a *Boys in the Band*, sunken-ship type: a man, a *famous* man, who had destroyed himself over the guilt and disappointments of homosexual life. He became popular as an ikon for all the self-indulgent semi-alcoholic gays who loved to gossip about the big movie stars who "were," and what they had done to themselves as a result. It was moronic, vacuous talk, unfair to the man Monty was and had been. They reduced him, in their own minds, to just another sad faggot.

Bob Evans used to invite Monty to his parties on Fire Island. There was always a lot of liquor. Monty would sit on the couch drinking, and then suddenly fall on the floor in the middle of a crowd heavy with homosexual chitchat. Someone would pick him up. He would fall again. This would happen three or four times. Eventually, the guests just let him lie there, stepping over him as if he were a sleeping dog.

271

With all the pain and boredom he felt, he was still somewhat aware of how to manipulate his essential image, the product of a lifetime of self-involvement and intellectual deliberation. One could say that he was still a calculating actor, but only at the risk of oversimplifying his psychic processes. When he spoke, for instance, he stood and pointed a finger at an angle if he wanted to emphasize something; then he would shrink back to a hunched position. If approached, Monty would hunch up even further, a saintly posture of which he was obviously intensely proud. He talked with another person as if he expected to be hit, drawing sympathy without actually asking for it.

A new acquaintance of his, Ray Buckingham, whom he had met through Lorenzo, half mimics, "Monty spoke *very* . . . *very* slowly . . . it was almost like . . . a . . . considered act . . . when . . . he . . . spoke. He would emphasize it with his finger. But it was so incredibly slow it was unbelievable. I think it was an act, but may not have been conscious; that was his only way of delivering everything. The only time I ever saw him not be like that was one time when he was very depressed, and then he spoke at a normal speed. The rest . . . of . . . the . . . time . . . it . . . was always . . . slow. I think what he worked out for his acting, he carried out for his life, his method of communicating, his everything. When he was going to confront someone, he was going to confront them with a design: like . . . I . . . will . . . do . . . this . . . when . . . I . . . say . . . hello . . . to . . . Raymond."

Despite his condition, Monty talked constantly about his comeback plan. His big mistake, he said, was in devoting himself exclusively to films for so many years, and in neglecting the serious career he had originally wanted for himself on the stage. He was going to return to the stage, as soon as he could retrain his voice and learn how to project once again. He might also direct. He could do films occasionally. During this time, he would drive to the ocean with Jack Larson and read passages to the waves from the *Hamlet* he wanted to do with Myrna Loy as Gertrude and Peter Finch as Claudius. "Can you imagine Gertrude with that wonderful nose?" Monty enthused. He went to rehearsals of television and theater plays so that he could watch directors, for his own future work as a director.

In 1964 and early 1965, Monty did make two timid ventures out of the film world. In 1964, he played Tom in a Caedmon Records recording of *The Glass Menagerie* opposite Julie Harris, Jessica Tandy, and David Wayne. It was no small feat for the director, Howard Sackler, to get Monty to do it. For two weeks before the recording date, Monty complained that he wasn't ready to do it and perpetually threatened to go off on a sudden trip. It is difficult to believe that any actor could outdo Monty's seemingly casual, but subtle reading of Tom's introductory narration. In April of 1965, he did the voice-over narration for a documentary television show called *Faulkner's Mississippi*. Once again, Monty képt telling the producer that he just might not show up. The television critics applauded his two-hour narration.

On February 24, 1965, Monty's father, Bill Clift, died of a heart attack at New York Hospital at the age of seventy-eight. He did not die a happy man. His entire estate, which he left to his wife, Ethel, amounted to less than $50,000, a pathetically small amount of money in view of his career as a Wall Street broker and the large sums of money he had earned in his lifetime. Maria, who was too upset to go to the funeral, says "Bill could have done a lot more with his life. He was intelligent, but not aggressive enough." His unhappiness in the end was caused in large part by the feeling that his famous son had drunk his career away and was now wallowing in a self-destruction that Bill could never comprehend. The case of Brooks' daughter had also depressed him. After the funeral, Monty told Billy that he hated himself for having treated his father the way he had all those years. "He always thought of Bill as sort of weak and helpless compared to his mother. I don't think he much regretted not having seen her; Monty thought of her as strong and self-sustaining. But toward the end he had a lot of regrets about his father."

The days, weeks, and months dragged. Monty remained in stasis. By mid-1965, he hadn't worked in films for a full three and a half years, despite Robert Lantz' diligent efforts to get him reinstated. Lantz always sent him plenty of scripts, but Monty complained that they weren't right for him. Most of them were degrading vehicles. One such was *The Last of the Late Great Jelly Bellies*, a "freak" genre film about a neurotic who falls in love with a fat whore, which Shelley Winters had agreed to do. Monty never would have done it, but he had so much time on his hands

273

that he kept tantalizing the young screenwriter with the idea that he would do the picture if the right revisions were made. The poor writer made the revisions, imagining that Monty and Winters would elevate his freak film into possible box-office magic, and then Monty rejected the revisions. Most of these shoddy things were low-budget enough not to require Monty's insurability, but Monty had always been proud that he could say, "I've never done a film that I was ashamed of," and he still clung to his self-respect. Any vehicle of quality, naturally, required both bankability and the confidence of producers and directors, neither of which Monty had.

The "big plan" to move into the theater was clearly chimerical. In 1965, he actually had a chance to go to London with Lee Strasberg's fine production of *The Three Sisters*, but he turned it down. He could hardly get up in the morning without Lorenzo carrying him to the shower to wake him out of a semi-coma caused by sleeping pills. How on earth could he have flown to England, gone through rigorous Chekhovian rehearsals, and then given eight performances a week? Monty knew it was impossible.

When it became too cold to go to Fire Island, he poured all his energies into renovating the town house. He hired Boak and Paris, Inc., to blueprint alterations on the house, shopped all over the city for different fabrics, a new sofa for the living room, totally different furniture for his bedroom. He became fanatical about having things done immediately. Once, he decided to convert a spare bathroom into a walk-in bar. For a few days, he waited impatiently for the carpenter to come and tear it down, and then he just took an ax and started whacking at it himself. Then he called the carpenter back and said, "You'd better come over now, because I've just done your work for you." The house became like the Temple of David, that everlasting project—always talked about but never quite finished.

Monty could startle you with such bursts of violent, incredible strength. He once tore a sturdy table apart with his bare hands. What did the rest of his body look like underneath the loose clothing he wore? Ray Buckingham found out one summer afternoon. He and Monty took Ray's boat for a cruise on the Long Island Sound. Coincidentally, Frank Sinatra used the same boat basin for his cruiser, and by the time Monty and Ray arrived, photographers were already there. One of them said: "Oh, my God, here comes Montgomery Clift!" and flashbulbs started going off in Monty's face. His cataract operations had left his eyes sensitive to such bright light, and Monty put up his hands in a defensive gesture against the flashbulbs. It turned out that one of these photographers had already been assaulted by Sinatra, and started crying that Monty had assaulted him, too. The next day's papers ran items that the photographer was going to sue Sinatra *and* Monty! Poor Monty, as usual, was the one who had been assaulted!

Once on the sound, Ray said, "Let's go swimming." Physical exercise? Appalling. "No, I don't want to go in swimming. I'm not wearing a bathing suit." Ray insisted, "So who's watching? Take your clothes off and jump in." "Ah, come on . . ." Monty whined, stripping to the skin. Ray pushed him in. "Now swim for ten minutes and I'll let you back in!" Monty had been complaining about feeling groggy before Ray pushed him into the breach, but after the swim he felt wonderful. He stood naked on the boat: "He had the physique of an Indian fakir, almost suffering from malnutrition. He did not weigh much more than a hundred pounds. His bones stuck out. There was no muscle tone left." It was not at all surprising: Monty now ate nothing but a piece of nearly raw meat once a day and some canned baby food.

Monty's depression lifted dramatically when, in the early months of 1965, he found out that Elizabeth Taylor, whom he considered just another ex-friend, had made a surprisingly loyal gesture. She had not closed her eyes to Monty's desperate situation. For several years, she had known he was trying to get back into films, and had never given up on him, even after he made several unfriendly remarks about her to the press. As John Springer, her friend and publicist, notes, "It's hard to become Elizabeth's friend, but once you are one, Elizabeth never forgets you." Rex Kennamer corroborates: "If you ever got into Elizabeth's small circle of friends, you always stay there."

After *Cleopatra*, Elizabeth, a freelancer, had more power in Hollywood than any studio head. Warner Brothers wanted her for their multi-million-dollar production of Carson McCullers' *Reflections in a Golden Eye*, a sensitive story about two neurotic Southerners—a colonel, who is a suppressed homosexual, and his dissatisfied wife. Elizabeth had played enough crazy Southern ladies and didn't want to do *Reflec-*

275

tions, but the part of the sexually terrified colonel seemed absolutely perfect as a comeback part for Monty. Elizabeth was not a reader, but her cinematic instincts told her that the vocal hesitations and peculiar mannerisms that had grown exaggerated in Monty were perfect for Carson Mc-Cullers. She agreed to do the movie, if Warners would agree to casting Monty opposite her. Naturally there was an uproar. John Huston had already been chosen as director! Suppose Monty could not get through *Reflections*? What company would insure him? And yet, without Elizabeth as box-office insurance, Warners could lose its shirt on such a strange mood piece. Warners and Elizabeth ping-ponged over Monty's casting until she finally ended the hassle by making one of the most magnanimous gestures ever made by a star of Elizabeth's caliber. She offered her own fee, her usual one million dollars, as insurance for Monty. Monty was cast. It was a part so perfect for his present skills that he could easily have walked off with another Oscar nomination, and certainly a completely new career.

Monty felt totally overwhelmed by Elizabeth's act. It was as if some old friend had found and rescued him from a solitary life raft on which he had been adrift for three and a half years. He told everyone what Elizabeth had done. He talked of her goodness, her generosity, how unfair the public had been to her during the ordeal of her marriage to Richard Burton. No one dared breathe a word against her now, even though Monty himself, in the just recent past, had moralized self-righteously about her succession of marriages and divorces.

Elizabeth had three other movies to complete, so *Reflections* could not begin until September 1966—more than a year and a half away. The waiting was murderous. Now that Monty felt wanted again, he longed to get out of that town house and prove himself instantly. He would call Elizabeth long-distance to make sure that Warners hadn't changed their minds, and she would tell him that they had nothing to say about it; this was *her* deal. If they wanted their film, he had better be in it. Monty became childish with frantic enthusiasm and insecurity, but she patiently put up with all of his calls. As far as John Huston went, she said, he would not dare treat Monty with anything but cultivated kindness while Elizabeth was around. Oh, Monty *was* excited, and for the first time in years, he felt loved.

The Burtons came to New York in August 1965, and checked into the Regency with a platoon of secretaries and half a dozen enormous trunks of clothing. In those days, they had more money than royalty, and certainly lived more lavishly. Monty came over to greet them. Burton liked Monty, just as Michael Wilding had; Monty, of course, could speak of nothing else but the plans for *Reflections*. He sat in their bedroom, going on and on about the movie, while Elizabeth um-hummed him and got under the bed with Burton to try and retrieve their little dog. Monty became fidgety and frustrated. For her, it was just another film, but for Monty it was St. Peter's gate. He left the hotel feeling upstaged by a dog.

Between 1964 and early 1966, while Monty played the waiting game, he began to see a plastic surgeon named Dr. Manfred Graf von Linde. The operations were infrequent and minor, such as removing the bags under Monty's eyes, and were designed to get rid of his sickly look.

Monty's main interest in Manfred von Linde however, was not medical. He was Lorenzo's friend, an eccentric, cherub-faced, blond six-footer, and a *poseur extraordinaire*. There were insidiously criminal overtones to his character which Monty, living in his prison of boredom, thought just wonderful. Manfred had been tossed out of the Army on grounds of homosexuality, performed illegal abortions, was being sued by actress Joann Dixon for a botched-up double breast-lift, and claimed to be a wealthy German count ("Graf" means count), forced to leave Germany because of the Nazis. His real name, however, was Robert Dent, and his birthplace was Birmingham, Alabama. He had replaced a Southern cracker accent with a German one, and rounded out his act with hammy "genteel" manners.

By the time Monty met him, the whole charade of von Linde's life had already been exposed to the public. All the New York papers had had splashy headlines about his possible indictment for the murder of a wealthy widow, Mrs. Lucille Rogers. The story read like installments of a clever Perry Mason mystery. At Christmastime 1961, the doctor's thirty-year-old roommate, Swen Swenson, introduced von Linde to Mrs. Lucille Rogers, fifty-two. At the time, Lucille was not wealthy but she stood to inherit her eighty-year old Aunt Polly's four million dollar estate. Poor Lucille was taken in by von Linde's continental act, and when he proposed marriage the unattractive widow immediately accepted. Shortly after, Aunt Polly conveniently and mysteriously died—a suspicious gaseous odor was detected in her hotel room. A few weeks later, Lucille and von Linde married, but von Linde would not move out on Swen Swenson. He told Lucille that the two of them could not consummate their marriage until their "honeymoon," which he planned for several weeks later. Meanwhile, von Linde convinced the vain, foolish Lucille to change her will, making him the beneficiary, and made reservations for the two of them to fly to Haiti for their official "honeymoon." She couldn't understand why he had chosen such a bleak place. She suggested Palm Springs, but von Linde insisted that he had business to conduct in a Haitian hospital. If she had checked, she would have discovered that Haitian law concerning autopsies and burials was most conducive to sudden death and foul play. Lucille then began getting telephone death threats from a young man who warned her that if she flew to Haiti with von Linde, she would never return alive. She didn't. Three days after their arrival in Port-au-Prince, she collapsed and died as mysteriously as had Aunt Polly. Von Linde then paid a "white-coated man" eighty dollars for what, he told the authorities, he thought was an autopsy. Von Linde claimed that the man did not understand him and instead embalmed Lucille. A quick Haitian autopsy revealed the astonishing fact that Lucille, who had been healthy as an ox before leaving New York, had died of a sudden heart attack. She was buried right after the autopsy, and the family notified. Under Haitian law, once a corpse is buried, it cannot be exhumed for eighteen months. Von Linde was due to inherit four million dollars.

Lawyers hired by Lucille's shocked family revealed the whole story to the papers, and the Haitian authorities were so embarrassed that they did exhume Lucille's body for a second autopsy, which showed that there had not been a heart attack after all, and held von Linde for possible indictment for murder. No poisons, or injected air bubbles, were found in Lucille's body; but it is a fact that embalmment can conceal such foul play. In the end, however, von Linde was released, went back to living with Swen Swenson in New York, somehow managed to continue practicing medicine, and did not receive a single penny from Lucille's estate. Because von Linde had married Lucille under false pretenses, the family was able to get the marriage annulled.

One wonders why Monty was not more wary of him. Monty was worth well over half a million dollars, but God knows what von Linde thought he was really worth. Monty still talked indiscriminately about how much he was going to leave this person or that person in his will. Monty and Lorenzo spent many evenings with the doctor and Swen Swenson, both at von Linde's house and Monty's, and sometimes Billy would join them. Billy liked von Linde, too—he was such a complete poseur and raconteur, still claiming to be a "Graf," despite the fact that whenever anyone addressed him in German, he could not understand a word. But Elizabeth, Monty's cook—who had seen a lot of perverse goings-on in Monty's house and had learned to take these things in her stride—did not trust von Linde's interest at all.

Von Linde, however, was only a symptom of Monty's disaffection with people who judged and tried to change him. The colorful doctor was at least sympathetic to Monty's indulgences and accepted his dissipation without a thought. Another such was a woman by the name of Irmgaard "Ischy" Gassler, who had met Monty while he was filming *Freud,* and who had made several trips from her home in Salzburg, Austria, to seek him out and declare her undying love. She was quite a silly character, gushing with schoolgirlish romance, and at any other time in his life, Monty would never have paid any attention to her. Ischy's pursuit, however, and her flood of love letters, must have been at least a break in the monotony. She took him out to dinner and plays, and even proposed marriage, though Monty had made it clear that he had no interest in taking a woman to bed. In the end, Monty wrote to her in Austria and told her that he had to "break it off." Even in his current state, he was capable of humoring somebody.

Monty also became deeply involved in astrology. He and Lorenzo visited the famous astrologer, Maria Crummere, and Doris Langley Moore sent Monty frequent reports on his horoscope from a friend of hers. (Monty was a Libra, a balanced but undecided type, just on the cusp of Scorpio, a complex, often tormented sign.) When the horoscopes started portending doom, however, Doris immediately stopped forwarding them. Monty shuddered, yet begged Doris not to protect him from the "ugly truth."

Meanwhile, Monty waited. And waited. It was killing him. Toward the end of 1965, Jack Larson visited him and saw that something had to be done, so he called Monty's old friend Salka Viertel, who now lived in Switzerland, and told her about Monty's state of mind. Monty, he said, was feeling good and he wasn't drinking, but he needed to work—otherwise he was liable to come apart. Salka was moved. She met with her friend, Flemish director Raoul Levy—famous as the discoverer of Brigitte Bardot and the director of most of her biggest-grossing films, including *And God Created Woman*—and suggested Montgomery Clift for his new spy film, *The Defector*. Salka already knew the movie was going to be dreadful; Levy had lost his touch and was more interested in his problems with mistresses than in the subtleties of filmmaking. The way Levy talked about *The Defector*, his own adaptation of a novel called *The Spy* by Paul Thomas, it was to be a Grade B picture with big box-office stars. Monica Vitti had already agreed to play the female lead, and he liked the idea of Monty, as long as Salka could promise that he wasn't drinking. Salka called Jack at Monty's house and told him that Levy would cast Monty in this second-rate film. "But get down on your knees and promise me that Monty will be able to get through it," she added.

As soon as Monty read the script, he knew exactly what he was in for. Yet he needed to work, and right away, so when Raoul Levy came to New York, Monty told him that he would do the film, as long as he could rewrite his part. Levy agreed.

Meanwhile, Monica Vitti had dropped out, after seeing the script, and Levy had gotten an even bigger fish to replace her: Leslie Caron. The bait for Caron was ten percent of the world's gross plus a high fee. Dollar signs swam in front of Levy's eyes—he had made fortunes in the past from the ingenious casting of certain stars in poor scripts. This one should be another moneymaker.

Monty should have made up his mind simply to give the movie the amount of effort it deserved: to fly to Munich, learn his lines quickly, shoot the scenes fast, and forget it immediately. Other top stars have made such garbage without significant damage to their reputations. But Monty couldn't do that. Jack listened to Monty talk about the script and he could see the problem. "I couldn't see how Monty was ever going to memorize his lines, he was so interested in the minutiae of lines and words and what emotional truths he was going to reveal. Working with him on *The Defector* script was like working with a small child: He wanted to talk about little words and things, instead of just learning his cues. And so I knew that the only person Monty could work with was Mira. The same evening that I brought it up, Monty called her."

Monty hadn't seen Mira Rostova for several years, and she had not actually worked with him on a film since *I Confess* in 1952. Mira had never held a grudge against Monty for dropping her. When he called to ask if she would come with him to Munich, she instantly agreed, as if all the trouble of the intervening years hadn't happened.

She also took a realistic attitude toward the script. She knew Monty needed to return to work, so instead of shaking her head about Levy's mess, she simply agreed with Monty that the two of them could rewrite it into shape. After all, they had done that once before, and their efforts had helped gain Monty his first Academy Award nomination. What they didn't know was that Leslie Caron, independently, had had the same idea. She had taken it upon herself to rewrite the entire screenplay, giving herself a fatter part, of course. When Raoul Levy turned down her changes, she immediately quit the film. Two weeks later, Levy replaced her with Nicole Courcel, a French actress. Monty was furious.

But that was only the beginning of the problems. By the time Monty arrived in Munich, forty-three-year-old Raoul Levy was apparently on the verge of a nervous breakdown. Roddy McDowall, who had a few scenes in the movie, felt that Levy behaved like a "comic opera idea of a movie director." Mira says, "He was no director—he was a joke." Levy's main problem was his floundering romance with the young, married script girl, Isabel, who lived with the rest of them at the Ambassador Hotel in Munich. He simply couldn't keep his mind on the work. Well after shooting had been wrapped up, Isabel was about to leave him to go back to her husband; Raoul became hysterical and went to her door at the hotel with a double-barrel shotgun and yelled, "Isabel, I've got to see you. I've got a gun." Then he began to pound on the door with the shotgun, but instead of pounding with the barrel he pounded with the butt and the barrel lodged in his chest and blew his stomach wide open.

Levy was just a part of Monty's mounting troubles. He also suffered from a bad case of "comeback fright." He would blow one take after another. He couldn't get his voice to operate properly. He stood near-paralyzed in front of the camera. Levy was too disconnected to be of any help, and Mira, seeing Monty's state, abandoned all interest in trying to rework the script, or even in attempting to improve his performance. All she cared about was having Monty memorize his cues and blocking well enough so that she could get him home.

The spring in Munich that year was cold and rainy, and all the outdoor shooting contributed greatly toward undermining Monty's health. He became weak and exhausted. Lorenzo always seemed to be half-carrying him from the sets at the end of each day's shooting. The accumulated results of four years of drinking and wasting away in solitary confinement could not be swept away by just a few months of cold-turkey.

The film's plot, if anyone cares, had to do with a scientist, who turns amateur spy for the C.I.A., which wants to aid a Russian physicist to defect to the West. In attempting to aid the physicist escape from East Germany, he tarries with a lovely counter-spy. That first part of the movie was the usual spy-flick stuff, with lots of revelations about who was spying for whom and why, but the second half constituted Levy's crazy idea of one, long, almost wordless escape sequence. It had Monty climbing walls, swimming in the Danube at night in freezing weather and jumping insanely from one boat to another—with little regard either for story logic or audience patience. Even Levy, on the verge of a collapse himself, could see that Monty was in no shape to do all that climbing and swimming, and wanted to use a stunt man, but Monty would not admit that he was sick and insisted on doing it all himself. He would be palpitating and ashen after those awful, freezing night plunges. Mira begged him to stop; the film just wasn't worth it.

But Monty was driven by fear. After Warner Brothers-Seven Arts had agreed to his casting in *The Defector*, solely as a "test" for *Reflections*, they were anxious to hear reports about his reliability to allay their worries about how he would do in *Reflections*. Monty was well aware of Warners' interest. He was also aware of how bad he looked in front of the cameras, and that he wasn't functioning properly. If reports got back to Warners about his blowing lines and his sickliness, they might use the opportunity to dump him. He *had* to get through the film, no matter what Levy told him to do; and in the end, through sheer force of will, he made it.

By the end of May, *The Defector* was finished, but Monty had to spend several weeks in Paris dubbing lines that he had either blown or misread in the film. When Mira parted from Monty in Paris for a little trip of her own, she had no idea that she would never see Monty again.

Monty and Lorenzo flew on to London, where they stayed at the Royal Garden Hotel and for a week made the rounds of parties, plays and old friends. Monty was exhausted but not angry, as he had been after *Freud*. He did make random comments, indicating some disgust with himself for having made *The Defector*, but there was no hint of the real revulsion he had felt at seeing a run-through of the rushes. Surrounded by the English friends he loved, his essential mood was one of sentimentality. He and Susannah York went to Stratford to see a Shakespeare play, and he cried so much one of his contact lenses literally washed onto the floor. Then he went to Oxford to see Fred Zinnemann on the set of *A Man for All Seasons*, in which York had a part, and Zinnemann was radiantly happy to see him. Paul Scofield came over to pay homage. At Leslie Caron's, Warren Beatty and Richard Harris openly idolized him. John Springer happened to call Caron's the night Monty was there, and made a date to meet Monty in New York the minute they both got back in town. None of them knew that they would never see Monty again.

When Monty and Lorenzo returned home at the beginning of July 1966, the self-loathing that had been building inside of him over his failure in *The Defector*, and his worries about Warners reneging on the *Reflections* deal, surfaced into a cavernous depression. At the house in The Pines, Ray Buckingham and his wife Ann had never seen Monty so down. All he would say about *The Defector* was: "Nothing went right. I had never been through such a bad time in my life." He looked slightly heavier than he had before leaving for Munich, but it was a "bloated," edematose heaviness; it was not a healthy look.

Monty had never made a truly bad film before this last, seventeenth one. Even in *Lonelyhearts*, the performance he gave would have been passable for a lesser actor. He never put it into words, yet it was obvious that he had passed judgment on himself during and after the making of *The Defector*, and what the critics would say about it when it came out was trivial compared with what he was telling himself right now.

At twilight, he and Ann walked on the beach near the house. "While we were walking, I had the distinct feeling that he just didn't want to stay around anymore, that he wanted to leave his body. He was so distant." It was as if everything was dying simultaneously: the sun had begun to turn into a smoky corpse, the ocean to disappear from the shore into the shadows, and Monty's voice, no longer alive with that calculating, slow hesitation, drifted on in an odd, monotonous way. They walked slowly; he talked, saying little.

When they came back to the house, Monty approached Ann and Ray from behind and hung over their shoulders. It was suddenly frightening. Monty said to them in a voice that wasn't his own, "I do love you. You know that, don't you? I love you both." Later, Ray told his wife what a shudder went through him when Monty addressed them both like that.

Monty did not want to be alone. Ray and Ann were supposed to come to Fire Island the next weekend of July 16, too, but they had just had a quarrel, and Ray called Monty to cancel their date. Monty called back and started to cry. "I wish you'd come out here. I was looking forward to it . . ." Then he lapsed into a sorrowful monologue. He kept Ray on the phone for two solid hours. Ray says, "I couldn't believe it. He went on and on and I got very scared. I had never heard him go on like that on the phone. He was usually very brief, or he would tell a little joke, or if he had something to say, he would get it over with. He was obviously desperately lonely and afraid . . . Suddenly, I realized I had to try to pacify him and we ended up making a date for the following week, saying 'Look, it's going to be beautiful weather and you'll catch a big fish from my boat and maybe we'll take a long walk on the beach.' Finally, he said good night and hung up. I turned to my wife and said, 'God, he's so depressed. We should have gone out.' "

Monty returned to the city and talked with several old friends the next week. Rick called him, and they made a date to have dinner the following Wednesday. Nancy Walker had not talked to him in months, and when he picked up the phone, she screamed, "You creep! This is the first time I've known how to get you since God knows when!" She said she was going out to Fire Island, and Monty was happy and said he would meet her there when he went out during the weekend.

Friday night, July 22, Monty drifted off, quite late. On Saturday morning, Lorenzo tried to wake him in the bedroom of the town house. Some hours later, Lorenzo told the police and a member of the Medical Examiner's office: "I was watching television at five A.M. and then I went to check on Mr. Clift because he had a habit of falling asleep with his glasses on and also because he hadn't been feeling well." Monty had been getting sick from his liquor again.

Monty, indeed, was still wearing his glasses when Lorenzo found him naked in bed at 6 A.M. He didn't seem to be breathing—but then Lorenzo was used to Monty's comatose states in the morning. It seemed to be taking a very long time to get Monty's eyes open and Lorenzo finally said, "Come on Monty, let's go to the showers!"—the usual ritual when Monty wouldn't awaken. He scooped his charge up and started toward the bathroom with the light, limp body in his arms. But something was terribly strange. Before Lorenzo got to the showers, it suddenly struck him that Monty had never been *this* bad. He carried him back to the bedroom. He checked the pulse. It was gone.

A stunned Lorenzo tried to call Dr. Ludwig, but he was out of town. Dr. Kline, Dr. Ludwig's associate, received the frightened call and rushed over to the town house. He examined Monty, who still had his glasses on, and pronounced him dead.

Monty had died sometime during the night.

Mrs. Clift was notified. Despite the wishes of the family, Dr. Kline was compelled to call the Medical Examiner's Office for an official autopsy, since Dr. Kline was not Monty's physician and could not, therefore, write the death certificate, circumventing autopsy. Dr. Kline called the Medical Examiner's office at 11 A.M. Jack Clareman, Monty's lawyer, arrived. At 1:45 P.M., Dr. Schmidt of the coroner's office and Detective Walter Little made their official calls. Kline told Schmidt that Monty had probably died of "convulsions due to alcoholism," but that he couldn't determine (from Lorenzo, who was either too confused or to reluctant to be specific) how heavily Monty had been drinking in the previous two weeks.

By 3 P.M., a private ambulance had brought the still naked boby—except for the eyeglasses—to the Medical Examiner's on the Lower East Side. Dr. Michael M. Baden started the autopsy at four, because the family was anxious to get the body back. He found no evidence that Monty had died of "convulsions due to alcoholism." Instead, there was every indication that Monty had died of a heart attack. "I immediately found one infarct of the left ventrical which was a few days old. There was severe arteriosclerosis of the three major coronary arteries. Eleven sections of the right coronary artery and eight of the left circumflex part were sclerotic . . . We were able to clearly demonstrate that there had been a fresh myocardial infarction—what most people would call a heart attack."

There was no evidence of foul play or drug overdose. Many of Monty's friends were suspicious of the infamous Dr. Manfred von Linde and thought he might have sneaked into the house while Lorenzo was unaware and pumped Monty full of something. Hadn't Lucille Rogers and Aunt Polly died mysteriously? But no traces of liquor or pills were found in his body. Monty had died of indisputable natural causes.

Meanwhile, Lorenzo took it upon himself to reach Monty's close friends, before they read the news in the papers the next morning. He told Roddy, who had just returned to New York. At three or four in the morning London time, John Springer woke up to the sound of a telephone ringing. He had just left a rousing party at the Dorchester thrown by Elizabeth and Richard. Roddy identified himself in a trembling voice. "Roddy, what's the matter?" asked John. "I wanted . . . to tell you . . . you've got to tell Elizabeth and Fred Zinnemann that Monty's dead." John was destroyed. He immediately called the Dorchester and Richard took the call. He sighed and said that he would tell Elizabeth privately. One by one, Monty's remaining friends heard the news.

The Clifts made a to-do about the funeral arrangements. Whenever the subject had come up, Monty had explicitly said that he wanted nothing more than a simple Quaker service, no pomp and fuss. Mrs. Clift told "Roberta" and Brooks that she also wanted what Monty had wanted, but Monty's twin, paralyzed with grief, shocked at the very idea of not having a wake and a church service with minister, flowers, pews and eulogy, would hear no arguments. She took over and made all arrangements with Lorenzo.

Three days later, on July 26, they held an early morning wake for Monty at Campbell's funeral parlor, and later on in the day St. James Episcopal Church held a service. More than one hundred and fifty people attended at St. James; yet there was a peculiar look of vacancy about the church while the brief service was held. People seemed alienated from one another; they sat either entirely alone or in small groups. The family—Mrs. Clift, Roberta, Brooks, others members—sat in the first row, with Lorenzo James conspicuously among them. How odd that Monty had cut most of his family off years before with the lame excuse that they were "bigots," and here they were sharing their most intimate grief with ebony-black Lorenzo—almost a living portrait of their desire to appease Monty's tormented spirit.

Libby Holman sat at the very back, next to her grown adopted sons, Tony and Timmy. She had suddenly grown very old. Her face, always prematurely wrinkled, was now that of Methuselah. She wore a dried-up, painted expression, entirely uncharacteristic of her, throughout the ceremony. Billy LeMassena sat, of course, with the family. Jerome Robbins and Jose Quintero sat alone. Ray Buckingham found himself next to a weeping Lauren Bacall. He frankly admits that he took Monty's death harder than the death of his parents, because he had been in a "playing-God role" with Monty's career and spirits, and it had all ended so abruptly, and *damn* it, he asked himself, *why?* Nancy Walker sat in the back pew. A young woman, who she thought must have been one of Monty's friends, came over to her and pulled out a pad and pencil: "I'm from the New York *Times*. I'd like to get your view." Nancy was horror-struck and told the miserable reporter to get away from her. It was the sort of thing that had always happened to Monty, and it was going on still, even here.

In a way, the scattered, alienated, uncommunicating nature of the audience was a striking reflection of Monty's life. Nancy didn't know Billy, Billy hardly knew Ned Smith,

Ned had never met Mira Rostova, and so on. Monty could only relate to individuals, not to a group, and so his friends, old and new, found themselves in a church full of unspeaking strangers.

The absentees were conspicuous. Not present were Elizabeth Taylor, who was in London; Kevin McCarthy, out of town in a play; Roddy McDowall, who had to fly to Hollywood to finish a work commitment; and Rick, who simply couldn't bring himself to come. Elizabeth sent two bouquets of large white chrysanthemums. There were also flowers from Roddy—who was still calling all of Monty's friends in Hollywood, in case they hadn't heard—and from Myrna Loy, Raoul Levy (who was just about to join Monty), and Lew Wasserman.

The coffin, which had remained closed at Campbell's, was carried into the church by pallbearers who were employees of the funeral home, attended by organ music that Monty had particularly liked: Bach's "Sinfonia," "Cathedrale Prelude," and "Fugue in E Minor." Outside, a July day had turned gun-metal gray, and it was beginning to pour. An enormous number of curiosity seekers clustered about the church. They were dressed in shorts and sports shirts, carried cameras and autograph books, and looked ready to pounce on the first celebrity to exit the church. They were not there for Monty; they were much too young to be his old worshipers. The greatest actor of the post-World War II generation lay dead inside, but these people were interested in living faces.

The service lasted barely half an hour. There was no eulogy, only a few prayers and a benediction. "Whatever you are doing, whether you speak or act, do everything in the name of the Lord," read Canon William Chase from the Psalms. It was over.

Lorenzo, Billy, Mira, Ray Buckingham and one or two others were the only outsiders to come with the family to the graveside. The Clifts owned their own plot at the Friends Cemetery in Brooklyn's Prospect Park. Mira, who did not show her emotions easily, could not stop crying. In the manner of Quaker burials, no headstone was placed to mark the grave. To find the place where Monty is buried, you have to ask the cemetery caretaker. Says Nancy Walker, "His grave was so like him."

Monty's death was a shock, and yet not a shock. Publicly, Elizabeth Taylor told the press: "I am so shocked I can barely accept it. I loved him. He was my dearest friend. He was my brother." And yet, when she called Rex Kennamer from England to talk about Monty's death, she said she knew it was going to happen soon, one way or another. As Roddy McDowall had put it, they were all, the ones who had remained—and there were so few of them in the end —just holding Monty's hand till the grave.

Fittingly, Marlon Brando replaced Monty in *Reflections in a Golden Eye*. Brando performed the part well, and for it earned his first million-dollar fee.

Warner Brothers-Seven Arts earned more money than it deserved from *The Defector* when the movie finally came out. Films whose stars die right after shooting always gross better than they would ordinarily. But it was such a dreadful way for Monty to be seen for the last time. Critics went out of their way to be kind to it and to him, but kind words could not hide the deathly scarecrow they saw on the screen. His lines were gasped, not spoken; his manner, disconnected. The film served as a reminder more of what Monty had become than of what he had achieved.

And he had achieved a great deal.

He left half a million dollars: approximately sixty percent to his twin sister and forty percent to his mother. He also left $12,500 to his brother, Brooks; $2,000 to Mira Rostova; $5,000 to Marge Stengel; $3,000 to Lorenzo; and 500 each to Anne Lincoln and Elizabeth Guenster. It wasn't a lot of money, in view of Monty's fame. But then Monty had never in his life worked for money.

A month after the funeral, a Quaker memorial service was held for Monty at the Friends meeting house on Fifteenth Street and Rutherford Place, in keeping with Monty's wishes. Attending were Mrs. Clift, Billy LeMassena, Ned Smith, Kevin McCarthy, Brooks, Robert Lantz and his assistant Helen Merril, and a handful of others. They all sat on plain wooden folding chairs. A man stood up and said, "We are all here to remember our friend, Edward Montgomery." Then there was silence as, according to Quaker custom, people stood up to say a few words in memory of the departed. It was gently sad, for only a few people stood up to say anything about Monty. Ned Smith spoke for a very long time about the days when he and Monty went fishing and hunting together, about what a great outdoorsman Monty was, and many other things that had absolutely nothing to do with the Montgomery Clift that most of the people in that room knew. Mrs. Clift kept glaring at Billy; she so wanted him to stand up from his plain wooden chair and recall the early days. But Billy couldn't. He couldn't forget that Monty was only forty-five and dead. He was so young, such a "victim."

But didn't any of them know? Montgomery Clift was "the oldest person in the room."

Appendix

THE SEARCH. MGM-Loew's International, 1948*. *Fred Zinnemann*. Jarmila Novotna, Aline MacMahon, Ivan Jandl, Wendell Corey, Mary Patton, Leopold Borkowski, and William Rogers.

RED RIVER. United Artists, 1948.* *Howard Hawks*. John Wayne, Walter Brennan, Joanne Dru, Noah Beery, Jr., John Ireland, Coleen Gray, Harry Carey, Harry Carey, Jr., and Paul Fix.

THE HEIRESS. Paramount, 1949. *William Wyler*. Olivia de-Havilland, Ralph Richardson, Miriam Hopkins, Vanessa Brown, Mona Freeman, Ray Collins, Betty Linley, Selena Royle, Paul Lees, Harry Antrim, Russ Conway, and David Thurdby.

THE BIG LIFT. Twentieth Century-Fox, 1950. *George Seaton*. Paul Douglas, Cornell Borchers, Bruni Lobel, O. E. Hasse, Danny Davenport.

A PLACE IN THE SUN. Paramount, 1951. *George Stevens*. Elizabeth Taylor, Shelley Winters, Anne Revere, Raymond Burr, Keefe Brasselle, Sheppard Strudwick, Frieda Inescourt, Ian Wolfe, and Herbert Heyes.

* Dates given indicate when films were released. *Red River,* made in 1946, was actually Monty's first film, and *The Search,* fimed in 1947, was his second. But *The Search* was released three months earlier than *Red River* in 1948.

I CONFESS. Warner Brothers, 1953. *Alfred Hitchcock.* Anne Baxter, Karl Malden, Brian Aherne, O. E. Hasse, Roger Dann, Dolly Haas, Charles Andre, Judson Pratt, Ovila Legare, and Giles Pelletier.

FROM HERE TO ETERNITY. Columbia, 1953*. *Fred Zinnemann.* Burt Lancaster, Deborah Kerr, Frank Sinatra, Donna Reed, Philip Ober, Mickey Shaugnessy, Harry Bellaver, Ernest Borgnine, George Reeves.

INDISCRETION OF AN AMERICAN WIFE. Selznick-Columbia, 1954*. *Vittorio de Sica.* Jennifer Jones, Dick Beymer, Gino Cervi.

RAINTREE COUNTY. MGM, 1957. *Edward Dmytryk.* Elizabeth Taylor, Eva Marie Saint, Lee Marvin, Rod Taylor, Nigel Patrick, Agnes Moorehead, Walter Abel, Jarma Lewis, Tom Drake, Rhys Williams, Russell Collins, DeForest Kelley.

THE YOUNG LIONS. Twentieth Century-Fox, 1958. *Edward Dmytryk.* Marlon Brando, Dean Martin, Hope Lange, Barbara Rush, May Britt, Maximilian Schell, Dora Doll, Lee Van Cleef, and Liliane Montevecchi.

LONELYHEARTS. United Artists, 1959. *Vincent J. Donehue.* Robert Ryan, Myrna Loy, Dolores Hart, Maureen Stapleton, Frank Maxwell, Jackie Coogan, Mike Kellin, Frank Overton, and Onslow Stevens.

SUDDENLY LAST SUMMER. Columbia-Horizon, 1959. *Joseph L. Mankiewicz.* Elizabeth Taylor, Katharine Hepburn, Albert Dekker, Mercedes McCambridge, Gary Raymond, Mavis Villiers, Patricia Marmont, and Joan Young.

WILD RIVER. Twentieth Century-Fox, 1960. *Elia Kazan.* Lee Remick, Jo Van Fleet, Albert Salmi, J.C. Flippen, James Westerfield, Barbara Loden, Frank Overton, Malcolm Atterbury, Robert Earl Jones, and Bruce Dern.

THE MISFITS. United Artists-Seven Arts, 1961. *John Huston.* Clark Gable, Marilyn Monroe, Thelma Ritter, Eli Wallach,

---

* *Indiscretion of an American Wife* was completed before filming began on *From Here to Eternity.*

Estelle Winwood, Kevin McCarthy, Dennis Shaw, Marietta Tree.

JUDGMENT AT NUREMBERG. United Artists, 1961. *Stanley Kramer*. Spencer Tracy, Burt Lancaster, Maximilian Schell, Richard Widmark, Marlene Dietrich, Judy Garland, William Shatner, Ed Binns, Kenneth MacKenna, Werner Klemperer, Torben Meyer, and Alan Baxter.

FREUD. Universal-International, 1962. *John Huston*. Susannah York, Larry Parks, Susan Kohner, Eric Portman, Eileen Herlie, Fernand Ledoux, David McCallum, Rosalie Crutchley, and David Kossoff.

THE DEFECTOR. Warner Brothers-Seven Arts, 1966. *Raoul Levy*. Hardy Kruger, Macha Meril, and Roddy McDowall. Released after Monty's death.

Index

The triumphant biography of a Queen!
The intimate story of a dynasty

MAJESTY

ELIZABETH II AND THE HOUSE OF WINDSOR

By Robert Lacey

"Highly entertaining ... an astute blend of gossip
and uplift ... a phrase I thought I would
never use describes it:
It is a good read."
Newsweek

"The best book on the fascinating
subject of 20th-century royalty"
Clifton Fadiman

MAIN SELECTION OF THE BOOK-OF-THE-MONTH CLUB

With 32 pages of photographs

 Avon/36327/$2.25

AVON ◆ THE BEST IN
BESTSELLING ENTERTAINMENT